THE SIEGE OF THE PEKING LEGATIONS

A DIARY

LANCELOT GILES

EDITED WITH INTRODUCTION

CHINESE ANTI-FOREIGNISM AND THE BOXER UPRISING

BY

L. R. MARCHANT

FOREWORD BY SIR ROBERT SCOTT
GCMG, KCMG, CMG, CBE, JP

UNIVERSITY OF WESTERN AUSTRALIA PRESS

First published in 1970 by
University of Western Australia Press
Nedlands, Western Australia

This book is copyright. Apart from any fair dealing for the purpose of study research, criticism or review as permitted under the Copyright Act no part may be reproduced by any process without written permission. Enquiries should be made to the publisher.

© University of Western Australia Press 1970

National Library of Australia card service number and
Standard Book Number 85564-041-3
Library of Congress Catalog Card Number 78-123328

Printed in Western Australia by Frank Daniels Pty Ltd, Perth, Western Australia
and bound by Stanley Owen and Sons Pty Ltd, Alexandria, New South Wales

Registered in Australia for transmission by post as a book

THE SIEGE OF
THE PEKING LEGATIONS

北京使館被圍日記

'Diary of the Siege of the
Peking Legations'
CALLIGRAPHY by LIU WEI-PING

*This book is respectfully dedicated
to the memory of
Lancelot and Marjory Giles*

CONTENTS

	page
Preface	xvii
Foreword by Sir Robert Scott	xix
Introduction: Chinese Anti-Foreignism	1
Diary of the Boxer Riots and of the Siege of the Legations	105
Notes to the Diary	179
List of Selected Works	193
Indexes	
Introduction	205
Diary	209

FIGURES

IN THE INTRODUCTION

1 South China: locations of major anti-foreign outbreaks, 1886-1895   16

2 The Peking-Tientsin railway   33

3 Seymour Expedition and Relief Expedition   65

4 Peking City gates   74

5 Operations against Taku forts, 17 June 1900   77

6 The Manchu royal family 1821-1912, showing Boxer affiliations   80

7 Legation Quarter in 1900   85

8 Operations around Tientsin   89

FIGURES

IN THE DIARY

1	General position of Legations	111
2	The defence of the British Legation	116-17
3	The Ch'ien Men catching fire from the Chinese City	118
4	A Chinese attack on the Fu and the Allied counter-attack	132
5	The operation designed to take the the big Chinese gun to the north-east of the Fu	138
6	The author's encounter with the Chinese in the Fu	149

ILLUSTRATIONS

The photographs reproduced in this book were taken by Lancelot Giles during the siege of the Legations, many of them under fire from the Chinese positions.

facing 105
1   Lancelot Giles at the age of 21 (Aug. 1899)

between 112 *and* 113
2   Lady MacDonald's fancy-dress ball, 1900: a group of Students Interpreters
3   The Students' Corps
4   Chinese troops crossing the North Bridge on the Imperial Canal before the siege
5   Converts taking refuge in the Fu
6   Boxer handiwork before the siege
7   The barricaded front of the British Legation
8   Enemy loopholes across the Imperial Canal
9   German marines
10 Russian barricade in the Legation Street
11 Chinese positions opposite the Germans
12 A Chinese barricade on the city wall
13 British marines

between 120 *and* 121
14 British non-commissioned officers
15 British staff
16 The first Boxer prisoner
17 Kansu (Tung Fu-hsiang's) soldiers
18 A Boxer temple in which forty Boxers were shot by the Allied rescue party

(xiii)

ILLUSTRATIONS

19 Those who shot them—the rescue party
20 The Ch'ien Men before burning
21 The Ch'ien Men catching fire from the Chinese City
22 The Ch'ien Men burning
23 The Ch'ien Men enveloped in flames
24 Ruins of the Ch'ien Men from the west
25 Ruins of the Ch'ien Men: a fragment
26 Ruins of the Ch'ien Men from the south
27 A balcony of the British Minister Sir Claude MacDonald's house
28 Through a loophole
29 Italian gunner and gun

page 122
30 A page from the diary in Giles's handwriting

between 128 *and* 129
31 Italian gunner in the Hanlin
32 The Nordenfelt
33 Colt automatic gun
34 The front line of defence in the Fu after shelling
35 'Boxer Bill'
36 The second line of defence in the Fu
37 The gate leading to the Mongol Market
38 The Mongol Market gate barricaded from inside
39 Germans commandeering Chinese labour
40 The last, improved, Russian barricade
41 Students' Quarters seen from the Hanlin
42 Daily food of the besieged
43 The Hanlin: the ruins of the main building
44 The Hanlin: the library

between 136 *and* 137
45 The ruins of Customs Lane
46 Under a flag of truce
47 A Chinese messenger, Liu Wu-yüan (age 16), who went to Tientsin and back
48 A scene in the German Legation
49 The Legation Street in ruins
50 The relief

ILLUSTRATIONS

51 Soldiers of the 7th Rajputs, the first to enter the Legation Quarter
52 The march through the Imperial palace: the British staff with Gen. Gaselee
53 The march through the Imperial palace: the British Marine Corps
54 The march through the Imperial palace: Graf von Waldersee reviewing the Allied troops
55 The march through the Imperial palace: the Japanese
56 The march through the Imperial palace: the Russians
57 *In memoriam*

between 144 *and* 145

58 Departure of Gen. Gaselee
59 Prince Ch'ing's arrival for the signing of the Protocol in Peking
60 Signing of the Protocol in Peking, 1901: the Allies
61 Signing of the Protocol in Peking, 1901: the Chinese
62 Students Interpreters before the siege
63 Students Interpreters: the survivors

endpapers

Chinese Empire, 1900

PREFACE

Revolutions, civil wars, riots, disturbances and other events in history will always be reappraised. This is not only because of man's shifting interests and viewpoints. The discovery and release of hitherto unsighted historical documents also stimulates new studies and interpretations.

An extensive amount of historical material on the Boxer Uprising is in existence. The event was witnessed by a variety of people, some of whom had their observations published in the form of diaries kept during the crises, or in the form of reminiscences written later. Foreign diplomats in Peking in particular had a good view of the Uprising. They saw the Boxer problem emerge and were besieged in the Peking Legations from June to August 1900. As far as British diplomats are concerned, their personal observations have never been fully revealed. The Uprising and the siege of the Legations were described in an official version presented by the British Minister, Sir Claude MacDonald and other diplomats. Selections of these reports were later published in British *Parliamentary Papers,* which like other government accounts and papers, reflected the policy of the government in power. British diplomats were not encouraged or permitted to publish private accounts or observations without them being vetted. They were servants of the Crown and views they expressed could have been used or misconstrued by opposition elements at home and abroad.

Lancelot Giles's diary of the siege of the Peking Legations is significant. He was one of the few British officials who wrote a day by day account of events. He did not hold an elevated position in the British civil service. He was a new recruit serving as Student Interpreter in the British Consular Service. However he was not a normal type of trainee. His father, Herbert Allen Giles, had served as a British Consul in China, and in 1900, some years after his return to England, he was a most eminent sinologist. Lancelot Giles wrote the diary specifically to inform his learned father of the events in China. This added to the author's perceptiveness and gives the work an added quality. His transcriptions of the posters put up by those conducting the defences in order to keep the besieged foreigners informed of events, and his observations on the conduct of the siege and the behaviour of the besieged indicate that he used his position to advantage.

An expurgated version of the diary, approved by the British Foreign Office, was published in 1900 in *Christ College Magazine,* Cambridge. The original diary, with three volumes of photographs, many of which were taken during the siege of the Legations, remained in the possession of Lancelot Giles's family who came to Perth, Western Australia. The diary was found in 1962 after my return from the London School of Oriental and African Studies, and was prepared for publication.

The book consists of four parts. There is an introductory essay on Chinese anti-foreignism and the Boxer Uprising, which puts the siege of the Peking Legations in perspective. Then follows Lancelot Giles's diary of the siege. This is supplemented by explanatory notes which clarify points made for Herbert Allen Giles who knew a great deal about Peking, the British Consular Service and the Chinese. Finally, there is a select bibliography of Western works on the Boxer Uprising.

I wish to thank in particular the late Mrs Marjory Giles, and her daughters Mrs R. Pickford and Mrs M. House for permission to use material in their possession and for their assistance. I also thank Dr Isobel Durack of the University of Western Australia for bringing to my notice the existence of the Giles family in Perth. Special thanks are also due to Sir Robert Scott for his contribution; to Dr Liu Wei-ping of the Department of Oriental Studies at the University of Sydney for his calligraphy; to my wife Gunhild for her invaluable help with preparing the manuscript for publication; to Mrs R. E. James of Floreat Park W.A., and to Mr F. D. Marchant of Claremont W.A. for their help with the proof copies, and to Dr N. Marchant of Cambridge University for his assistance with the photographic plates existing at Cambridge University library.

Nedlands, Western Australia   LESLIE R. MARCHANT

FOREWORD

For generations the name Giles has been known to students of China throughout the world. The diary now published is yet another contribution to sinology by a member of the Giles family.

Young Lance Giles was finishing his first year in Peking when the siege of the Legations took place in 1900. He recorded his impressions and activities during the siege in a letter to his father, written in diary style. This came into the hands of Leslie R. Marchant of the University of Western Australia, sixty-five years later.

Professor H. A. Giles

Herbert Allen Giles, to whom the letter was addressed, went to Peking in 1867 at the age of twenty-two to enter Her Britannic Majesty's Consular Service in China, in which he spent the next twenty-five years. Too much of an individualist to settle easily into a civil service mould, his career as a consular officer was not outstanding. But he was fascinated by the Chinese people, their language, and their civilization; a fascination that in later years became an obsession. Once he had mastered the language, much of his time was spent on lexicography. He resigned from the Consular Service in 1892 when he had completed his monumental *Chinese-English Dictionary*. He was then Consul at Ningpo. He never revisited China.

The first edition of the dictionary, which was to become a standard reference work for generations of students of Chinese, appeared in the same year. From China, Giles went to Aberdeen. But, on the Chair of Chinese at Cambridge University falling vacant a few years later, he applied for it and became Professor of Chinese there in 1897, an appointment he held for thirty-five years, retiring in 1932 at the age of eighty-seven.

Punctual, methodical, hardworking, fond of controversy, Giles set out to transform current European ideas about China as a country of mystery and barbarism, and peopled by a race whose ways, habits and beliefs were illogical, ridiculous and unimportant, to the view that China was a country with an unsurpassed record of civilization and culture, where scholarship was revered, and where the language, though constructed on a pictorial instead of an alphabetical system, was nevertheless as flexible, as precise and as subtle as any other.

When he went to Cambridge, the university did not rate Chinese studies highly, nor was the subject popular with undergraduates. But, if the stipend was small, the teaching load was light. With abundant energy, ample leisure, and the facilities of the university at his disposal, Giles pursued his chosen task of revealing and explaining China to the West. In 1922 the Royal Asiatic Society awarded him their Gold Medal on the grounds that he 'beyond all living scholars has humanised Chinese studies'. The tribute was deserved. This was the man to whom the letter was sent. The writer was his sixth son, Lancelot—usually known as 'Lance'—born at Amoy on June the 6th 1878.

Herbert Allen Giles married twice; first in June 1870 to Catherine Fenn, daughter of a surgeon in Suffolk. She died at Pagoda Anchorage near Foochow in 1882, worn out by repeated pregnancies and the strain of looking after her children and her brilliant but already somewhat eccentric husband in a strange land with strange customs, lacking many of the things she had been brought up to believe were essential to child welfare: doctors, medicines, and even milk and drinkable water. There were few European women in China at that time, and fewer with small children. Moreover the family was constantly on the move from one place to another. In her twelve years of married life Catherine lived in Tientsin, Ningpo and Hankow; went back to England on leave; and returned to China to live at Swatow, Amoy, and finally Foochow. In that time she bore eight children, two of whom died in infancy. The six surviving children, four boys and two girls, were all under the age of nine when Catherine died. Giles took them back to England a year later and there he met and married his second wife, Elise Edersheim who accompanied him back to China.

The four boys were sent to a Jesuit school in Liège, and from there to Stella Matutina, the Jesuit College at Feldkirch in Austria, where they stayed until their father left China when they joined him at Aberdeen. In due course the eldest son, Bertram, joined the Consular Service in China; after attending Oxford University, Lionel, the second son, secured a position in the British Museum, becoming well known in later years as Keeper of the Department of Oriental Printed Books and Manuscripts and as translator of Chinese classics. The third son, Valentine, had a distinguished career in the British Army in the Royal Engineers. Lance, the youngest of the brothers, accompanied his father, stepmother, two sisters, and half-sister to Cambridge in 1897 and embarked on classical studies at Christ's College where his tutors formed a high opinion of his abilities. Professor Giles, however, cut short his son's university career, probably because he could not afford the expense.

The Consular Service

The British Consular Service in China was founded in 1842 and came to an end, as a separate branch, in 1935. Till 1834 the East India Company had possessed a monopoly of British trade with China. The monopoly withdrawn, new independent British traders appeared on the scene. Between these and the Chinese authorities there developed increasing friction culminating in the Anglo-Chinese war of 1839 to 1842, better known as the 'Opium War'. By the Nanking Convention of 1842 five ports were opened to foreign trade and China conceded the right for foreign powers to appoint consuls at them. Subsequent treaties with Britain and with other powers opened other cities with the same concession. All of these consular places were known as 'treaty ports' even though some were far inland.

The difficulty of the language and the special qualifications required, soon led to the formation of a 'close' service, the members of which were all salaried and restricted from trading, with entry by competition among nominated candidates. By 1872 this requirement had been dropped, and anyone could compete.

By the end of the nineteenth century there were twenty-seven British consular posts in China, staffed by two Consuls-General, twenty-one Consuls, three Vice-Consuls, eleven First-Class Assistants, twenty-two Second-Class Assistants and twenty-five Student

Interpreters. This last category, the most junior grade, was made up of new entrants who spent their first two years in Peking studying the language with only minimal office work.

Lancelot Giles

Given the family background, an environment permeated by the influence of China, this Service was the obvious choice for Lance provided he could pass the entrance examinations without a university degree. Apart from this drawback his qualifications were good. He had a sound general education and a good knowledge of French and German.

He passed the examination and was accepted for the China Consular Service as a Student Interpreter; his letter of appointment, July the 19th 1899, stated:

> You will, whilst holding this appointment, receive a salary of £200 a-year, to commence ten days previously to your departure from London to your post. You will be provided in addition with official quarters (or an allowance in lieu thereof) suitable for a single man, the Regulations of the Service not admitting of any provision being made for married officers of the rank of Student Interpreter.
>
> A passage to Shanghai will be provided . . . at Shanghai you will apply to Her Majesty's Consulate-General for directions and full particulars concerning the continuance of your journey to the capital.
>
> You will be expected in the first place to devote yourself principally to the study of the language of the country. But you will not fail, at the same time, to take advantage of such opportunities as you may have for acquiring an insight into the manner in which the business of Her Majesty's Diplomatic and Consular establishments is conducted.

The system had not changed much when I went to China as a Student Interpreter in the same Service in 1927, by which time Lancelot Giles was a senior and much respected colleague. By then a few posts had been upgraded to Consulates-General. One or two other posts had been closed. The salary of a Student Interpreter had gone up to £300 per year. The warning that no provision was made for a wife had become a prohibition on marriage on pain of forfeiture of a bond for £300 and liability to dismissal. But the British Consular Service in China was still, in 1927 as it had been in 1900, a small corps whose members joined intending to spend their whole working lives in that country. At neither date was it the only specialized branch in Britain's Consular Service. There were also the Consular Service for the Ottoman Dominions (known later as the Levant Service) and the Consular Services for Japan and for Siam. When these four special branches were merged with the General Consular Service in 1935, the China Service had twenty-two posts and sixty-three members of whom six were Student Interpreters.

Marriage

At the end of the letter to his father, Lance said: 'There is some talk of our being sent home on leave.' As he probably realized, these rumours were unfounded. Home leave for Consuls in the China Service was infrequent though generous when it came. He had been in China less than a year when the Boxer Uprising occurred. Consequently he finished his studies in Peking and was posted to Hankow. A long and dangerous journey from Hankow (whose consular district covered an area larger than that of the United Kingdom) to investigate the murder of a British missionary, introduced him to an aspect of consular work with which most members of the Service in those days were familiar. He was promoted Second-Class Assistant and went on leave in 1905. By that time he was twenty-six. His stepmother and sisters thought it time for him to marry, and with this in mind they collected the names of suitable damsels. Soon after he reached Cambridge his stepmother happened to fall off her tricycle and was helped to her feet by a girl named Marjory Scott, an undergraduate from Newnham College. Mrs Giles invited her to tea and she met Lance. He told the family to throw away their list of prospective brides, as he intended to marry Marjory. Theirs proved to be a very successful marriage. To the end of his life the two were inseparable save for brief and unavoidable interludes such as her journey to England to take one of their two daughters to school.

Consular Career

Lancelot Giles spent much of his career in what were known as the 'outports', which were situated on the China coast and in the Yangtze valley. A man of remarkable calm and considerable personal courage, he came unruffled through crisis after crisis; civil wars, riots, anti-British boycotts and demonstrations. His widow and daughters (Rosamond is now Mrs Pickford, Marjory Mrs House) now live in Perth, Western Australia. They recall many occasions of living under fire, of sandbagging windows, of the children being sent indoors when it was too dangerous to be outside ('though tennis and croquet went on just the same, so long as the firing was not too intense'), of anti-British demonstrations with thousands of students marching on the Consulate shouting: 'Kill, kill. Cut off their heads.'

He was stationed in Swatow when the communists, who had been terrorizing the countryside, decided to move away, causing further troubles as they did. His wife and elder daughter, as always, were with him. He never believed in the policy of evacuating women and children in a crisis any more than he believed that they should conform to the normal practice of European residents in China and go to a hill-station or the seaside to avoid the summer heat. Communist intentions were at first unknown (it was in fact the early stage of their long march to the northwest), and for the only time in his life he thought it prudent to show his wife and elder daughter how to load the rifles stocked against emergency by most British consulates in China. Rosamond pulled the trigger instead of the bolt. Her father decided that she would be better employed bringing food and water to the defenders than in loading their rifles.

Estrangement from his father

Lance's later years were clouded by a rift with his father. As Professor Giles grew older he became more and more cantankerous both with other sinologists and with his own sons. By the early 1920s he had broken with both Bertram and Valentine. A few years later Lance also found himself estranged. He had always written regularly to his father, ever since his first arrival in China. But Professor Giles did not wish to hear about the civil wars, the chaos, anti-British demonstrations, rioting, and general disorder endemic in China in the 1920s. These had no place in the image of China which Herbert Allen Giles had conceived for himself. In 1922 the Royal Asiatic Society had acclaimed him for humanizing Chinese studies. To him in fact the Chinese became more than human: they could do no wrong. Lance began to find that his letters were being returned to him embellished with savage and critical comments by his father. The correspondence stopped. There was a complete break between father and son. Professor Giles never broke with Lionel who was at the British Museum, a man with whom it was hard to quarrel because he was unusually slow to take offence whatever the provocation—and moreover Lionel was a person whose translations from the Chinese classics portrayed a China that conformed to the image cherished by his father.

Death of Lancelot Giles

Apart from this rift, Lance's family life was exceptionally happy. He and his wife had wide and shared interests in the arts, horse racing and literature. They enjoyed their social life as leaders of the British communities in their various posts in China, and had many Chinese as well as other foreign friends in the cosmopolitan world in which they lived. He liked China and his work, and his services had been recognized by the award of a C.M.G. (Companion of the Order of St Michael and St George).

I had been in China three or four years when I first met Lance. I had heard much about him and indeed hoped to serve under him at some future date, for he was known in the Service as a good chief, a man of wide experience, sound judgment, cool in a crisis, fair and helpful to his juniors. But it was not to be. I saw him several times on visits to Tientsin where he was British Consul-General. It proved to be his last post. He died there on November the 21st 1934 after a long illness.

Professor Giles maintained the feud with his son to the end, though he had been told by his granddaughter that Lance was dying of cancer. He replied to Rosamond that he was sorry; but sent no message to Lance or to his wife in Lance's last days.

The diary

The diary now published in full for the first time (an expurgated version was sent to the *Christ College Magazine,* Cambridge, by Professor Giles in 1901) had long since come back into Lance's possession. After his death, his widow, who decided to remain in China, kept it with her. By chance she happened to be in India in December, 1941 and so avoided Japanese internment in China. The diary went with her to New Zealand and finally to Western Australia. There, in 1965, she made it available to

FOREWORD

Mr L. R. Marchant, Senior Lecturer in Chinese History in the University of Western Australia.

Its importance was immediately perceived. Mr Marchant set about the task of preparation for publication by annotating the text and by setting the siege of the Legations in the general context of the rise of anti-foreignism in China.

A great deal of work has been done by others on nineteenth-century China, on the Boxers, and on the siege of the Legations. The theme to which Mr Marchant addresses himself, however, has hitherto been comparatively neglected. Giles's lively and readable journal is an appropriate peg on which to hang a study of anti-foreignism. It is also a document worth publishing for its own intrinsic merits.

The Boxers and the Red Guards

Mr Marchant's work is timely. Never has the outside world taken such interest in events in China as in recent years, climaxed by the Red Guard movement, with so much still unexplained about the movement and with its repercussions still unpredictable.

Vastly different as the circumstances then and now are, there are nevertheless some intriguing and perhaps significant features in common between the Boxers and the Red Guards. Both emerged at a time when Chinese intellectuals were ideologically confused, when China confronted difficulties at home and pressures from abroad and when the prestige of China was on the wane—in Boxer times as a result of defeat by Japan; in Red Guard times, as a consequence of the collapse of China's Indonesian alliance and the setbacks to the world ambitions of Chinese communism. Both periods were marked by mounting anti-foreignism, in Boxer times against all foreigners, now primarily anti-Russian. Both wanted changes but both were basically Chinese racialist movements favouring Chinese isolationism. And both were against modernization copied on an alien pattern. In Boxer times an effete Manchu dynasty was nearing the end of their 'Mandate from Heaven'. In Red Guard times, the momentum of the revolution has been running down though its tasks have not been completed. Whether the Red Guard leaders were at first aware or not of the real strength and nature of their appeal, the movement seems, like the Boxer movement, to have been initially

FOREWORD

a protest against the regime or some of its policies, and evidence of discontent or at least disillusion. In both cases the more reactionary elements in the regimes, which in both cases were led by an aging ruler seeking to assure continuity of policy and to harness the forces of discontent to that end, were successful for a time in subverting the movements and exploiting them for their own political purposes against more cautious or moderate elements.

Whether the rulers of China today will in the end be any more successful than the Manchus in controlling the forces they connived at releasing, remains to be seen. For all their customary outward placidity, the Chinese are from time to time victims of mass hysteria. Lancelot Giles experienced it first during the siege of the Legations. Years later he saw it again, when mobs shouting 'kill, kill' advanced on his Consulate. The symptoms are now evident again, however different the target and the circumstances.

Peebles, Scotland
January 1967   R. H. SCOTT

INTRODUCTION

CHINESE ANTI-FOREIGNISM

DIATHESIS

It is wrong to view the last two decades of the nineteenth century primarily as an age of unbridled colonialism, which saw European powers extending almost effortlessly beyond their 'national' borders to swallow up large tracts of territories in the populous Afro-Asian world. The period, and especially the latter decade, the 1890s, was marked by violent anti-colonial agitation and outbreaks of opposition to Western 'aggressions'. The non-Western peoples did not sit idly and let the frontiers of European empires roll over and past them. Like any other peoples they had traditions, lands, livelihood and beliefs to defend, and they had no more inclinations to let the new white invaders from overseas control their societies and doctrines, than they were willing to submit to ambitious neighbours. The resistance which they put up was not as noticeable or as successful as that of the Balkan states against the Turkish overlordship at the time, but it was sufficient to reveal that European expansion into the non-Western world was fraught with the dangers of rejection and subversion.

Although the resistance offered to the colonizing West was multifarious and made up of a variety of isolated outbreaks involving a great diversity of cultural types, the records left by observers, missionaries, military men and civilian administrators who experienced the struggles at first hand, indicate that two types of opposition in particular were resorted to in an attempt to check the progress of the 'expansive' West. There was violence in the form of armed conflict and insurrection, and there was covert resistance.

Armed risings, frontier wars and other violent outbreaks aimed at eliminating the white man, came as no great surprise. They were, in fact, half expected to occur. Nevertheless, the resistance offered to the colonial powers at the end of the nineteenth century by the Ashanti in West Africa, the tribes in East and Central Africa, by insurrectionaries in Indonesia, North Borneo and northern Vietnam, as well as in a variety of other places, put the powers on the alert and tested their mettle, bringing the realization that colonial settlements would not be imposed easily in many of the territories in the non-Western world.

More disturbing and more difficult to counteract, were the covert attempts by non-Western peoples to resist the invaders. These attempts invariably began with the formation of a cult or a secret society, and ended in violent outbursts of anti-foreignism and barbarous ritualistic murders. In Central and East Africa the cult of the Leopard Men and Crocodile Men arose, aimed at ridding tribal territories there of white men and native heretics. In German East Africa there emerged an even more incomprehensible water cult among the Maji Maji who sprinkled their bodies with 'holy water' to render them safe from the bullets and shots of Westerners, whom they could then attack with impunity. In India also, neo-Hindu cults appeared, and bands practising gymnastics rose under Bal Gangadhar Tilak in a new attempt to subvert British rule; and magical cults appeared in other threatened territories.

It was in China that the most notorious anti-foreign group emerged, the Boxers, who engaged the assembled allied colonial powers in what was virtually a full-scale war. Their late appearance on the scene, just before the turn of the century, at the end of the period of large scale colonial expansion, was not accidental. Significant changes in the world situation led to rising anti-colonialism. In particular it was seen that Britain, the greatest power of all, had been humbled by a handful of Boers in South Africa, and this revealed to a wide audience that imperial powers were not invulnerable. It was as good a stimulus as any that could be offered to Asians and others.

This is an account of the Boxers and their rise to prominence against a background of anti-foreignism that swept China in a decade of imperial expansion, the 1890s, and in particular of their convergence on the foreign settlements in Tientsin and in Peking, and the siege of the Legations in China's capital; the events of which Lancelot Giles describes in his diary.

INTRODUCTION: CHINESE ANTI-FOREIGNISM

ANTI-FOREIGNISM IN CHINA

The Tradition

For the greater part of their long history, the Chinese people have always preferred to live a secluded life in their East Asian empire. They did not, of course, object to visitors coming to see them at home, and to worship the glories of Chinese civilization. In fact they expected this sort of tribute to be made. But what they did not welcome was foreign advice, and the type of newcomer who brought new ideas and ideologies and alien practices to force on the Chinese. Confucianism and the rich culture it stood for was good enough for them. Like the cultured ancient Greeks, the Chinese viewed anything which came from outside their borders, as 'barbarous' in origin, and second-rate.

This was all very well prior to the nineteenth century. China then had the power to resist. There was no state nearby that could force China to accept Indian Buddhism, or early Christianity, or Western science, each of which took time to permeate. However, in the nineteenth century significant changes took place. Chinese power declined, and the West moved into the area. It was not the old Europe, but a new one that contacted China after the Napoleonic wars. The nations that had emerged as the victors in what was really the first world war, together with their rehabilitated victims, spread into Asia with a confidence and arrogance that matched China's. They were no more willing to pay tribute to China, than China was to admit them as equals. Western might soon settled the issue. After two wars fought from 1839 to 1842 and 1856 to 1858, China submitted and engaged in new-styled treaty relations. This in itself was not disturbing. What upset matters more than anything else was that China's inland territories were opened to foreign merchants and protestant Christian missionaries, both of whom were intent on creating their own types of 'new Jerusalems', and the Chinese felt threatened. Their civilization and culture, their villages and cities were in danger of being honeycombed by 'subversive' elements on a larger scale than had ever been experienced before.

As cultural importation spread when foreign settlements and mission stations were established about the Chinese countryside, reactions came. During the 1860s and 1870s a series of violent riots, directed against Christian missionaries in particular, broke out in the various provinces. This culminated on the 23rd of June 1870 in a large-scale massacre of Christians and their converts in Tientsin, a foreign treaty port in north China. This movement was not only anti-Christian; it was also anti-foreign. Five years later the general nature of the opposition was clearly demonstrated. A British official, Margary, who was surveying a new trade route which Britain hoped to establish from India to China, was murdered in south China, apparently with official connivance; and other incidents occurred to indicate that foreign innovators were not welcome.

There is no need to trace and describe the whole course of anti-foreignism in China in order to understand the Boxer Uprising. That would take far too long, and in any case the Boxers rose in the midst of special circumstances, as will be seen, and these had few links with earlier rebels. However, if one wishes to see the Boxers in perspective, it is necessary to note that the historical records of China's dealings with 'the barbarians' indicate that anti-foreignism had certain characteristics. They show that all strata in Chinese society from top Confucian officials to uneducated peasants were involved in the incidents. Also, just as there was a variety of people involved, so was there a diversity of causes; economic, cultural, and political, inciting people who felt that their livelihood, traditions, beliefs and country were being threatened by invaders who were bringing foreign commerce and new ideas. The Chinese did not oppose foreign penetration merely because of xenophobia. Finally the records indicate that anti-foreignism was demonstrated in a number of different ways.

Causes

There were sound reasons for Chinese of all strata to become increasingly hostile to foreigners in the nineteenth century. The main cause for the rising hostility, of course, was the growth of foreign 'immigration' into the Empire. The treaties China was forced to sign with the various powers between 1842 and 1860 opened the country to a foreign invasion. Missionaries, merchants, concessionaires, arms dealers, travellers, engineers, advisers, do-gooders and a variety of others flocked to China in mounting numbers, so that by the end of the nineteenth century there were few areas left in the Empire where people had not seen 'foreign devils'.

Physical presence of unwanted people in a community is not always a constant cause of hostility. If a person feels sufficiently strong about an alien or aliens who come to stay in or visit their locality, it is quite easy to draw away from contacts and remain aloof, as many Chinese did, to avoid disturbing emotions. But in China after the treaties this was not always possible. When foreigners flocked into the country they began to leave more permanent and tangible evidences of their presence than their strangely costumed bodies. Along the coast and along China's great rivers, where treaty ports were opened, large foreign-style cities modelled in stone and concrete and lit with gas and electric light rose, like Shanghai, to contrast with the traditional walled Chinese cities that lay close-by, affecting aesthetic values. Even in the countryside, inland, where some of the more injudicious missionaries and merchants took advantage of their treaty rights to build churches and warehouses, foreign-style roofs and buildings rose to affect the architectural balance of streets and towns, and to alter skyline vistas. Missionary records, which recount the stories of the destruction of many of the foreign churches, reveal that there were widespread feelings of hostility among the local gentry about these aesthetic changes, as well as about the growing number of books on Christianity and westernization, which began to flood the country, and which were regarded by Chinese as heretical writings.

Also penetrating the country from the centres of foreign influence, and affecting wider strata of the Chinese, were the foreign trade goods that came into the markets, protected by the treaties. Steamships and steam launches and the steam locomotives and iron railroads similarly spread out from foreign commercial cities. In particular increasing imports of cotton goods from Indian, European, American and Japanese spinning mills caused rising hostility. The Chinese merchants who handled the goods, of course, were only too glad to deal in a new commodity which seemed to sell well, but the influx of foreign cloth had an effect on farmers who received some of their small incomes from selling home-spun cloth made by women-folk in the cottages. Moreover, the steam boats and steam launches which plied on the rivers and canals, and the steam trains posed a distinct threat to the livelihood of Chinese boatmen and overland porters who carried the bulk of the commercial and trade goods about China. This type of labour could of course be offered jobs constructing the railways, but they, and the Chinese gentry who were responsible for their well-being, were sufficiently clear-sighted to see that the task of rail construction would not last for the next generations, and not even for their own. Consequently some felt every reason to rebel against mechanization. The construction of railways naturally became the important issue, raising widespread reactions. There were not only economic issues involved, but cultural ones as well. The iron tracks constructed under foreign guidance were pushed through the provinces, with little regard being paid to local feelings and traditional beliefs about the spirits, and superstitious Chinese reacted to the permanent way with as much fervour as the Indian sepoys had reacted in 1857 to the suggestion that the bullets issued to them had been dipped in animal fat. There was, in fact, a lot for the Chinese to adjust to: the new noises, the new sights and the strange new smells that came with westernization.

Underlying all these causes were deep-rooted racial feelings. Little has been written about this as yet, because the facts are few. When the Boxer Uprising occurred social psychology and sociology were in their infancies and no scientist or investigator since then has attempted to make a survey of mob-violence and racial tensions in China. However, there are plenty of illustrations in nineteenth-century literature and records which indicate that there were intense and widespread racial feelings among individuals on both sides. No one party was to blame. Both Chinese and foreigners were as bad as each other when it came to racial attitudes.

WESTERN ATTITUDES TO THE CHINESE

By the mid-nineteenth century, when China was opened to foreign intercourse, the idea long held in Europe that the Chinese led a life very much like that pictured on the then fashionable willow pattern plates, had died. The Chinese from that time were no longer viewed as being highly sophisticated and cultivated scholars, with a philosophical attitude to life, as Oliver Goldsmith, Jesuit missionary writers and the French encyclopedists had portrayed them in the past. They were increasingly regarded, instead, as a static, decadent and backward people, slightly above the level of heathens in Africa and the Pacific, but who had nevertheless somehow missed out on the spirit of progress. The Chinese Empire came to be regarded by Westerners not so much as the country which produced Confucian scholars but coolies for export.

Some Western intellectuals were attracted to the Chinese and their ways of life, but these were exceedingly few. When this did occur, and the foreigner increasingly absorbed himself in Chinese things, the general consensus of opinion among his countrymen was, at the best, that he was eccentric, and at the worst that he was a traitor to the group. Unless the Chinese-attracted person resident in China was a scholar of renown, or a prominent person, he found foreign social life soon closed to him. Most of the foreigners lived their own secluded lives at their clubs, playing tennis, joining in the social whirl, cutting themselves off from overmuch intercourse with the Chinese and Europeans who had 'gone native', though not of course from the missionaries who were expected to live the lives they had chosen to lead—those of the Chinese people. The bulk of the foreigners lived in the treaty ports, and these were foreign enclaves and, at the time, were kept as such.

Feelings of racial superiority were naturally held by foreigners right throughout the treaty period, from the 1840s. Towards the end of the century, however, they intensified. There is no doubt that the changed attitudes among Europeans were contributed to in the 1890s by the influence of popular Darwinism and readable works about the origin and nature of the species, which had become a popular literary fashion as a result of the writings of atheistic scientists such as Huxley. Nations and peoples and races were seen by many as being distributed up and down a scale at the top of which was modern urban-industrial man, and in particular the Anglo-Saxons, and at the bottom of which were the Tierra del Fuegians and Australian aborigines.

This whole issue was raised in the treaty ports in 1897, on the eve of the Boxer Uprising. On the 27th August an article on 'Darwinism and China' was published in the *North China Herald*. Discussions about man's origins actually had been going on for some time before this, and Westerners on the China coast, who always wanted to be as up to date as possible, were not unaffected. They were kept constantly informed in the journals and papers they read, of scientists' and explorers' attempts to discover the 'missing link' between men and apes. In 1895 an apparent great advance was made in the quest. In that year it was revealed that a dutch scientist, Eugène Dubois, claimed to have discovered man's ancestor in Java, where he found an erect ape-man. His discovery was widely publicized at the time, and played a considerable part in sustaining the theories of the evolutionists.

Stimulated by Dubois's report, the anonymous author of 'Darwinism and China' turned the eyes of treaty-port Europeans in China closer to home than Java. Dubois's findings, he claimed, could be verified by Europeans any day on a daily walk in China. The article is worth quoting extensively, for although it reads today as if the author were participating in a glorious but ill-conceived joke, it was written in earnest. Westerners in China at the time had reasons to regard the Chinese as barbarians. Just before the article was written there had been a particularly bad series of anti-foreign riots and murders of women and children, which horrified Westerners and caused many of them to throw doubts on China's claim to being 'civilized'.

Although the author admitted that he had no evidence of the mental capacity of Chinese, which was a vital factor always looked for by those seeking the 'missing link', he drew attentions to the physical features, which were also regarded as an important characteristic. The Chinese, he pointed out, had a flat nose, and flat nose in Latin was *simus*, which summed up the most important feature of 'primitive' man. Moreover, he pointed out, the Chinese lack the sense of pain, and swim in the dog-paddle style, both of which are held in common by 'lower creatures'. More important, he went on to say:

> Many Chinese have retained vestigial control of the feet which Europeans have lost. The natural space between the great toe and the next is more marked, and the muscular power of the toe more under control. Not only can a Chinese boatman hold his oar by the toe, but he can bring enough lateral pressure to bear to be able to give a hard punch; and his baby, if the chance were given, could play five-finger exercises on his toes. Similarly the habit of walking on the outside of the foot, so noticeable in the anthropoid apes and traceable in all races of men, is very well marked in the Chinese. Observations of barefooted coolies on a damp road will prove plainly enough that the innerpart of the sole never touches the ground at all.

Moreover, apart from these physical peculiarities, the author observed to further make his point:

> Man is never nearer to the beasts than when he is angry, and probably no civilized man ever exhibits the animal nature in China more clearly under those circumstances than a Chinaman who is thoroughly infuriated. His simian ancestry have returned for the time being—it is a true case of transmigration—and transformed him into a raging beast whose eyes glare, whose mouth foams with almost as poisonous a secretion as that of a mad dog, whose snarling lips disclose the old time weapons, and whose face is redder than the glow of health ever made it. Watch him half bend himself downwards and then spring up with a jerk, his gesticulating arm and twitching fingers hardly under control: he is the very picture of an enraged anthropoid ape.

If there were 'foreigners' who read this and similar articles with a critical eye, there was, nevertheless, a widespread belief among them at the end of the nineteenth century that the Chinese were markedly different from themselves, and that there was plenty of scope for Chinese to change for the better. Indeed, feelings among foreigners in and about the treaty ports ran high and racial attitudes had hardened so considerably that by the time the Boxers appeared on the scene, the stage was set for bitter racial troubles. Many of the foreigners had little hesitation to chastise the Chinese, whom they appeared to like and respect no more than the earlier Christians liked the Moors and the Turks.

CHINESE ATTITUDES TO WESTERNERS

Feelings of superiority and racial antipathy were not confined to Europeans in China. If these people attempted to place the Chinese on the evolutionary scale, and regard them as examples of 'primitive' and 'backward' races, the Chinese, for the most part, had already fixed foreigners in their position among the ranks of peoples seen in the Middle Kingdom. Europeans were regarded as 'barbarians', uncouth in manner, strange in appearance and believing in what appeared to be little more than weird doctrines; and as such they were naturally viewed as an inferior type of person.

There is no need to look at all the racial incidents in China to see how deep and widespread the feelings of suspicion about foreigners were throughout the nineteenth century. Chinese contempt can be readily measured by the uncomplimentary names they used for Westerners. In the streets, and in placards and books it was the usual thing for foreigners to see and hear themselves referred to as 'barbarians', *i jen,* or 'foreign devils', *yang kwei tzu,* or even 'red-headed', *hung mao,* 'big-nosed', *ta pi,* barbarians, to illustrate their physical peculiarities. The Western powers, of course, insisted in their treaties that such terms be dropped, but they were only successful in preventing their use in official documents. The children in the streets and the disturbed populace were more difficult to control, as the British were finding out for themselves at home, when residents in Limehouse developed their own hostile reactions to the Chinese emigrants there.

One of the best indications of what the Chinese felt about Europeans has come down not in street name-calling, but in the permanent phrase for Europe in the Chinese dictionary. There was no term for Europe when the modern West came to China. In such cases, when a term has to be invented, the Chinese take a phonetic which sounds like the name of the country, or just the first syllable of that name, and then add to it the term *kuo,* for country or nation. Thus England or Britain became *Ying-kuo* (Heroic Country), America became *Mei-kuo* (Beautiful Country) and so on. Each of the national states seemed to have watched their own interests in this regard, getting a name that suited them. But, in the days between the Holy Roman Empire and the present Common Market, there did not seem to be any nation or European patriot who was prepared to watch the interests of Europe as a whole. In any case, whatever the reason, the Chinese selected and used a vile term, *ou,* meaning vomit or diarrhoea, as a phonetic, so that Europe became *Ou-kuo,* the meaning of which was plain to everyone. Admittedly, in Chinese there are few words which have the sound *ou* or *oo,* but the Chinese did have some choice and all of them were more acceptable in meaning than the one selected.

Name-calling of this sort, and general demonstrations of contemptuous feelings, according to reports of travellers, merchants, missionaries and diplomats in China, were widespread and deeply affected Europeans who found it difficult in the age of imperialist and jingoist sentiments to shrug the matter off.

By far more scurrilous descriptions of Europeans and attacks on their way of life and their standing in human society were made in the series of anti-Christian publications that became increasingly numerous as the century progressed. The bulk of the anti-Christian and anti-European works drew their inspiration and ideas in particular from a vile publication known as *The Death Blow to Corrupt Doctrines (Pi-hsieh chi-shieh)*. This work presents a very weird and derogatory view of Europeans. The author does not only seek to attack foreign beliefs, but also endeavours to explain the peculiar qualities of the Europeans, which descriptions were as wide off the mark as were the suggestions made by the author of 'Darwinism and China'. The peculiar smell that Europeans have, the book stated, comes as a result of European men's practice of drinking women's menstrual flow. Other even stranger and more scurrilous descriptions were given of other European characteristics. The work claimed that medicines used and sold by Europeans were made from children's eyes and testicles. Moreover, when describing European moral behaviour, the author of the book stated that it was the normal custom in Europe to place a plug in the anus of new-born babies, not only to retain a 'ritual essence', but also to dilate the orifice and facilitate sodomy.

The most serious attacks, however, were made on Christian beliefs and ritual. The most prevalent attack was on the name 'Jesus'. In Chinese the term used for the Christian Son of God, *yeh*, is homophonous with the term for pig and it is invariably the latter character that was used for 'Jesus'. Christian liturgy was also ridiculed. There is a long descriptive passage in the book describing Christian liturgy and revealing that after the chants the congregation broke up to copulate together. It was widely circulated views such as these that affected Chinese villagers and town people and aroused their hostility to encroaching missionaries and Europeans.

One might find basis for several of the stories which circulated. Any Chinese who read the rudimentary translations of the Old Testament, which is not noted for its description of pure living, could see that this was not a classic to be followed in the manner of Confucius' moral works. The Christian Church left the compilation of a fully annotated Bible quite late in China, and suffered as a result a great number of literary attacks by intellectuals and the not so wise. Moreover, foreigners in the treaty ports did not always live a life of moral rectitude. They had their weaknesses and sinned. But they were no more as weird because of this, as the anti-Christian works claimed, than the Chinese were 'primitive' because they swam in the dog-paddle style.

It was this type of prejudice, passed on by means of rumour and chatter, and based on misinformation that led to the increasing friction between the Chinese and the Westerners. This does not mean, of course, that racial tensions were building up consistently throughout the century in such a manner that a bursting point was reached. Outbursts were more associated with pressures that were imposed on China rather than being the result of some natural law of progress. What the prejudices and racial views did was to intensify racial feelings and provide a ready made situation for a bitter struggle between anti-foreign Chinese and national-minded Westerners when the time came.

TYPES OF CHINESE ANTI-FOREIGNISM

Chinese reactions to the variety of pressures and changes made by Westerners in China were not confined to any one course. During the nineteenth century, in fact, there were three distinct types of anti-foreignism in China. The most positive and noticeable manifestation was, of course, in the form of violence and terrorism directed against individual foreigners, groups of foreigners or the foreign community as a whole. Besides this, as has been indicated above, there was a more sophisticated type in the form of literary attacks in books and pamphlets and placards, which for the most part was confined to the scholar class of Chinese. Finally, there were passive methods of resistance. Methods of this sort of resistance are legion. There are any number of ways a person can deal with an unwanted guest. Turning a cold shoulder, a sly glance, a smirk, a rude gesture, a boycott and the cautious avoidance of any physical contact can all play a part, and all were used in China by anti-foreign elements to make Europeans feel uncomfortable in their new environment.

INTRODUCTION: CHINESE ANTI-FOREIGNISM

PRELUDE IN SOUTH CHINA

Although increasing foreign pressures in the northern part of China after 1895, as will be seen below, led to a rise of anti-foreign feelings and increasing disturbances, it was in the south that the real prelude to the Boxer Uprising occurred. There in the populous provinces in the Yangtze River and West River basins, early pressures by European colonial powers gave rise to widespread and bitter movements throughout the decade from 1886 to 1896, aimed at eliminating the encroaching foreigners. Of course, there had been troubles before this in Tientsin in 1870 and in Yunnan where Margary was murdered in 1875, as has been indicated. But the risings which occurred in the next decade, which saw mounting imperialist expansion in Asia, were of unprecedented magnitude and revealed to foreigners in general the precariousness of their position in China.

Much the same sort of causes stirred up the Sino-Western conflicts in the south as later led to the trouble in the north. The main reason for trouble, in the first instance, was European colonial expansion at China's expense. Between 1884 and 1886 both Britain and France absorbed territories that were traditionally in China's 'sphere of influence'. Tongking, now part of northern Vietnam, was conquered and added to the French Empire after a war with China between 1884 and 1886, and further west Britain, not to be outdone by France, conquered and absorbed Upper Burma, thus bringing both expansionist powers to reach China's southern borders. Not content with colonial expansion, economic penetration followed. Treaties and agreements gained by both countries from China gave Britain and France the right to build railways in China, to open new trading stations, to develop mines, to exploit China's mineral resources and her overland and river trade routes. Moreover, at the same time, there was growing pressure being exerted by Christian missionaries who were taking an increasing interest in China's social and political reformation. Chinese resistance naturally followed, at first on the border areas where the threat was greatest, and then, as Western pressures and influence grew, trouble spread inland. Although each disturbance had its own local causes and its own characteristic form, there were, broadly speaking, two sorts of anti-foreign uprisings in south China:

those directed against foreigners in general and those directed in particular at Christians and the Christian faith.

Anti-foreign riots

The first major disturbance in the south during the age of imperial expansion occurred at Chungking, Szechuan province, in July 1886, when the British Consulate and other foreign buildings were destroyed by a mob. Although some diplomatic officials at the time felt that the Consulate was lost because it had been built too close to Christian missions, the evidence suggests that although Christians were attacked, the reasons for this riot were political. Rumours were circulating about Chungking at the time that foreign merchants were coming to open up the province in accordance with new treaty rights acquired by the French, and the Szechuanese took action to see that the area stayed closed. The troubles soon simmered down when it became apparent that the rumour was not a fact. Indeed, it was not until the end of the nineteenth century that foreign pressures became noticeable there. But this was not the case in the lower Yangtze. Before the memory of Chungking died away other more startling outbreaks occurred. In February 1889 the foreign concession and consulates at Chinkiang were destroyed and plundered. There was no loss of life on this occasion, but this was only because the foreigners were quickly evacuated on to British ships in the river. Evidence about the causes of the riot is conflicting, but there is no doubt that it was brought about by the British use of Sikh police and British police methods in the concession area which they wanted to keep free of Chinese.

Shortly afterwards a similar outbreak occurred at Hankow. On this occasion the rioters were led by students who objected to the foreigners' policy of preventing Chinese citizens from freely entering the concession areas, which they claimed was Chinese territory. This disturbance which broke out under the very eyes of the Governor-General of the two Hu provinces (Hunan and Hupeh), who lived across the river in Wuchang, was put down with little more than feelings being injured. Elsewhere, however, new riots occurred which had a somewhat different complexion and purpose.

Anti-Christian riots

Already before the consulates and concessions were attacked, anti-foreign elements in south China were directing their attention to Christian converts and missionaries. The basic causes of the trouble were two-fold: the spread of unfounded anti-Christian rumours and the establishment of Christian orphanages.

In 1888 a significant rising occurred at Canton. The main object of the Chinese mob was the French Catholic orphanage which was saved from destruction by quick action by Chinese and French officials. There was perhaps some justification for Chinese concern about this and other Christian orphanages at the time, although, of course, there was no need for mob violence. Christian orphanages in Europe and China at the end of the nineteenth century were not noted for their public relations, and their secretiveness and their insistence on working behind high closed walls encouraged the growth of wild stories. Moreover, the actions of missionaries engaged in orphanage work in China were carried out in a highly suspicious manner. Children were gathered up in questionable circumstances, sometimes without parental consent. No doubt this was the best for the child concerned, but such practices did lead to trouble. More important, many of the children who were taken into orphanages seemed to have been in bad health, and as a result the death rate was high. Chinese observers, such as in Canton in 1888, were consequently concerned about seeing Chinese children going into a foreign mission, disappearing from view, and baskets of bodies coming out the back way. It gave some sort of credence to the views presented in anti-foreign works such as the *Death Blow to Corrupt Doctrines*, that children's organs were being used to make the medicines sold in the prescription rooms attached to the Christian mission stations.

The Christian attraction to orphans was not the only cause of trouble in the south, although orphanages and children were the cause of most of the riots. The Chinese also demonstrated and rioted, as on other occasions, in order to protect their culture from missionaries who were pressing foreign ideas and a foreign ideology on their congregations and on crowds of Chinese in the Empire. There is also evidence to suggest that secret societies, in particular the anti-Manchu *Kao Lao Hui* (Elder Brothers' Society) were at work, organizing attacks on foreign missionaries

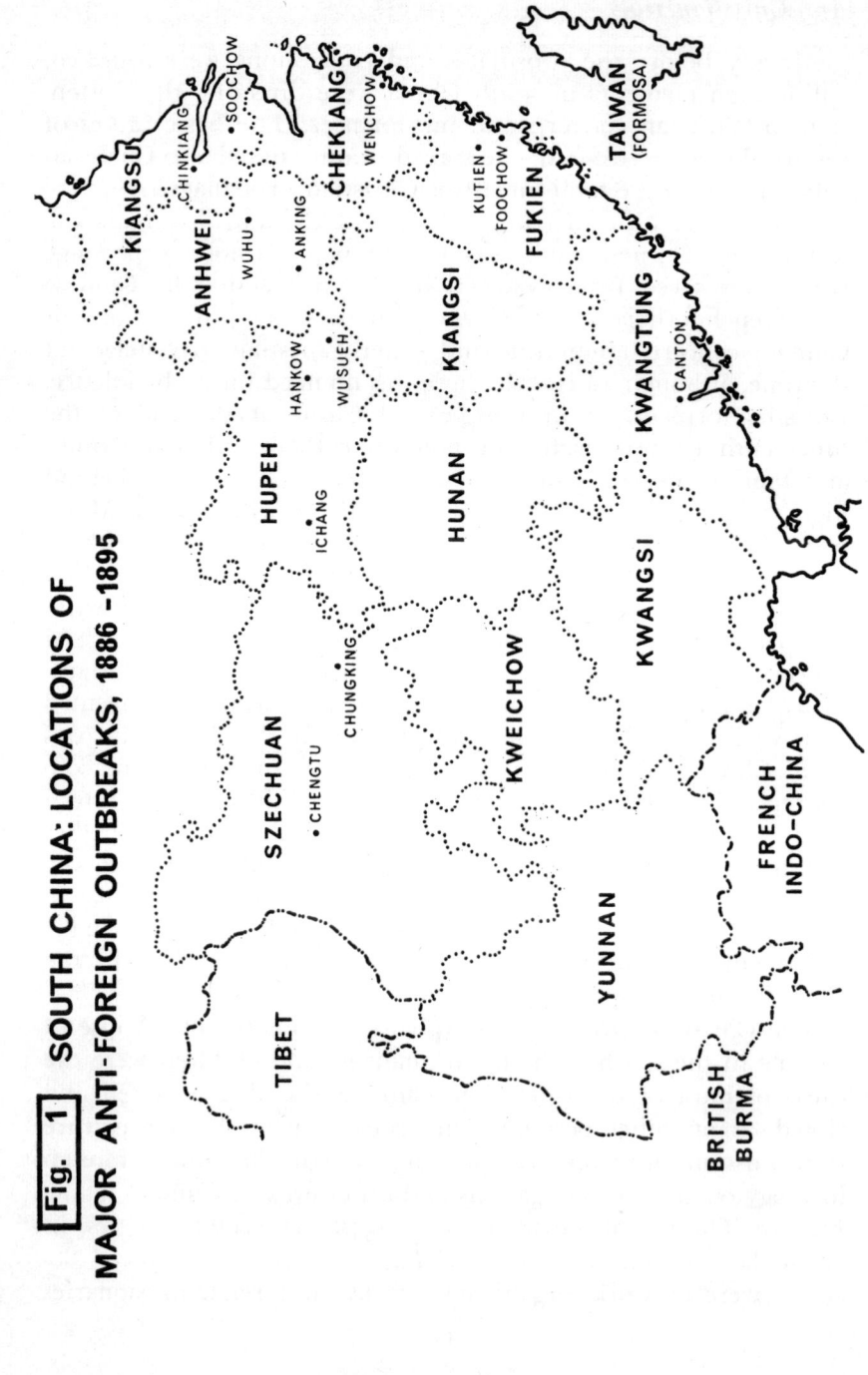

Fig. 1 SOUTH CHINA: LOCATIONS OF MAJOR ANTI-FOREIGN OUTBREAKS, 1886-1895

and converts, so as to embarrass the Chinese government in the eyes of the foreign powers, and thus hasten the fall of the dynasty.

Whatever the causes, the riots spread and became increasingly violent. In May and June 1891 there were uprisings in Christian mission districts on the Yangtze from Ichang to the coast. In the June of that year a particularly bad outbreak occurred at the port of Wusueh where the first British lives were lost, again starting over the question of orphans and their treatment. The situation for the rest of the year seemed so serious that the British Admiral in charge of the China Station wrote home warning his government that the Yangtze seemed about to erupt in a 'general conflagration', and called for naval reinforcements to help him preserve peace and protect the treaty ports. Riots continued in 1892, in Szechuan and lower down the Yangtze River, and in 1893. In the following year there was some respite, but in 1895 a further considerable anti-foreign rebellion broke out in Szechuan and a large-scale massacre of Christian missionaries occurred at Kutien, Fukien province, where anti-foreign feelings were stimulated in great part by the Japanese victories over China together with the fear of increased foreign pressure. This had similarly moved the Chinese at Chungking on a previous occasion, nearly ten years before, when the French and British made their gains at China's expense.

Results of the troubles in the south

The rise and then the suppression of anti-foreignism in the south brought to notice four important facts about disturbances and riots that were occurring in the age of imperial expansion, which help pave the way to an understanding of the later Boxer affair. First, the southern provinces found that rioting did not pay. Officials there were forced to make considerable reparations when the incidents were over, and this knowledge, that anti-foreign provinces and territories would be forced to make amends, played no small part in keeping the south quiet at the time the Boxers rose. The southern provinces, in fact, remained peaceful until the rebellion of 1911. Second, to further encourage tranquillity, the Western powers who sent significant naval reinforcements to patrol China's rivers in the early 1890s, revealed that they would not hesitate to move forces into Chinese territory to protect their interests, if China failed in that task. Third, the various Western powers further revealed that despite differences that existed between them at home, they were more than ready to submerge these in East Asia and form a united front to deal with China. Finally, in the face of these changes, there emerged in China a group of Chinese officials who sought to suppress anti-foreignism in its more violent forms in order to avoid the impending dangers, and who sought to impress on their colleagues the virtues and gains that could be had from moderate policies. It was moderate officials of this type in the north who, drawing on these experiences, later tried—unsuccessfully as we shall see—to control Boxer and Manchu hotheads.

THE TROUBLES IN THE NORTH

While rioters were on their final rampage in the southern provinces, trouble was already flaring in the north. From 1894 onwards there were disconcerting reports of serious and persistent outbreaks of anti-foreignism in and about the metropolitan provinces which were situated in the proximity of the capital city, Peking.

Prior to this the north had been relatively free of anti-foreign disturbances. There had been demonstrations of anti-foreign feeling, but the only serious large-scale outbreak to occur was the Tientsin affair in 1870. This absence of trouble was not because Chinese in the north were quieter and more tolerant, or because they were closer to the watchful eye of officials in the capital. There were Chinese in the metropolitan provinces as anti-foreign and as xenophobic as groups in any other part of China. The real reason for the small-scale size of early outbreaks, which before 1895 were in the main in the form of personal attacks on individuals, and their infrequency, was that the greater part of the north had not then been opened to foreign intercourse as were the southern provinces, and the pressures there were fewer. There were, for instance, only three relatively small treaty ports north of the Yangtze in 1897—Newchwang in Manchuria, Tientsin in Chihli province, and Chefoo in Shantung province—compared with twenty-one open ports and a number of other consular stations in the south. Moreover, besides there being few open ports, there were also few Christian mission stations north of the Yangtze. Like the merchants, Christian missionaries up to the 1890s confined the greater part of their attention to the southern provinces, which provided sufficient work.

Emergent anti-foreign problems, 1894-95

Two events brought a sudden change to this situation and led to a large-scale foreign 'invasion' of the north, which paved the way for the rise of anti-foreign elements such as the Boxers.

First, and most important as far as anti-foreignism was concerned, the protestant Christian churches decided to hold a celebration in 1895 to mark the centenary of their establishment among the Chinese. This celebration took the form of 'a great forward movement' which had the aim of taking the Christian message to within the reach of every Chinese in the Empire. Preparations for the movement were already made in 1892. Special funds were collected and earmarked; missionaries were recruited and widespread interest was raised. In 1895 and during the following years, Christian missionaries who were eager to help China strengthen itself and reform, poured into the previously unexploited territories in north China. Every stratum of Chinese society was affected: the poor, the unhealthy, the educated and the rich. Most significantly some of the protestants who were engaged in the expansion took an active interest in China's social and political problems, engaging themselves in reform movements. Not unnaturally, both the educated and illiterate strata in China saw the new foreign preachers as the vanguard of foreign powers who were seeking to destroy Chinese culture in the political centre of the Empire, the metropolitan provinces.

Second, in 1894 Japan went to war with China and badly defeated her. On the 17th of April 1895 China signed a humiliating peace treaty. By this, concessions were made to Japan and these were subsequently claimed by the other foreign powers under the most-favoured nation clauses in their treaties with China, thus paving the way for further foreign penetration in the northern provinces, where the different powers commenced to base themselves.

There was also a third change in the situation in the north which is worth noting. The Sino-Japanese War was confined to the metropolitan provinces. Britain, which had significant interests in south China, made it quite clear to Japan that she would take action against her if hostilities were extended below the Yellow River, and consequently the armies of warring China and Japan at least were confined to the north. Large areas in the region as a result were devastated by the forces which fought and which had to be fed and maintained. Besides this, the northern provinces were subjected to occupation troops. Economic dislocations in north China soon followed as happens in the case of the aftermath of most wars. Commodities were scarce, food was hard to obtain and inflation set in. There seems to have been an increase of some 15 per cent in prices in north China in the war years, which may not appear much on paper, but these caused considerable hardships among the subsistance farmers and wage earners who were no more happy with the changing economic situations than they were with defeat and occupation. Few Chinese had cause to thank the foreigners who were coming into the country.

The anti-foreign feeling that emerged in 1894 and 1895 was not directed solely against the 'yellow dwarfs', as the Japanese were called. There certainly was a great deal of anti-Japanese propaganda and boycotts, but some of this feeling was displaced to other non-Chinese races.

It was the foreign Christian missionaries in particular who became a butt for anti-foreign agitators both during and after the war. To many of the local inhabitants in the north coastal provinces, where attack was threatened, there seemed to be little desire to make a distinction between Japanese and European Christians. They were both alien. Missionaries, in fact, were regarded on a number of occasions as the advance guard of a foreign invasion. There was no foundation for this belief. The missionaries may have been imprudent enough to preach to the Chinese about the coming of the 'new Jerusalem' and of the coming occupation of their country by 'the soldiers of Christ', which were currently fashionable sermon themes, but they certainly did not consciously encourage any military attack on the Chinese Empire. However, there were many Chinese who seemed to be ready to believe the wild rumours that spread, and to make up some of their own. In Shantung, for instance, stories spread about Christian missionaries importing and concealing cannon, and stockpiling straw for the use of cavalry forces which would invade the country. Such charges were always investigated by Chinese officials on the spot and invariably proved foundless.

The cannon turned out to be the new-style galvanized iron stove pipes, and the straw which was taken into mission stations was for thatching, and for use in Christian handicraft industries; but the suspicions and anti-Christian feeling continued unchecked even after the occupation by Japan was over.

Post war anti-foreignism, 1895-97

If it was events in the Sino-Japanese War that established the basis for an upsurge of anti-foreignism in north China, it was happenings in the post-war years that brought matters to a head, and created the situation where Boxers could flourish and spread.

Peace and normal living did not return readily in the north China provinces. The main problem was the Chinese armies which had fought the Japanese, and were no longer needed. With the establishment of peace these were disbanded, as was the Chinese custom. Consequently, from the early part of the northern summer 1895, when the armies were dispersed, there was in the area a large number of former soldiers with their pay in arrears and little money, and few prospects for a quick return home or assistance to resettle themselves. As a result there were outbreaks of brigandage, an increase in the crime rate, outbreaks of attacks on foreigners, and an upsurge of activities in secret societies which had taken advantage of the large gatherings of men in the armed forces to recruit members and spread ideas. These dissident elements did not hesitate to turn their attentions to the growing problem of expanding Christianity whose missionaries were multiplying rapidly in north China in the years of peace. Ex-servicemen have always been a problem in China, and the years after 1895 proved to be no exception.

Besides the problem of disbanded armies, made worse by a series of bad farming seasons, there was an added worry for Chinese officials and people. When Japan made peace with China the Western powers began to press for concessions. Once China was defeated and her weaknesses revealed, the Western powers led by France made a series of demands for trading rights, special privileges, railway and mining concessions and changes in the Chinese government. Attracted by the spoils, the powers were soon fighting like jackals about a corpse. Taking advantage of differences among the powers, and playing a skilful diplomatic game, China managed to resist these for several years. But in

1897 and 1898 China suffered what appeared to be a second collapse.

The heightening of tension, 1897-98

Although the apparent threat by colonial powers to dissect China had passed by 1897, in the following two years there was a resurgence of diplomatic activity and pressure in Peking, and an increase in foreign penetration which revealed the inability of the Ch'ing government to stave off effectively a 'quiet' invasion. This increase in foreign activity again affected the north in particular, and made certain that the provinces there could not readily return to a state of tranquility.

The most important event was the murder of two German Catholic missionaries in the village of Yen Chow in Shantung province on November the 1st 1897. Shantung, the birthplace of Confucius, had been the centre of anti-foreign and anti-Christian activity ever since the Sino-Japanese War (1894-95), and the murders came as no surprise. Reactions were quick and startling. Germany demanded a concession of territory as compensation.

The German Admiralty for some time had been trying to establish a naval base in East Asia, to meet the needs of their growing navy and empire. The closest base they had to China in 1897 was in South America, and this was too distant to be of use in the growing power struggle in East Asia. Opportunities to secure territories, however, were limited. There were few vacant lands. The murder of the German missionaries came at an opportune moment. On November the 14th, with the Kaiser's approval, Rear-Admiral von Diedrichs occupied Kiaochow Bay in Shantung province, and ordered the Chinese to withdraw. This was a skilful diplomatic move as far as Germany was concerned. She did not only gain her naval base in a strategic part of China, in the metropolitan provinces, but also dealt a blow to the French monopoly of protecting Catholic missions, which France had been charged by the Vatican to do. But although clever, it was not wholly wise. The Chinese were touchy about Shantung, as touchy as Christians were about the Holy Land, and they had no desire to see 'infidels' established in the historic old state of Lu, where Confucius' ancestors had been born and lived. As a result there was a rising tirade of hate and violence against Christian missionaries and the Germans. This anti-foreign feeling soon developed as other powers joined in a race for naval bases in China. Russia grabbed Port Arthur, Britain took Weiheiwei in Shantung province to balance the naval power, and Italy was hovering while France took a base in the south, at Kwangchowan, each causing protests and disturbances.

The situation was actually not so bad as anti-foreign elements in China pictured. When naval bases were grabbed the West was not 'carving up' China, nor were they intending to do so at that stage. Politicians in Europe realized that any attempt to make a colony out of China or parts of it, except in the case of some of the outlying tributary states, would be difficult and exhausting. Consequently their territorial demands were minimal. Moreover, the bases they gained in China were not real concessions. Unlike on previous occasions, the powers in 1897 and 1898 could not get territory alienated to them by China. They had to accept leases which had rather stringent conditions. The Chinese government at the time, in fact, was sufficiently strong and purposeful to lay down terms which showed that the areas 'conceded' were no more than new treaty ports which remained Chinese territory in which there was maintained some form of Chinese administration. In Kiaochow, Weiheiwei and the other places, however, foreign forces, ships and administrators flocked in, giving ample evidence of a foreign invasion to the local populace, who were not interested in the subtleties that existed in the legal documents and treaties.

Besides the grab for bases, there was at the same time a noticeable increase in foreign economic penetration by Westerners in the northern Chinese provinces. After the Sino-Japanese War, in an attempt to make China strong, reconstruction was commenced, and side by side with this development foreign commerce grew.

As soon as peace was established, foreign businessmen began to move in to take advantage of the newly opened and growing markets. Foreign trade in the treaty ports grew enormously. Between 1896 and 1900 foreign trade at the port of Newchwang almost doubled and there were increases that were almost comparable at the ports of Tientsin and Chefoo. The major increase was in foreign imports into China, in particular cotton goods. This resulted in disturbances in areas where Chinese manufactured cotton, and in farm areas where cotton spinning was a cottage industry.

In such rural areas the farmers, on the eve of the Boxer Uprising, were having a hard enough time as it was, trying to contend with rising living costs and inflationary tendencies, without having to feel that they were competing with foreign imports.

Equally important, as far as foreign economic penetration was concerned, were the concessionaires. When the north was opened after 1895, and Chinese officials turned to strengthen their country, foreign investors crowded into Tientsin and Peking, seeking to secure contracts to open mines, build railways, construct industries and exploit the resources of the north in general. Chinese officials soon succumbed to the pressures brought by the concessionaires and the governments of the foreign powers who backed them up, and a battle for concessions quickly commenced, with many of the newly arrived promoters emerging successful with attractive contracts to build up the metropolitan provinces. Railways were started, mines were opened, warehouses were constructed inland side by side with engineering works to keep the lines of communication in motion, which soon stretched from the foreign settlements in Tientsin and Shantung to the inland.

Railways caused most of the trouble and upsets in the north of China. These did not only disturb those with national sentiments. Local transport workers were also worried about the coming competitions of the railways; superstitious farmers and villagers were concerned about the iron roads which affected the spirits and the graveyards of their ancestors, and those who worried about foreign invasion saw the new railway lines as a deep-laid plot to make inland China quickly accessible from the foreign bases on the coast.

The foreign impact on the capital

But what also affected the northerners was the fact that Peking after 1896 rapidly became the centre for Western concessionaires. Peking had never been an open city. For more than forty years the Chinese had resisted attempts to convert the capital into a trading centre or treaty port.[1] All that had been allowed there officially, as a result of the treaties, was a Legation Quarter inhabited by diplomats and their dependants, although missionaries soon moved in and established themselves about the city.

[1] All foreign concession areas in China, whether inland or on the coast, were called treaty ports.

The influx of successful concessionaires after 1896 served as a further indication of China's plight, and further revealed the inability of the Ch'ing government to cope with the foreign problem and maintain China's dignity.

There were other evidences of Western intrusion into the capital, which caused more anxiety than economic pressures. After the war of 1895 many Chinese showed a desire to reform the country and strengthen it to meet foreign threats. This reform movement, as has been related, provided many protestant Christian missionaries with an opportunity to establish themselves, and they gathered in Peking where they felt better able to influence matters at the national level. There, in the capital, translations of Western books and pamphlets were circulated, Western knowledge and sciences were taught, discussion clubs were opened, journals and newspapers were started and sermons with political themes were given, all of which affected traditional life in the city. The most active of these protestant Christians was the Welsh missionary Timothy Richard. He epitomized the then new type of Christian mission worker appearing in China at the time. Like the early Jesuits he aimed at the top officials, working on reform-minded bureaucrats and the young Emperor himself. The trouble was men such as Timothy Richard made no secret of the fact that they aimed not only at reforming the Chinese state, but also at replacing it with a Christian version, which, they claimed, was the only way to meet effectively the challenges of modern life. There was naturally a number of Chinese who did not whole-heartedly share this view, and who viewed with alarm the apparent rise of Christian influence in the Imperial City.

REFORM AND REACTION

By June 1898 the apparently foreign-inspired reform party was well entrenched in Peking. The conservatives centred about the Emperor's aunt, Tzu Hsi, the Empress Dowager who was without doubt the most important political figure in China at the time. Acting imprudently and ignoring the desires of the Empress Dowager, the Emperor Kuang Hsu together with the reformers led by a modern Confucian thinker, K'ang Yu-wei, issued a series of reform decrees that startled bureaucrats, moderates and conservatives throughout the Empire. These came out without cease for three months, seeking to sweep away the old and replace the new. Early in September the reformers made an ill-advised move. They arranged for Timothy Richard, the Baptist reformer, to come to Peking where he urged the reform party to take foreign advisers. Events then proceeded rapidly. Rumours were spread about the reformers and their foreign views, and the Christian threat to the Empire. The conservatives then gathered closer about the Empress Dowager, and overtures were made by them to the powerful northern army under Yuan Shih-k'ai, who himself seemed to be a reformer, to come to the aid of the Empress Dowager's party, with the result that on September the 30th a successful coup was made by the conservatives in Peking and the young Emperor, Kuang Hsu, was removed from power, and the reformers were hunted down and executed or exiled.

Foreigners gained little from this exercise in reform and reaction. Christians obviously emerged from the situation with a bad name. There was also a deep suspicion among Chinese officials about the Western powers and Britain in particular. The Empress Dowager had never been a favourite with foreigners. They had always shown a marked preference for the young reform monarch, and there was a genuine fear by conservatives in Peking that the West would move to re-establish the Emperor on his lost throne. As a result of this fear there was a rise in anti-foreign agitation about the Legation Quarter and throughout the capital in the latter part of 1898, and matters became so serious that the treaty powers moved up armed guards to protect their Legations and officials. This was the first time that armed forces of the foreign powers had moved to Peking in times of peace. Admittedly they were few in number. There were no more than 115 guards involved.[1] But they were certainly not welcome and their presence in Peking did not temper feelings, although it was reported by foreigners that the sight of foreign bayonets served to restore some semblance of order and brought a halt to anti-foreign attacks.

THE RISE OF THE BOXERS

However, even though news about the capital was disturbing, it was in Shantung, the front line between China and the foreign

[1] Sixty-six Russian, 30 German and 25 British guards arrived in Peking in October 1898 on special duty.

powers, where the Boxer sect rose. There is no need to go far back into the history of the movement, as some historians do, to understand the Boxers at the end of the nineteenth century. They certainly had likenesses to other secret societies existing in previous centuries. But the modern Boxers stood out as a special group which rose to prominence as a reaction to events occurring in China in the late 1890s. If the fortunes of the Manchu dynasty and of China had not deteriorated in so marked a manner in that decade, it is doubtful if Boxers would have appeared on the scene in such a dramatic manner.

The *I Ho Ch'uan*, or Society of Harmonious Fists, or as Westerners called them, the Boxers, was one of a number of secret societies which appeared in the northern provinces in the disturbed period after 1895. They seem to have been connected in some way with two older and more famous societies, the Big Sword Society, *Ta Tung Hui*, and the White Lily Sect, *Pai Lien Chiao*, which were patriotic, pro-Chinese and anti-Manchu, for the ruling dynasty in China, we must remember, was foreign just like the Westerners.[1] In any case, whether or not they were linked with other more famous secret societies, Boxers appeared on the scene after the Sino-Japanese War and were mentioned as existing and stirring up trouble in Shantung from the early months of 1898.

Boxers and their practices and beliefs

There is no conclusive evidence to show the composition of these forces. Some Buddhist and Taoist priests who were inclined towards mysticism were involved, but the bulk of the adherents appeared to have been illiterate rural and town people of lower strata, who were concerned with local problems. According to accounts of observers who experienced Boxer attacks, and who surveyed bodies in the field, the bands were made up mostly of youths. There were only two other noticeable characteristics about the Boxers. First, unlike the case of most other major rebellions in China, there was no one clear leader standing out as a rallying point. The cult seemed to spread like a plague, infecting villages and localities in turn. Second, unlike other secret societies, there was a great emphasis placed on public ritual

---

[1] The Manchus, a non-Chinese people from north of the Great Wall, conquered China in 1644 and ruled the Empire until 1912 when they were overthrown.

and exercises which helped secure the *I Ho Ch'uan* their Western nickname of Boxers.

Ritual and magic played a significant part in the Boxer sect. It was in this way, by means of public trances and magical displays that the Boxers gained their widespread support among the superstitious population. Consequently, in order to better understand their success in getting adherents, it is as well to look at Boxer methods of initiation.

The Boxer recruit, once he was attracted to the cult, was put through two set stages before he became a fully fledged society man. First he became 'an initiate', learning the incantations and tricks of the trade, and then, when sufficiently entranced, he was regarded as being 'under the spell'. Once this stage was reached he was regarded as being immune from bullets and shells, which it was claimed would bounce off the true Boxer's body. Thus equipped, he was ready to join the fight to save China and its traditional beliefs from foreigners and native 'heretics' such as Christian converts.

Methods of induction varied according to the locality. But invariably large initiation and induction meetings were held in assembly halls, *lu,* which were rather akin to Buddhist temples, and in public squares. At these meetings, which must have had quite a magical effect on those attending, it was claimed that divine powers descended on all present, so that 'the spirit soldiers' would multiply. It was difficult for anyone to stand aloof. Unbelievers seem to have been regarded as little better than traitors, and significant pressures by Boxers were brought to bear on local peoples, which paved the way for a widespread reign of terror. In the late 1890s it was virtually impossible for any Chinese in the north to raise his voice against the new cult.

Boxer members were easy to detect. They donned a special garb, rather like that of another secret sect, the Red Lantern Society. On their head they wore red turbans or caps, and to this they added a sash or scarf of the same colour, which gave a bloodthirsty appearance. They were armed with primitive weapons, mostly consisting of knives and long swords and old fashioned firearms. But of course, armed as they were with magical powers, there was no reason for them to fight the Westerners on the Westerners' terms, with modern arms.

The Boxers' main aim was to rid China of foreigners and foreign influence. Although they always opposed Christianity and Europeans, their prime purpose, in the first instance, like many other Chinese political secret societies, was to evict the alien Manchus from the Dragon Throne, and bring an end to the Ch'ing dynasty which seemed incapable of preserving the Chinese Empire intact. By 1899, however, due to encouragement given to them by the Manchus to save their own skins, the Boxers were turned to direct their attacks solely against the 'foreign devils' from overseas. These, they increasingly believed, were the source of China's ills.

Boxer anti-Christian beliefs and anti-foreign attitudes from that time on are well described in a number of placards and poems which were circulated in the north between 1898 and 1900. Foreigners were blamed for a number of evils: the poor state of the crops in China, the constant droughts which were occurring in the north, the poverty and a number of other bad happenings. The following wall placard, which was pasted up in Shantung, gives as good a description as any of their general feelings:

> The Roman Catholic and protestant religions have ruined and destroyed Buddhism. Their adherents have insulted the gods and holy areas, and do not observe the law of Buddha. They have irritated heaven, and in consequence no rain has fallen. Eight millions of spiritual soldiers will be sent down from heaven to sweep away the foreigners. There has only been a fine rain. It will not be long before the soldiers will be aroused to action, and there will be a calamity among the military and people. The Buddhist religion and the society of 'Righteous Harmony' can protect the Empire and give peace and tranquillity to the people. Whoever sees this placard and distributes six copies of it will thereby prevent a calamity to one hundred. The circulation of ten copies of it will prevent a calamity to a village. Those who see this placard and do not circulate it will commit a crime punishable by decapitation. If foreigners are not swept away no rain will fall. If there are any who have taken the foreigners' poisonous medicine they should eat seven black plums, and take five mace [ounces] of *tu chang* [a climbing plant with black spotted stalks and leaves] and seven mace of *mao tsao* [a medicinal herb]. This spiritual prescription should be steamed in water and then taken.[1]

Thus with the help of the gods and popular characters in Chinese historical fiction who were regarded almost like gods,

---

[1] United States 56th Congress. *House Documents.* I Foreign Relations 1900, pp. 123-4.

the Boxers aimed to exterminate foreigners, remove the railway tracks, pull up the telegraph poles and destroy the steamers that were coming in, and preserve the old ways of life.[1]

Boxerism in Shantung, 1898-99

It was Shantung, the province where foreign pressures were the greatest, that first experienced Boxer violence. There is no evidence that the sect was responsible for the murder of the German missionaries, which took place before the German occupation of Kiaochow. But the situation deteriorated swiftly after that incident. German punitive expeditions were sent out and Western pressure in a variety of other forms continued in the province, with the result that a series of 'bandit' incidents were reported. By 1898 no Christian settlement in Shantung was safe from attack, in particular by the newly emerging Boxer sect.

There is no doubt that this state of affairs was greatly contributed to by Chinese officials who made no moves to stamp out the rioters and disorders. Shantung, in the troubled years between 1895 and 1899 was administered by two succeeding governors and there is every reason to believe that their policy of encouraging Boxers, whom they regarded as anti-foreign patriots, was greatly to blame for the rise and spread of the sect in north China.

Li Ping-heng who ruled the province down to 1897, admittedly made some attempt to suppress rioters, but he was noted for his anti-foreign views and did little to make peace between rioters and Christians, and to remove the basic cause of the trouble, the rumours and stories about 'the foreign devils' that circulated about the province and caused bad feelings.

Li was succeeded in 1897 by a violently anti-foreign Manchu official, Yu Hsien, who gave such active support to the Boxer sect, protecting them from punishment and repression, that it was openly said he was himself a Boxer. Although there is no evidence to support this charge, the suggestion was not unbelievable. Quite a number of high Manchu officials who did not have the same educational advantages as Chinese bureaucrats, were associated with the movement. In any case, in Yu Hsien's period of office as governor, there were a series of particularly vicious

---

[1] There is a Boxer poem about this in A. H. S. Landor, *China and the Allies*, vol. I (London, 1901), pp. 15-16.

attacks on Christian mission stations and on communities of Christian converts. Neophytes were murdered, Christian churches were destroyed and the position of Christian missionaries and their converts was made exceedingly uncomfortable. By 1899 the situation had become so bad that foreign eyes in China were turned to the north, which appeared to be in an imminent state of revolt, and Yu Hsien's encouragement of the Boxers seemed to be greatly to blame.

The turning point in Shantung, as far as the emergence of Boxers as a powerful force was concerned, came at the end of 1899. Already the treaty-port press had been warning readers about the serious state of affairs in the province, although to then no foreign lives had been lost, but only property destroyed and native converts killed. On December the 31st this was suddenly changed when a British missionary, the Reverend S. P. Brooks of the Society for the Propagation of the Gospel in Foreign Parts, was murdered in the village of Chang Shia Tien in Shantung. Subsequent investigations carried out by Chinese officials proved that the murder was for revenge rather than as part of a movement to exterminate foreigners. The ring leader of the attack, Meng Kuang-wen had had a brother killed earlier that year during a Boxer attack on Christian converts who, on that occasion, were protected by Chinese soldiers. The bereaved brother, when the opportunity arose, attacked Brooks's mission to get his own back, and succeeded in killing the mission leader. The only fortunate aspect about the incident was that Brooks was a British subject. If he had been German there is no doubt that large-scale reprisals would have been made by the German forces who had done the very same thing in the past, and had used occasions such as this to make large demands on China.

British officials when they heard of the news, confined their activities to diplomatic protests. Together with the European powers they merely made a demand for China to put her house in order and guarantee the protection of foreign lives, and to punish those responsible for the murder. Diplomatic pressure finally secured the arrest and trial of the murderers and their punishment, which took place in the following March.

By that time there was every hope that an early end would come to confrontation that existed between Chinese and foreigners in Shantung. Just before the murder, in early December 1899, following months of Western pressure about the matter, the violently and openly anti-foreign Governor Yu Hsien was removed, and this seemed to herald a coming period of peace. More important, Governor Yu was succeeded by an anti-Boxer strong man, Yuan Shih-k'ai, who led one of the most modern and well-equipped and foreign-trained armies in north China. Hope for the future, on the news of this appointment, was high. All that was needed for peace in the province, many believed, was a firm policy and a strong hand.

Although Yuan seemed to some Westerners to be something of a 'trimmer', changing from one side to the other whenever it suited his interests, he soon curbed the troubles in Shantung province and made the hopes a reality. Taking a firm line he acted to ban the Boxers and stamp out the cult and prevent riots in Shantung province. By the first months of 1900 his policy had succeeded. The province was quiet and safer for foreigners than it had been for a long time. Like the southern viceroys who had had to deal with similar troubles, Yuan Shih-k'ai rightly came to the conclusion that direct confrontation with the foreigners did not pay.

Yuan Shih-k'ai's actions in Shantung did not settle the Boxer problem. The secret society, far from being suppressed, merely moved out of Shantung into adjoining provinces where the authorities were not so harsh on them. By April 1900 it was apparent that large groups of Boxers had entered Chihli, the metropolitan province. There they appeared to move in two directions. One group headed towards Tientsin, the only treaty port with a large foreign population, and the railhead for the line from the coast to Peking. The other group made north towards the capital city itself, where the Manchu ruling group appeared to grant the sect increasing favours. It was this displacement of Boxers and the migration north to eliminate foreigners in the foreign centres there that placed Peking and the foreign Legations in peril.

Boxers in Chihli

It took some months for the Boxers to reach the vicinity of the two 'foreign' centres. Reports of increased Boxer activity in the metropolitan province started to appear in January 1900, when they spilled over the Shantung border, attacking Christian com-

INTRODUCTION: CHINESE ANTI-FOREIGNISM

munities in their path as they made north. In the following six months, to the time the siege of the Peking Legations commenced, they multiplied rapidly and spread, affecting areas as far as Manchuria in the north.

Recruitment to their ranks and the incitement of disturbances against 'foreign devils' was not difficult. There were three influences which led to their successes in motivating an anti-foreign uprising in Chihli province about Peking in 1900.

There is no doubt that drought and famine played a considerable part in the spread of Boxerism in Chihli during the first year of the present century. The two previous seasons had been very bad and caused a lot of economic hardship and local discontent among subsistence farmers in the province. The year 1900 started off with little promise, and as the months wore on and no rain fell, despite the presence of cloud and overcast skies, it became apparent that further poor harvests were in the offing. By early summer 1900 the province was in the grip of a drought. It was the failure of the weather that gave the Boxers their opportunity to incite superstitious peasants to find scapegoats among the Christians for the blight. If foreigners and Christians

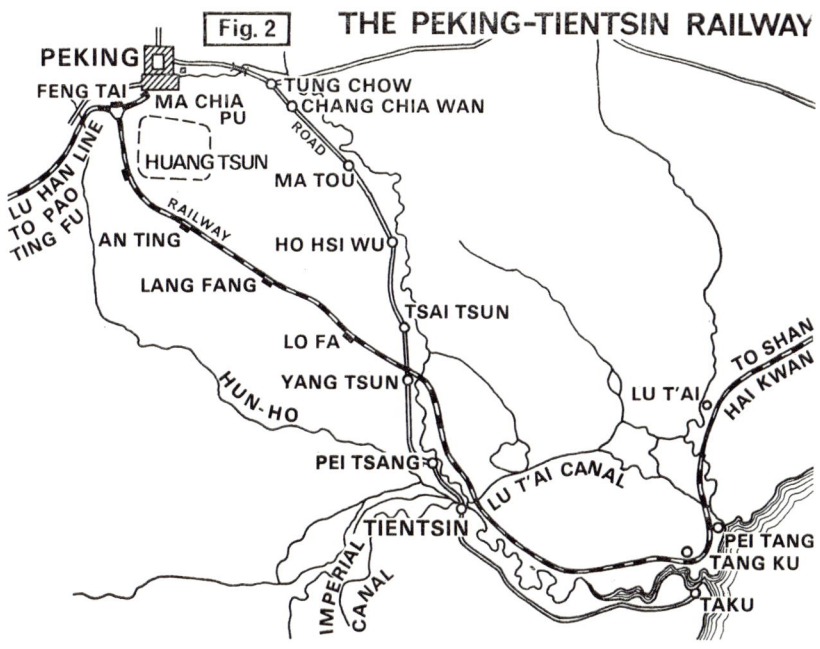

were exterminated, the Boxers preached, the rain which foreigners held off, would fall.

Foreign diplomats, in particular the British Minister MacDonald, were firmly convinced that the drought was the main cause of the trouble. Once rain fell, they continually claimed, the trouble would be washed away. This view, in fact, was not very sound. Adverse weather conditions and drought certainly played a part, but it was not the most significant cause of the trouble. There were other issues disturbing the population and the Boxers.

In particular, foreigners in Chihli had paved the way for an upsurge of anti-foreignism in the province by making specific demands and advances which caused bad feelings. After the war with Japan, while the powers were battling for bases and concessions, the foreign consuls in Tientsin, which had become somewhat of a boom town, demanded large extensions of foreign-controlled territory in the town. Consequently China conceded four new concession areas. Britain in particular took a large slice of the Chinese City, measuring some 1,630 *mou*[1] to add to her area. In 1900 the argument about removing Chinese residents and houses in the concessions to make way for Europeans still raged, and this served as a bait for Boxers and other anti-foreign elements, who quite rightly saw that as far as Chihli was concerned, the battle for concessions was a reality, and the threat to China's territory was not to be under-emphasized.

Besides this there was the question of a railway from Tientsin to the capital. This was built in the face of considerable opposition by people who did not want to see Peking made easily accessible from the coast, and was opened on September the 30th 1897. Two other controversial lines were built. One went north from Tientsin along the coast to the port of Shan Hai Kwan and then into Manchuria. The most important line, however, was a further one known as the Lu Han line, which went from Peking south to join the capital with the important Yangtze city of Hankow. All of these lines were built by foreign engineers, which naturally caused apprehension. More important for local peasants, who seldom had a chance to see foreigners, there were continued reminders of foreign presence in the sights of the newly laid steel rails which stretched across the parched lands, and the foreign-style railway stations and large brick 'go-downs' which dominated

---

[1] A *mou* equals approximately 1/6th of an acre.

the countryside. It was along the Lu Han line that the Boxers moved to Peking, tearing it up, sleeper, spike and rail, as they came north.

This does not mean that missionary causes of the Boxer Uprising are to be ignored. The Boxers in Chihli province were certainly not solely anti-railway. They were also at the same time violently anti-Christian, although it is quite wrong to believe, as some historians do, that Christian missionaries were mainly to blame for the troubles in Chihli. Engineers and developers must also share the blame. It was the railway lines converging on Peking that served to draw the Boxers in the direction of the capital, not the new Christian mission stations.

There was a third factor which drew them to the same place and which played a great part in giving a free hand to Boxers in the province, allowing them to spread and prosper. That was the growing anti-foreignism of the Chinese Court.

The attitude of the Court

On January the 2nd 1900, before the news of the Brooks's murder reached Peking, Conger, the Ambassador for the United States, wrote home about a change in Peking policy which seemed to be getting firmer towards foreigners. He did not make an issue of the matter, as to him it seemed relatively unimportant. However, two Chinese documents came into his hands which he thought sufficiently significant to comment on in a special despatch.[1] The first was a circular sent by the Court to top Chinese officials in the maritime and riverine provinces of China, which were specially susceptible to foreign attack. This decree warned the officials of foreign desires for conquest and the possibilities of increased pressure, and urged on them the need 'to exercise the utmost vigilance and watchfulness to guard against sudden aggression and to be always prepared to resist an enemy'. The second document, an edict dated the 21st November 1899 and sent to high provincial officials, was just as revealing on the matter of the foreign threat. This document again warned officials of 'the tiger-like nature of the foreign powers' and urged them to call on united local forces to defend the territories of the homeland, promising that Peking would never talk peace, and

---

[1] U.S. 56th Congress. *House Documents.* I Foreign Relations 1900, p. 85.

making it quite clear that they were not to succumb to foreign demands and pressures. Conger and the Americans made no fuss about this as these Chinese aims were not very different from what the United States hoped China's policy would be. The United States government did not wish to see China's territorial integrity threatened any more than patriotic Chinese did.

There is no evidence that these documents were seen by the representatives of the other major powers. They were certainly not passed on by the United States. If they had been, they could have added to the alarm, for they indicated in no uncertain terms that there was a group at the Court who was prepared to go to any length to preserve the Chinese Empire.

It was not the decrees such as these which revealed to the world at large a hardening of opinion in the Court towards foreigners, but the news of the Brooks's murder which reached the capital on the 2nd of January.

The British Ambassador, MacDonald, had already issued a warning to the Chinese government about the seriousness of the situation in Shantung province on December the 29th. On the 2nd of January he took a new initiative. Chinese officials at the Chinese Foreign Office in Peking, when the news was known, were immediately contacted. They in turn acted swiftly, calling on the Shantung authorities for information and explanations, and finally, on the 5th January 1900 a decree was published expressing China's regret and promising that those involved in the murder would be captured and punished. There is no doubt that the Chinese authorities made genuine attempts to patch up the difference and meet Britain's demands and restore tranquillity. All the messages were conveyed speedily by telegraph with no delays, which was unusual in Peking at that time. However, the matter was not over. The criminals were not caught and punished, and British officials well knew that that would be the real test for the Chinese government and not the issuing of a promissory decree.

On the 11th of January there was a sudden change in the situation which took the foreign diplomats by surprise and revealed the depth of anti-foreign feeling at the Court. On that day a decree was issued which countermanded the previous decree of the 5th. The new document, issued in the name of the Emperor, asked the officials and people to differentiate between outlaws and patriots, and far from urging the protection of Christians, it recommended that they be treated the same as any other sect that caused trouble and that they should be subjected by local officials to the same scrutiny as outlaw groups. Moreover, in the spirit of the earlier decrees commented on by Conger, which encouraged national sentiments and defence, the decree of January the 11th suggested in no uncertain terms that local groups with patriotic purposes would be encouraged to serve as local militia units to protect the country. This system of local defence, incidentally, was quite the normal procedure in China. Standing armies alone were not meant to defend the country. Local militia units, or 'train bands' as they were called, were supposed to work with regular forces to protect villages and local areas against the ravages of bandits and the threat of invaders. After the defeat by Japan the Manchu authorities had already encouraged the development of local 'train bands' to improve defences in the north. When the Boxers came to Chihli these groups, which offered great scope to sects such as the Boxers, were infiltrated by them, and from January the 11th Boxers could read between the lines of the decree and find that they had the approval of the Court to organize for patriotic purposes. Even if this was not the intention of the Chinese government, a number of rumours started to circulate, indicating that the Court was giving active support to the Boxers.

Although it was not readily apparent at the time, the two different decrees of the 5th and the 11th were issued because of divided opinions in the Court. There were in Peking two parties, one anti-foreign and one moderate. The anti-foreign group was made up basically of conservative Manchus such as Jung Lu and Prince Tuan who were close to the Empress Dowager, having come to her support in the latter part of 1898 to save her from the reformers. In this group Prince Tuan seemed to have played an increasingly dominant rôle. Born as Tsai I, the Prince inherited his rank in 1860 and spent the period from then until the late nineties in political backwaters. The events of 1898 gave him the opportunity to advance. Seeing the Empress Dowager's position threatened, he rallied with the conservatives to defend her status and was foremost in leading the purge of the reformers. He subsequently emerged as the Court favourite. He was not only politically acceptable to the Empress Dowager, but was also linked with the royal family having married her niece. After the coup of September 1898, when the Emperor Kuang Hsu's political fortunes declined, Prince Tuan's eldest son, P'u Chun, who was of imperial rank, was chosen to succeed the unwanted reforming monarch. There was considerable opposition to the latter move by the foreign powers at the time, as has been indicated, when they called up guards to protect diplomats against rioters. Whether foreign pressure and preferences were the determining factor in saving Kuang Hsu's position is immaterial, for there was internal opposition to the selection of P'u Chun as Heir Apparent as well. In any case, no formal declaration of succession was made and Prince Tuan and his family consequently had a real grievance against the foreigners and foreign powers. Whether it was this reverse, or a quality of mysticism in his character that attracted him to the magical cult, he and two of his brothers assumed an active leadership of the Boxer sects about Peking.[1]

Opposed to this clique was a moderate Chinese party. Prominent among these was Prince Ch'ing who controlled the Chinese Foreign Office, with the possible addition of Jung Lu, the army commander in the north of China, who seemed more to 'sit on the fence' than act as a moderate. This group was by no means reformist in sentiment, nor did they press for appeasement. They were above all cautious, and were well aware of the dangers of giving free rein to sects such as the Boxers, who could bring trouble to the nation. The decree of January the 5th which sought to indicate to the foreign powers that China was capable of keeping her own house in order, gives a fair summary of their views. They did not approve the use of 'bandits' to keep the foreign powers at bay.

Further deterioration of the situation in Chihli

The issuing of the January the 11th decree began a bout of diplomatic negotiations aimed at banning the Boxers, which lasted until the outbreak of war in the following June. Before firm approaches were made by the foreign powers, however, there was a further deterioration in the situation in Chihli province, which indicated the power and strong position of the anti-foreign clique. What the foreign diplomats had failed to grasp was the fact that the former anti-foreign Governor of Shantung,

[1] Fig. 6 on page 80 shows the Manchu imperial family, indicating the relationship of the Boxer princes with the monarchy.

INTRODUCTION: CHINESE ANTI-FOREIGNISM

Yu Hsien, was in the capital, and rumours suggested that he was advising the conservative Manchus. Far from being censured for the Brooks's murder and the anti-foreign violence in Chihli, he was rewarded by the Court. On the 16th of January it was announced that the character *fu* (happiness) had been conferred upon him by the Emperor in audience. The foreign powers protested, but these complaints were swept aside by the Chinese government who said that this was normal procedure for a retiring governor. In fact this was not the case at the time. Other governors who had faced similar troubles in their provinces, especially during the Yangtze riots, had been severely dealt with.

Just over a week later there was a further indication that the anti-foreign clique was gaining strength. On January the 23rd an announcement was made in the name of the Emperor, calling all the high officials in the capital to an audience the following day. There was an air of expectancy in the city throughout the 23rd. Then on the 24th a decree was issued announcing that both the Empress Dowager and the Emperor were ill, and that as the Emperor had no issue, Prince Tuan's son, P'u Chun had now been officially nominated as Heir Apparent. Although this seemed to indicate that the conservatives were getting what they failed to achieve in 1898, the move was quite in order. The Empress Dowager who was responsible for the matter, acted very wisely. In 1875 when she upset the dynastic laws by having Kuang Hsu placed on the throne out of his generation,[1] she had promised to find a prince who would be made the adopted son of the dead Emperor T'ung Chih, thus carrying on the line in succession. P'u Chun was to fulfil this function. The most important effect this announcement had was that it not only secured the Empress Dowager's position in Peking, dealing a blow to the power and future of the Emperor Kuang Hsu, but it also placed the pro-Boxer anti-foreign Prince Tuan in a more favourable position in Court. He was from that time not only the Court favourite, but the father of the Heir Apparent, and moderates who opposed his policy had to think carefully before they raised their voices in opposition to him. From then on, as Prince Tuan and his anti-foreign colleagues consolidated their positions, the situation for

[1] He was the same generation, that is the Tsai generation, as the previous Emperor. See Fig. 6 on page 80. The next Emperor after T'ung Chih should have been a P'u and not a Tsai.

foreigners in the north became increasingly precarious. Boxers multiplied, the areas of disturbances expanded, and threats to exterminate foreigners grew. Although the situation seemed perilous, there were no reports of attacks on foreigners in Chihli after the Brooks's murder. Anti-foreign elements seemed to concentrate their attention on 'second-class foreign devils', that is Christian converts, and Chinese who worked for foreigners or openly accepted foreign ideas, although there were threats and rumours of a general massacre of foreigners being put about.

In view of the fact that no foreign lives had been lost in Chihli the foreign powers did not act precipitately by moving in forces to protect their interests in north China, as some were pressing for them to do. Instead they began a round of diplomatic activity that lasted till the following May when the real crisis came.

THE DIPLOMATIC TUSSLE

There is no doubt that the diplomatic confrontation that became increasingly embittered as it drew on, was a serious miscalculation on the part of the anti-foreign element in the Court. They may have saved the Manchu regime from the wrath of the Boxers, but in so doing what China had always feared in modern times had come about. She was facing a growing united body of foreign powers who seemed bent on imposing their collective will on the country. Prior to 1900 the chances of this happening had seemed remote. The Western powers had previously acted together, somewhat reluctantly, to settle the Yangtze riots, but since 1895 the united front of powers existed in name only. It was rent by personal jealousies and national differences which allowed China to play off one power against the other and so escape the worst of the pressures made on her in the period of concessions. There was no reason why the powers should act together. Each was suspicious of the other. The British trusted the Russians as much as they would an anarchist, and the republican French even less. The Germans were wary of everyone; the French and the Russians worked only with each other, but always with hesitation. Each power was in fact quite suspicious of the other, and each foreign diplomat in Peking was jealous of his neighbour. The events of 1900 in China served to end these differences and paved the way for a united crusade against the 'yellow peril'.

INTRODUCTION: CHINESE ANTI-FOREIGNISM

The emergence of a foreign concert of powers against China soon became apparent. On January the 27th, after conferring, the foreign diplomats presented identical notes to the Chinese government to make sure that China could not resort to her old policy of playing one against the other. In these notes the diplomats made demands which were to be the constant points for discussion in subsequent months. They called for the punishment of the Boxers in Shantung who had not then been dealt with, and the publication of a new decree banning Boxers and anti-foreign sects in the Empire in general. To make their threats real the ministers talked of a united naval demonstration, although the Foreign Offices in Europe and in particular Lord Salisbury in London were hesitant to go so far. The diplomats further indicated that they would not relent until the new orders about Boxers were printed in the official Chinese government journal, the *Peking Gazette*.

Despite promptings on these matters no reply was received from Chinese officials until the 25th of February, and this only went part of the way, revealing that only local authorities in Shantung and at Tientsin in Chihli had been requested to issue proclamations against the Boxers. On the point of publishing a decree in the *Peking Gazette*—which circulated throughout China—the Chinese government remained obdurate. In view of this stand two more approaches were made by the foreign powers to the Chinese government on the 2nd and the 10th of March. Far from meeting the points of demand, the Chinese caused a further deterioration in the situation. The day before the second foreign note, a purge of Chinese officials in Peking was made. Five Hanlin academicians were involved and the director of the European-financed Peking Syndicate which was building railways and exploiting mineral resources in north China. The reason given for the purge was that they were members of the reform group which was still being hunted out of existence. In actual fact these men were moderates in politics, and their demise caused some comments in foreign circles who saw the move as being a further example of the rising power of the anti-foreign party. Moreover, on the 14th of March the foreign diplomats in Peking were shocked to hear that the anti-foreign Yu Hsien had been appointed to the post of Governor of Shansi province, which was a significant centre for Christian missions, and where foreign combines such as the Peking Syndicate group had extensive economic concessions. This seemed to the foreigners little better than a slap in the face and promised ill for the future of foreigners in Shansi province. The only bright news that came to hand was that action had at last been taken in Shantung against the murderers of Brooks. Of the five prisoners held, two were sentenced to death, one to life imprisonment, one to ten years and one to two years banishment. Besides this an indemnity of 9,500 *taels* was paid and a memorial tablet was erected on the scene of the crime to remind the local Chinese about what had occurred. This settlement, however, appeared to be the result of the personal initiative and wishes of the new Governor of Shantung, Yuan Shih-k'ai, instead of Peking's policy. The only other piece of hopeful news was that the Governor-General of Chihli province, who resided at Tientsin, took it upon himself to publish the Imperial decree issued in February, which asked provincial officials to proscribe the Boxer sect.

Although the foreign powers gave up their demands to have the anti-Boxer decree published in the *Peking Gazette,* they did not remain inactive. Protesting against the new anti-foreign moves made by China, they warned her that they reserved the right to take action by themselves to restore order. Naval reinforcements were called for and commenced to congregate about Taku, off the Pei Ho, or North River, which led inland from Tientsin to near Peking. Moderates in Europe, such as Salisbury, in view of the deteriorating situation after March, from this time were not opposed to a united show of force and to the despatch of foreign troops inland to guard foreigners and foreign interests. Both sides were now prepared for an escalation.

BOXER ADVANCES

From the end of April 1900 news of attacks on foreigners and of disturbances in Chihli became increasingly frequent. The real extent of these incidents and the subsequent troubles will never be fully known. There was no central agency or office collecting news in north China at that time. Reports of disturbances trickled in to mission centres in Peking and the treaty ports, and to officials and newspaper men. The total news coverage of the troubles was thus particularly poor. Most foreign correspondents' eyes, in fact, were turned towards the Russian threat in East Asia and the diplomatic imbroglio, and they ignored happenings about Peking. Consequently only the major incidents that occurred were reported, and a major incident as far as foreign news services were concerned, at that time meant the death of a 'foreigner' or an attack on foreign property.

Therefore, it is not possible to pinpoint all the Boxer targets in the months that followed. The evidence clearly suggests that there were two areas in particular on which they concentrated their attention; the region about Pao Ting Fu, a large provincial city that was both an important centre for Christian mission work and a base for railway engineers constructing the Lu Han line which had by then reached the vicinity of the city; and the region to the west of Peking, especially in the vicinity of Tung Chow, on the Pei Ho, which was also a 'Christian area', and which lay between the capital and the coast. These areas were to remain constant sources of trouble until Peking and Tientsin were besieged in the following June.

It was the Pao Ting Fu district that came first into the news with accounts of extensive anti-foreign outbreaks. On April the 24th a particularly bad incident was reported in Peking, which has occurred at the village of Chiang Chia Chuang about fifty *li* (seventeen miles) south of Pao Ting Fu. The bulk of the Chinese residents there were Roman Catholic, and they were suddenly attacked by Boxers who appeared to be moving along the railway line from the south towards Peking. A force, later estimated at 2,000 Boxers, was engaged in the attack on the village, but as the Christians had been warned in advance they had prepared themselves well, getting arms and building defence works. The result of the skirmish was that the poorly equipped Boxer force was soundly defeated with apparently a great loss of life, while the Christian casualties were reported as one dead and six wounded. This event did not cause a great deal of consternation among foreigners, despite the magnitude of the affair. After all no foreigners had been involved and no foreign property had been destroyed. In fact very few foreigners, apart from some missionaries who lived in the unsettled interior and who were regarded as alarmists, noticed the incident and they continued to believe complacently that the Chinese were engaged in some local skirmishes which would soon die down.

In early May, while other incidents of a similar nature were still occurring in the countryside in Chihli province, the Spring Race Meeting was held as usual at Peking, taking up the time and attention of most of the staffs of the foreign Legations. The membership register of the committee which arranged the meeting and attended it as dignitaries, read very much like a diplomatic corps list. Only two powers were not represented; the seriously inclined Germans and the French, who at that time, in the period of Toulouse-Lautrec, were not expected to indulge in that sort of organized sport. Despite some minor difficulties the race meeting was a success and was followed as usual by a round of invitation balls, picnics, tennis parties and theatrical evenings.

Further down the railway line to the coast, at Tientsin, a similarly successful Spring Race Meeting was held in mid-May, and work went on hurriedly to establish a swimming club and pool to provide better facilities than were offered by the Pei Ho which had fallen five feet as a result of the drought, recording one of the river's lowest levels in the memory of foreigners.

Thus in foreign official circles, in Chihli province at least, there was optimism in the air. Nothing untoward had happened to them to disturb their complacency, or personal safety. Foreign officials in the capital, in fact, had outlooks and views which were not unlike the London crowds who flocked to see the visiting mystic, the White Mahatma, who foretold the relief of Ladysmith, and the winner of the Viceroy's Cup, but who gave no warning of the impending troubles in the East. However, for those who looked close, there were already signs of trouble which lay not far beyond the dust clouds raised by the heavy ponies as they raced around the parched race tracks.

Early in May, to the consternation of some of the more perceptive observers, Boxers were seen both in Peking and Tientsin, although they did not remain there for long. Besides this sudden appearance of the ill-famed secret society close to the foreign enclaves, there were two other changes which revealed that the situation was deteriorating. First, commencing on May the 12th 1900, the *North China Herald* and later other newspapers, began printing articles warning about the impending dangers, revealing that the Manchu leaders and the Empress Dowager herself were involved in an anti-foreign movement and that the threatened outbreak was imminent. Second, it was obvious to any observer

INTRODUCTION: CHINESE ANTI-FOREIGNISM

that the Court was becoming increasingly bellicose in its attitude to foreigners. In May more anti-foreign officals were finding favour at the Court and were being promoted. For instance an Imperial Censor (a Civil Service Investigator) named Wang who was notoriously pro-Boxer, was raised two grades in the Civil Service and made Governor of Peking, which represented a direct threat to foreigners in the Legations and the city. Other extremists also rose to prominence while the moderates and 'fence sitters' such as Jung Lu fell from favour. There was, apart from this, a third indication of rising feelings among the Chinese. Reports came in during May that the old term of abuse for foreigners, *yang kwei tzu* (foreign devils) was coming into current use in the north, as it had in the region on the eve of the Tientsin massacre in 1870.

The tensions felt in Peking during the first half of May soon died down and matters were soon back to normal there and in Tientsin as far as foreigners were concerned. The more unruffled among the Westerners took heart from the turn events had taken, and seemed pleased to reveal that they had stood firm while some of the missionaries and newspapermen had sounded 'false alarms'. The Boxers who had come near the foreign settlements, it was pointed out, had disappeared without causing disturbances, indicating to those who wanted to believe it that the troubles were not that deep. The point missed was that there were real reasons for the Boxers to leave. It was subsequently reported that they left Peking and Tientsin to go down the Lu Han line to Pao Ting Fu to join in the large-scale trouble that was brewing there. They did not leave the vicinity of the foreign enclaves because they were frightened or because they had been appeased.

In other words, just after the Spring Race Meetings ended and while costumes were being prepared for the round of dances, the centre of trouble developed on the Lu Han line at Pao Ting Fu, where a general rebellion against foreigners broke out. News of this was slow in coming to Peking or elsewhere and there was a tendency among foreigners to pass it off. However, the incident was of such magnitude that it could not be ignored: in fact the Pao Ting Fu massacre proved to be the first significant turning point in the foreigners' reactions to the Boxers in Chihli. It caused them to take note of the movement.

THE FIRST MASSACRE AT PAO TING FU

In mid-May the long expected outbreak of violence occurred in Chihli. Boxers, who had gathered at the large provincial city of Pao Ting Fu, went on a rampage and attacked Christian converts and Christian missionary settlements. Reports about the damage and destruction vary, but there is no doubt that it was a very violent affair. Some seventy Christian converts were massacred and this and other Boxer attacks in the countryside surrounding Peking sent streams of refugees heading for the safety of the capital city. It seemed to missionary observers as if the promised rising had at last commenced and that only drastic action could restore order and tranquillity.

Although the massacre was bad, the foreign diplomats in Peking did not take immediate action. After all no foreigners had been killed or reported dead as yet, and the ministers were most reluctant to act hastily especially when the Chinese were involved. The matter did not blow over and the organized slaughter of Christians at Pao Ting Fu became a significant turning point in Sino-foreign relations in the north. Detailed reports of the horrors and the refugees served to galvanize at least some of the ministers to action.

It was the French representative in Peking, Pichon, who took the initiative and started events moving. He heard about the matter direct from the Roman Catholic missionaries whom he was charged by his government to protect, and was alarmed. The news actually came to him in the form of a lengthy letter from Bishop Favier of Peking who collated the reports coming in. In this letter the Bishop did not only describe the horrible massacre which had taken place, but he also revealed that the refugee problem was becoming so acute that he intended to close all schools and hospitals in Peking to accommodate them. In a final note of despair he advised Pichon that 'day had practically ended for all in Peking', and warned him that the same bitter placards were appearing and threats were being made as in the case of Tientsin in 1870 on the eve of the massacre of foreigners there.

What Bishop Favier wrote certainly impressed Pichon. The Bishop, after all, was one of the best informed foreigners in Peking at the time. His sources of information, which included foreign missionaries, native converts and Chinese officials reached far and wide into Chihli province. Moreover, the Bishop was not inclined to be an alarmist. He had lived through many bitter experiences in China, some of which were quite recent. If he had been an alarmist there were many occasions before May the 19th when he could have alerted the French and requested them to exercise their protectorate of the Church.

Pichon's first reaction was to call a meeting of the foreign diplomatic body in Peking to discuss the Bishop's letter and the situation, seeking to get united action with which to confront the Chinese government. But if Pichon was worried, his colleagues did not unanimously share his gloom. The Italian representative was the only one to agree that the situation had become alarming. The Russian Minister, to the contrary, ridiculed the idea that there was widespread unrest, and condemned Bishop Favier's letter as being alarmist. The British Minister, MacDonald, who had the final say, carried the others at the meeting with him by siding with the Russian, raising doubts about the imminence of the danger. Firm united action by the powers was thus decided against. It was merely proposed to give the Chinese government a warning, and to urge China to act to set her house in order and restore peace. Beyond this, all that the foreign diplomats demanded was an assurance that foreign lives and properties would be protected by the Chinese government and that action would be taken against the Boxers. If these measures should fail and the situation deteriorated, for they did not doubt Favier's words about the rise of violence, then at a later date, when the occasion demanded it, the ministers indicated that they would consider calling up more guards from the warships lying off the coast at Taku.

There were real reasons for the Russian and British views. Calling on guards to come to Peking, and issuing ultimatums to China, which would have meant a show of force, were large steps to take and could have lead to unforseen results. The Manchu government, the foreign diplomats realized, was shaky and firm demands could lead to its downfall and the rise of further political troubles which would only serve to worsen the situation.

Nevertheless, in acting this way, the British and Russian Ministers, as Peter Fleming states in his book *The Siege at Peking,* certainly performed like ostriches with their heads buried in the sand. It was pure arrogance bred from ignorance for them to pass judgment on Favier's letter and Pichon's plea. Both of them were far from being the most knowledgeable diplomats in Peking.

MacDonald in particular knew little about the situation in the province of Chihli. He had no consuls inland there; no-one on his staff had been sent out to collect information about impending troubles, as was usual in such cases, and there were no informative reports for him to read in *The Times*. That paper's correspondent, George Morrison, missed the growing revolt. His coverage of the Boxer crisis, in fact, was particularly poor. For most of the first months in 1900 he was chasing Russian bogeys about China, feeling they were more important than the Chinese ones that were appearing in what he felt was a crumbling empire. In view of this the British Minister and his Russian colleague made a serious mistake, and their mistaken opinions were accepted by the diplomatic body and acted upon. The proper course they should have followed was to have had a thorough investigation made of the situation before they pronounced on it.

The evidence was not hard to find out at the time. Some of it was being pasted up in the form of placards on the walls of the Chinese buildings beyond the Legation stables. These were markedly different in character from the earlier placards which had appeared in Shantung province. By May the foreigners were being told in no uncertain terms that they would be the target for attacks and would be exterminated, and were being informed about how this would be done. The following placard, which was pasted up in Peking, and which Sir Claude must have known about, is indicative of the type of material that was used to incite the population in north China.

> In a certain street in Peking some worshippers of the *I Ho Ch'uan* (Boxers) at midnight suddenly saw a spirit descend in their midst. The spirit was silent for a long time, and all the congregation fell upon their knees and prayed. Then a terrible voice was heard saying:—
> 'I am none other than the great Yu Tu (God of the Unseen World) come down in person. Well knowing that you are all of devout mind, I have now descended to make known to you that there are times of trouble in the world, and that it is impossible to set aside the decrees of fate. Disturbances are to be dreaded from the foreign devils; everywhere they are starting missions, erecting telegraphs, and building railways; they do not believe in the sacred doctrine, and they speak evil of the Gods. Their sins are numberless as the hairs of the head. Therefore am I wrath, and my thunders have pealed forth. By night and by day have I thought of these things. Should I command my Generals to come down to Earth,

even they would not have the strength to change the course of fate. For this reason I have given forth my decree that I shall descend to Earth at the head of all saints and spirits and that wherever the *I Ho Ch'uan* are gathered together, there shall the Gods be in the midst of them. I have also to make known to all the righteous in the three worlds that they must be of one mind, and all practice the cult of the *I Ho Ch'uan* so that the wrath of heaven may be appeased.

So soon as the practice of the *I Ho Ch'uan* has brought to perfection—await for three times three or nine times nine, nine times nine or three times three[1]—then shall the devils meet their doom. The will of heaven is that the telegraph wires be first cut, then the railways torn up, and then shall the foreign devils be decapitated. In that day shall the hour of their calamities come. The time for rain to fall is yet afar off, and all on account of the devils.

I hereby make known these commands to all you righteous folk, that you may strive with one accord to exterminate all foreign devils, and so turn aside the wrath of heaven. This shall be accounted unto you for well doing; and on the day when it is done, the wind and rain shall be according to your desire.

Therefore I expressly command you to make this known in every place.'

This I saw with my own eyes, and therefore, I make bold to take my pen and write what happened. They who believe it shall have merit; they who do not believe it shall have guilt. The wrath of the spirit was because of the destruction of the Temple of Yu Tu. He sees that the men of the *I Ho Ch'uan* are devout worshippers and pray to him.

If my tidings are false, may I be destroyed by the five thunderbolts. Fourth Moon, 1st day (29 April).[2]

We must avoid judging MacDonald and his imperturbable colleagues according to our knowledge after the event. We know the Boxer Uprising occurred and we should not expect those who lived in China in 1900 to see it coming. But set among his contemporaries MacDonald was blind, and disregarded the evidence which existed about him. The situation in Peking in 1900 was changing rapidly, as well-informed observers noted.

The placard quoted above sums up the types of wild rumour that suddenly began to spread about Peking in and after May. First, there were whispers that a date had been set for the extermination of foreigners. This is obscure in the placard. It is not

---

[1] The meaning of this is obscure.
[2] *United Kingdom Parliamentary Papers* 1900, cmd 257, p. 105.

clear what the reference to three threes and nine nines is. They obviously do not mean the day and month of the crisis. The third month in the Chinese calendar had passed, and the ninth month would fall late in October, well after the rains would have fallen. Rumours about the city suggested that June the 1st, the occasion of the Dragon Boat Festival, was the appointed day for the extermination of foreigners. Others with more reason, indicated that the rising would take place on the anniversary of the Tientsin massacre, which took place on June the 21st 1870. In the Chinese calendar this was the 23rd day in the 5th month. In 1900, however, due to calendar differences, the Chinese anniversary of the incident fell two days earlier than in the Christian calendar. That is the Chinese anniversary of the Tientsin incident fell on June the 19th. It was on this date, incidentally, that the major attack on foreigners was finally made, although, as will be seen, this came by accident rather than as the end result of a carefully organized and widespread plot, though the latter, of course, must not be discounted and its importance underestimated.

Other rumours circulated about the method of extermination. Telegraph and railway lines would be cut first, then foreign buildings would be destroyed, and finally foreigners and foreign-living Chinese would be exterminated. About May the 25th, further rumours began to spread to explain the Boxer withdrawal from Peking. These claimed that they were going to Pao Ting Fu, which was again starting to seethe with trouble.

In the meantime, following Pichon's appeal, the foreign ministers requested the Chinese Foreign Office to exercise restraint. This was difficult at the time. The summer holiday spirit seemed to be generally in the air. The Court had moved away from the dust and heat of the city to the Summer Palace near the Western Hills, and diplomatic intercourse was not easy. However, MacDonald himself saw Prince Ch'ing who was in charge of the Chinese Foreign Office on the afternoon of the 27th and received assurances that all would be well, and that action would be taken to preserve peace. Decrees condemning Boxer outrages indeed were issued. But there was no real reason to believe these would be any more effective than the one issued in January, which had been countermanded. The Court and high placed Manchus were still anti-foreign, and MacDonald did nothing to try to limit their power. He seemed far too ready to accept the assurances of moderates in the Foreign Office who told him the things he wished to hear and believe.

Already it was being clearly shown that powers of the moderate elements were limited. Jung Lu, the army commander in the north was in a bad position and vacillating more than ever. Rumours were spreading that he had poisoned the Empress Dowager's favourite eunuch, and this story seemed to frighten him into joining closer with the reactionaries. More important, new garrison troops from Kansu province, under the command of anti-foreign General Tung Fu-hsiang, moved into Peking where the soldiers proved to be as anti-foreign as their commander. Besides this there were other reports which indicated the inability of moderates and the imperial troops to keep the peace in the north. News sifted in towards the end of the month that a force of Chinese soldiers under a Brigadier Yang had been on their way to restore peace at Pao Ting Fu, but had been attacked and wiped out by Boxers at a place called Lai Shui on the 22nd of May. Thus whoever tried to restore peace at the time would certainly have found it difficult, especially in the absence of clear leadership from the Court. Further reports from Christian mission stations indicated that the troops which had been sent to protect them, far from carrying out their tasks, were openly fraternizing with the Boxers. It is difficult to understand why, at this early stage, MacDonald and the others did not make it quite clear that local officials and commanders would be held personally responsible if they failed to keep the peace—as had been done during the Yangtze riots—to make certain that all bureaucrats and soldiers would have a stake in maintaining tranquillity; or alternatively why the foreign diplomats did not order foreigners to evacuate the inland areas in the north as had also been done in the south when foreigners outside the treaty ports were refused protection during troubles.

FURTHER RIOTS

At the end of May, while the foreign powers were waiting expectantly for the Chinese government to take action to control the Boxers, the situation again suddenly deteriorated rapidly. Two violent anti-foreign incidents occurred that could not be ignored by either side. There was another large-scale riot at Pao Ting Fu and at other places on the Lu Han line on May the 28th, three days before the Dragon Boat Festival, resulting in the loss of foreign lives and the destruction of foreign property. And on the double fifth (the fifth day of the fifth month of the Chinese calendar) the day of the Dragon Boat Festival, two British missionaries were attacked in the nearby town of Yung Ch'ing, one being killed immediately, the other being put to death on the following day. There were other incidents in Chihli besides these two. Tientsin, the main foreign centre in Chihli province, did not escape. On the double fifth the Chartered Bank there was burnt down and Boxers were seen in the city. But this was a relatively minor affair. The first foreign blood had been drawn elsewhere in Chihli, and the chances of either side making a compromise after that grew increasingly remote.

Irritated by Chinese procrastinations about Pao Ting Fu, the foreign ministers on May the 27th had approached the Chinese Foreign Office to give the ministers there what was in actual fact an ultimatum. Anti-Boxer decrees had been issued by the Court as a result of pressure brought to bear since May the 22nd, but the proclamations were being torn down off walls amidst angry popular denunciations of the government for attacking 'patriotic groups'. The foreign ministers therefore decided to give China twenty-four hours to clear up the mess. If the situation was still unsettled on the 28th, they advised that then they intended to consider strengthening the Legation guards. MacDonald again saw the Chinese ministers on this occasion, and after speaking directly to Prince Ch'ing and the Superintendent of the Peking Police force, who was also a member of the Chinese Foreign Office, came away assured that all would be well.

THE SECOND ATTACK AT PAO TING FU AND ON THE LU HAN LINE

Before the foreign ministers reconvened on the 28th of May to consider the situation, news of a further serious attack at Pao Ting Fu and at other places along the Lu Han line came to the capital. The Boxer attack there followed the plan in the placards that had been pasted up, almost as if they were blueprints. First, the telegraph lines had been cut, then the railways had been torn up, and then foreigners were put to the sword.

It was not the missionaries and converts who were the prime targets for attack on the 28th. The bulk of these who lived south of Peking had moved in a steady stream of refugees who headed for the capital after the earlier Boxer outrages. The main aim of the Boxers who rioted on the 28th was to destroy the Peking-Hankow railway which was still being constructed in the vicinity of Pao Ting Fu. In contrast to the earlier massacre, this attack, which caused extensive damage to foreign property and loss of foreign lives, created general consternation among foreigners.

The attack actually began on the evening of Sunday the 27th when the new station being constructed at Liu Li Ho, between Peking and Pao Ting Fu, was destroyed. On the 28th riots broke out afresh and widespread destruction took place. Nearly thirty miles of line between Peking and Pao Ting Fu were torn up, two railway bridges were destroyed and as the Boxers moved north along the line, two other railway stations, at Chang Shui Tien and Lu Ko Chow, near the Marco Polo Bridge outside Peking, were set on fire.

The news of wholesale destruction was bad enough, but the most worrying thing as far as foreigners were concerned, were the foreign engineers who were constructing the line, and their families. These in the main were Belgians who were responsible for constructing the section of line from Feng Tai to Pao Ting Fu, and reports came in on the 28th that they were besieged on top of a hill by Boxers, with rescue seeming out of the question. Losing no time the Boxers followed the line to Feng Tai and on the same evening, the 28th, burnt and destroyed the railway centre which lay in sight of the capital, causing damage estimated at 100,000 dollars. Sleepers were pulled up and burnt, foreign warehouses destroyed, locomotives were stripped of brass and the houses of foreign engineers looted. Fortunately there was no loss of life. The engineers at Feng Tai had become aware of the threat and they had retreated down the line to Tientsin with plenty of time to spare.

There were now two disturbing thoughts to plague foreigners inland near the capital. First, railway services from the coast to Peking, which had to pass through the junction at Feng Tai, were disrupted. Trains stopped running to a normal schedule on the evening of the 28th. Second, the foreigners who had been cut off at Pao Ting Fu were still missing. They were cut off and no-one knew their fate. There were only rumours about their end and these did not make nice hearing.

It was left to private individuals to rescue foreigners besieged in the out-back districts. The diplomats had other problems. They still wanted to try to prevent a large-scale conflagration. They met as scheduled on the evening of the 28th to consider the question of their ultimatum. Without dissent they decided that matters had gone far enough, and that extra foreign guards would be called up forthwith. Their plan sounded heartening, but it was contrived bumbling. The ministers decided to call up to Peking the force which had been landed from the allied fleet off the coast. This force had already proceeded inland to Tientsin. The trouble was that not very many troops were involved. Most of the foreign forces remained on ships which lay in the bay off Taku. There were some hundreds of marines and soldiers in Tientsin, but that city was also threatened and in need of protection and consequently not many guards could be spared. In any case the Legations in Peking could not house and keep very many. The Legation area was small and cramped and not designed to be a military camp.

On the 28th, before the telegraph lines were destroyed, the guards were ordered up. In order to play the game squarely, the foreign ministers approached the Chinese government to get permission to bring up the forces. This was naturally refused. Constant pressure, however, wore the Chinese down and at 2 a.m. on the 31st permission was given for the foreign troops to travel inland. That evening, at 8 p.m., some 340 guards arrived at Ma Chia P'u station in Peking, and marched to the Legation Quarter. The numbers who arrived bore little relation to the needs of Peking. The main criteria used by the diplomats when selecting the bodies of troops to go to the capital was to see that no one power supplied more than another. The British force was kept down to seventy-five to match the members sent by France and Russia. The rest of the contingent was made up of 50 Americans, 40 Italians and 25 Japanese. To make matters worse the force was poorly equipped. They had no heavy armaments and were short of stores and ammunition. The British marines, for instance, were supplied with an 1887 model Nordenfelt five-barrel quick-firing gun, which repeatedly jammed after every fourth round. The only good feature about the expedition was that they arrived at Ma Chia P'u at night and walked to the Legations in the dark, out of sight of most of the Chinese population. This did not only keep to a minimum the chance of fraying tempers, but resulted in confused reports about the size of the force. Subsequent rumours that circulated about the capital had it that at least 2,000 foreign soldiers had arrived and were camped in the Legation Quarter, and this story could have deterred the more cautious anti-foreign elements from hurling themselves at the diplomats inside the city walls.

Although foreigners appeared to take most of the initiative when news of the destruction of the line reached Peking, the Chinese were not hesitant. After all the railway was theirs. The foreigners who were involved were only employed on the line as constructors. In order to get things back to normal as quickly as possible the line from Tientsin was repaired on the 29th of May and re-opened to traffic. On the same day, Jung Lu went to Ma Chia P'u and took a train to Feng Tai where he made a survey of the damage, although he did not alight from his carriage. Not that this mattered much as the destruction could be plainly seen from any position. Also, in order to give an impression of activity, Chinese troops were belatedly stationed at Ma Chia P'u. The only question that caused concern about this was whether these troops, who were from Tung Fu-hsiang's anti-foreign force at Peking, had been stationed there to keep the peace, or were there to stop further contingents of foreign guards from entering the city. Rumours about the city had it that the latter was the true purpose.

While these measures were being taken, the dominating question of who would rescue the foreigners missing on the railway line still remained. Although they acted in other ways to get matters back to normal the Chinese officials, to their discredit, played little part in this affair and seemed to have little interest in the fate of the foreigners residing outside Peking. In the meantime further reports had come into Peking and it appeared that there were two groups in particular who were in peril. One party of Belgian engineers and their families were at Ch'ang Hsin Tien, then the headquarters of the Lu Han line. Another group was reported to be holding out at Pao Ting Fu.

THE RESCUE AT CH'ANG HSIN TIEN

There was only one way for the foreigners at Ch'ang Hsin Tien to be rescued from their hill. A party would have to go down and extricate them. In view of the destruction of the railway, this would have to be done by road from Peking or from Feng Tai which was still open to the coast.

An attempt had been made to rescue the engineers besieged there on the 28th, the evening of the riots. Two French engineers had come in to Feng Tai from the south to raise the alarm about the Boxers and get assistance to rescue their colleagues. Consequently a locomotive was taken down the line to examine it, and see if it was possible to push south and make contact with the missing foreigners. The engine got as far as the village of Lu Ko Chow where the line crosses the river. Before reaching the bridge there, the line at Lu Ko Chow takes a wide sweep to skirt the village. As the engine went around this, the rescuers saw a large armed group make for the line behind them, as if to cut them off. In front they saw the destroyed station and line, and being few in number the foreigners saw nothing for it but to retreat. When they arrived back at Feng Tai they warned their colleagues about the advancing Boxers and pointed out that no doubt the same fate as had been met by colleagues further down the line, awaited them. Consequently on the 28th a general evacuation was made to Tientsin and safety, leaving Feng Tai open for the rioters.

Two attempts were subsequently made to rescue the engineers trapped south of the Marco Polo Bridge. On the afternoon of the 29th a group of volunteers, mostly French residents of Tientsin, set out from that place to go by train on the newly mended line. They returned on Wednesday the 30th empty-handed, having found that all rescues possible by railway had already been effected.

A more successful and stirring rescue was carried out by a small band of foreigners from Peking. It was led by an adventurous Swiss, Auguste Chamot, the manager of the Peking Hotel, who proved to be one of the outstanding heroes in the later siege, and who led a subsequent adventurous career elsewhere about the globe. Accompanied by his equally adventurous American first wife, for he did not lead a placid marital life, a young Australian named Dupree and four Frenchmen, he rode out along the road south with carts, spare animals, provisions, arms and ammunition. The party apparently met no opposition on the way and successfully evacuated the engineers and their families to Peking. Reports of the numbers rescued vary, but they consisted of seven children, about nine women and approximately a dozen men. As the party left Ch'ang Hsin Tien and retreated north they saw their houses and the compound they had been defending being destroyed. The most disturbing sight was that of the Chinese soldiers who had been sent by the local officials to defend them, participating in the looting, giving credence to the rumours circulating among foreigners that the Chinese army had joined the Boxers. The party reached Peking the same evening where they were afforded only momentary relief from danger.

THE HORROR MARCH FROM PAO TING FU

The rescue of the foreign engineers from Ch'ang Hsin Tien did not raise much interest. It was fortunately successful. The fate of the party at Pao Ting Fu was a different matter. Part of their group was massacred and the rest underwent a particularly harrassing march to escape. News of their plight and sufferings took some time to sift through. It was early June before the details were known, and a feeling of revulsion swept the foreign communities in China about the incident when it became known. It was from that time, after the survivors of the march came in, that foreigners began to talk about a reign of terror which did more than anything to harden foreign attitudes towards the Chinese and incite a bitter racial struggle.

The foreign engineers at Pao Ting Fu were attacked at the same time as the general attack was made on the railway line. With that and the telegraph destroyed they were cut off from the outside world and escape, and the hope of rescue seemed remote. It was consequently left either for the besieged foreigners or for the Chinese authorities to save them. In the circumstances, in view of the disturbed conditions, they decided to quit the city *en masse*. There were three ways of getting out of Pao Ting Fu. A traveller could follow the proposed railway line to the south and the Yangtze River, which was dangerous as it meant travelling through the anti-foreign provinces south of Chihli. Alternatively, a traveller could move north along the same railway line to Peking which was also dangerous as it meant going through known Boxer territory. Finally it was possible to travel to Tientsin in an easterly direction along the Tung Tien River which was used for navigation between the two places. As this was the shortest route to the coast and seemed the safest, the engineers decided to follow this.

The party of thirty survivors which included six women and one child, left Pao Ting Fu on May the 31st, making for the river under the protection of a Chinese official and a small Chinese military force. They took a boat down the river still accompanied by soldiers. For the first 150 *li* (fifty miles) there was no trouble. Then as they entered a narrow channel in the river they were confronted by Boxers who stood on the river banks and threatened the party with a wooden cannon. The party decided to push on and the foreigners were advised by the Chinese soldiers to close the windows of the boat and keep out of sight as they tried to sail past quickly. Unfortunately the boats ran aground at the narrowest part of the river and the Boxers attacked. Fire was returned by the engineers and a number of the attackers were killed. When the battle subsided the engineers jumped out of the boat and pushed it to the further bank which seemed free of Boxers, where the party took stock of the situation.

The leader of the party Assent, a Swiss, together with his sister and an Italian and a Turk separated from the group and, it seems, set out to return to Pao Ting Fu for safety. They did not reach the city. They were murdered in particularly brutal circumstances while on the way, and their bodies were mutilated by the Boxers.

Unaware of the fate of these four refugees, the rest of the party formed a square with the women inside and began the long march to Tientsin with little food, ill-clad and relying only on what water they could find on the way. They marched in that manner for three and a half days, avoiding villages and towns, taking a circuitous route, fighting their way to the coast against spasmodic attacks. The women were a particular worry to the party. One was near maternity, and she and the other women who were weak and exhausted, as well as the child, had to be carried by the men. The effort was too much for some. Five men broke away from the party when they were about forty *li* (thirteen miles) from Tientsin. Two of these turned up in Tientsin at 1 a.m. on Sunday the 3rd of June. News of the party's plight was thus made known, and a group of twenty-five armed men set out from Tientsin at 11 a.m. to shepherd them in. As something of an anti-climax, the armed patrol failed to find the large party of refugees but the Belgian Consul Ketels, and a doctor who went out unescorted found them and brought them in. A sweep was then made by Cossack troops to look for the three missing men, but without success.

THE MURDER OF ROBINSON AND NORMAN

At the same time as the march from Pao Ting Fu came to the notice of foreigners, news came of even more alarming incidents. Two British missionaries, Robinson and Norman, were murdered at Yung Ch'ing, about twenty miles north-east of Pao Ting Fu. There were few details reported about the matter. Yung Ch'ing was an isolated place, but the facts which did come to hand were disturbing to say the least. The attack was made, as in the case of the Pao Ting Fu incident, on the Chinese double fifth, the day of the Dragon Boat Festival. Robinson and five converts were killed straight away. Norman was captured and was killed in brutal and cold-blooded circumstances the following day, adding to the belief among foreigners in north China that they were living in the midst of a rising terror.

A major crisis did not occur immediately, however. The violence that broke out about the time of the Dragon Boat Festival died as suddenly as it began, and matters remained quiet as far as foreigners and foreign settlements were concerned. The worst that happened to foreigners in early June was that they found their 'boys' leaving them, and found Chinese acquaintances avoiding them or giving them whispered warnings to clear out while they could.

The two series of brutal murders at Pao Ting Fu and at Yung Ch'ing nevertheless had serious consequences. The incidents gave hot-heads on both sides an opportunity to incite trouble. Anti-foreign elements in China were given a fillip when nothing was done to punish the attackers, and foreigners in the treaty ports and at home commenced to demand revenge and firm action by their governments. There were even suggestions made by some foreigners for the foreign powers to capture high Chinese officials in the south and hold them as hostages, and to pour troops into the north. Although the more extreme demands were ignored, significant foreign forces began to assemble off Taku in early June, and more token forces of guards were landed at Taku to move inland to protect foreign settlements in Peking and Tientsin which began to take on the appearance of an armed camp. The foreign military display, if it was intended to be one, was a half-hearted affair. There were no more than 300 foreign troops ashore. The bulk of the forces still remained in the deep-draught ships which were anchored out of sight of the Chinese coast beyond the bar that guarded the entrance to the Pei Ho (North River). The foreign powers still did not intend to reveal their strong arms and frighten the Chinese government. They continued to hope that the Chinese government would come to its senses and take action to preserve the peace. In view of this the foreign ministers in Peking continued to work to end the confrontation.

FURTHER ANTI-FOREIGNISM IN THE COURT 4TH TO 9TH JUNE

In the face of the evidence there was really no chance for MacDonald and the other foreign ministers to hope for a return to peace. The real seriousness of the situation was brought home to MacDonald at a meeting he had with the Chinese foreign ministers on the 4th of June. When he called on them to protest about the murders of the British missionaries and the foreigners at Yung Ch'ing and Pao Ting Fu, one of the Chinese ministers fell asleep while MacDonald was talking, and the others remained unmoved. Consequently, he abruptly walked out of the meeting. The next day MacDonald went back to see Prince Ch'ing, the head Chinese Foreign Office official, and received nothing but what he now saw to be the conventional expressions of assurances. As regards the Boxers, the Chinese ministers appeared to be helpless and MacDonald at last became concerned. He had cause to be. While MacDonald was talking, the war party at the Court was further consolidating its position and the Imperial Army, as MacDonald and his secretary Cockburn feared, was not controlling Boxers, but appeared to be infiltrated by them. This was clearly revealed in a new round of anti-foreign and anti-Christian riots.

As a result of the foreign guards coming to Peking and the stories that others were about to follow, Boxer attention had moved away from the main Lu Han railway line and was directed at the Peking-Tientsin line. From the 4th of June considerable Boxer activity was reported along this line, and there were rumours that Imperial troops had been ordered to hold their fire and not attack Boxers who seemed to have achieved the position of auxiliary Imperial forces. The rumours now appeared to be fact. General Nieh who was in charge of the Chinese army based between Peking and Tientsin, had attacked a Boxer force at the outbreak of trouble on the 4th and defeated them, but had been ordered back to his base instead of being commended.

The anti-foreign Manchus were managing to neutralize the work of the moderates, and it was pointless for the ministers at the Chinese Foreign Office to do anything more than sleep or give blind assurances. Their power was exceedingly limited.

A meeting of Court advisers had taken place in the Court on June the 4th, and the moderates had been over-ruled by Prince Tuan and the other extremists on the point of whether or not the Boxers were to be regarded as patriots. This discussion in itself was not so important as the subsequent meeting of the Grand Council, which was held in the presence of the Empress Dowager on the 6th of June. The moderates there, putting forward what seemed to be sound arguments, managed to convince the Empress Dowager to appoint officials to go to the Boxer camps at Liang Shiang and Cho Chow, outside Peking, to intercede with the Boxer leaders and try to disperse the group. If their pleas failed, then the delegates were empowered to call in General Nieh's troops and use force to complete the task. This policy was agreed to at the Council meeting, but the disturbing thing was that the two officials appointed, Chao Shu-ch'iao and Ho Jun-sheng, were certainly not firm-minded about the foreign question, and also, on the same day, while the delegates were on their way, a new decree was issued which condemned Christian priests for interfering in Chinese village life and for causing trouble, which was not the wisest way for the Court to act in the midst of such an explosive situation.

Whether or not the Manchu anti-foreign party confined their activities to this, or actively interfered with the peace mission as well, is not clear. Unofficial reports indicated that some high Manchus went with the peace mission to the Boxers, and the attempts to make the Boxers see reason proved to be unsuccessful. The delegates returned to Peking on the 8th without actually finding any Boxer leaders to talk to, having done nothing but paste up some proclamations in the cities they visited.

Immediately after the projected governmental peace talks with Boxers in the vicinity of the capital failed, more troubles broke out. On the 8th Boxers were reported to have destroyed sections of the railway line between Tientsin and Peking while Imperial troops, who were charged with protecting the railway, were withdrawing. At the same time the whole countryside appeared to come under the control of Boxer forces. Massacres of Christian converts took place especially to the west of Peking. At Tung Chow, fourteen miles from the capital, an American school was destroyed and as on other occasions, Imperial troops were seen joining with the bands of incendiaries and looters, giving even further credence to the reports and rumours that the army had turned pro-Boxer. More disturbing for foreigners, the Boxers had not only moved in on Tientsin, but were gathering in force in the temple-studded Western Hills where the foreign Summer Legations were established. Added to this, Boxers were seen openly parading in Peking in increasing numbers, and the anti-foreign troops from Kansu province under General Tung Fu-hsiang, were strutting about the streets of the capital from the 9th. There now seemed every possibility even to the most optimistic of the foreigners, that the foreigners in the capital would be cut off from the coast.

PEKING THREATENED: THE ATTACK ON THE RACE COURSE

Peking itself, and foreign residents there had been free from attack and interference to the 9th of June. Down to that time there had only been veiled threats with nothing more violent directed at foreigners than invectives and spittle. The only sight that foreigners in Peking had of trouble at the end of the first week in June was the smoke from the burning railway outside the city walls and, for those who ventured into the streets, the existence of red-girdled and red-turbaned secret-society men. On the 9th this suddenly changed and feelings of alarm arose that overshadowed all previous crises. The Boxer target on that day was the Race Course. This was situated not far outside the southern city gates, near the first railway station outside Peking, on the railway line to Tientsin. On the evening of the 9th, which was a Sunday, a crowd of Boxers and anti-foreign rioters assembled at the Race Course, which had become a symbol of foreign intrusion, and burnt the grand stand, incinerating a number of

Christian converts who had been captured and hustled into the building.

This time it was the British Minister, MacDonald, who took the initiative in dealing with the matter, rallying his colleagues to act quickly to prevent a disaster. There was no real reason for Sir Claude to stir himself about this new act of destruction. His ponies had not done very well at the Spring Race Meeting, although no doubt he had a soft spot for Flying Fox which had come second in three of the races. Perhaps it was this, or his general sporting instinct, or a genuine fear that the Boxers were getting uncomfortably close to foreigners which moved him. In any case, no matter what the reason, when the reports of the destruction of the Race Course reached him, he burst into activity with as much alacrity as a Hindu who heard of the slaughter of sacred cows. Without waiting to consult his diplomatic colleagues MacDonald immediately sent a telegram to Sir Edward Seymour, the British admiral in command of the naval squadron at Taku, asking him to send a relief force to Peking. With this done MacDonald then met with the other foreign ministers. The reception he received there was not enthusiastic. This time it was Pichon who took a cool stand and advised caution and moderation, suggesting that the British minister was viewing the news in an alarmist manner. The ministers this time saw eye to eye with Pichon, who seemed to be well informed, and it was decided to hold back the proposed relief force sent for by MacDonald for a day in case the move incited further trouble. In the meantime preparations were made in Peking to receive refugees in the Legation Quarter, and the foreign powers and foreign missionaries took the precaution of handing over Christian mission property to the care of the Chinese government, informing them that they would be held responsible for its safe keeping.

It will never be known if Pichon, who urged caution, or MacDonald, who sent urgent appeals for a relief force, was correct in the interpretation of events. On the face value of the evidence there seems to have been less cause for panic than during the crisis in the latter part of May. Admittedly, in early June the Boxers were closer to the Legations and vicious rumours were circulating and anti-foreign placards were being pasted up about the city, but on the brighter side the telegraph system was still working and the railway line was not permanently out of action, and more important, no more foreigners had been attacked and killed since the earlier murders. What is certain, however, is that MacDonald's call for a relieving force caused a serious escalation of the struggle. The guards he called for set out from Tientsin as requested and as the large contingent moved inland, like an invading army, the general situation deteriorated and new waves of violence broke out.

ADMIRAL SEYMOUR'S RELIEF ATTEMPT

In order to understand better the rise of the new troubles inland, which culminated in the siege of the Legations, it is necessary to turn away from happenings at the capital and along the railway lines, and take note of the course events were taking at Taku, just off the coast of China, where the allied fleets were assembling.

Warships of the Chinese squadrons of the various foreign powers moved in on Taku at the end of May. When news of the destruction of the Lu Han line came to hand there were already fifteen vessels anchored and prepared for eventualities, not far from the mouth of the Pei Ho, awaiting any demands the foreign ministers at Peking might make of them. On May the 30th and 31st the first contingent of guards had been landed, as requested, and sent to Peking and as the situation deteriorated further reinforcements of vessels continually arrived from the various foreign naval bases that had been established on the different parts of the China coast two years before during 'the battle for concessions'.

The news of the Pao Ting Fu massacre and march, and the Norman and Robinson's murder, as well as reports of growing anti-foreignism at the Court, which came to the ears of the allies at the coast about the 3rd of June, brought a radical change to the situation. The admirals who were stationed at Taku, it should be realized, were not merely servants of the foreign ministers. They were significant officials armed with independent powers which they could use whenever they felt the need arose. On June the 4th, in view of the possibility of the ministers and other foreigners being sealed off and attacked, the naval authorities decided to use their powers. More troops were landed and sent to Tientsin to be at the ready, and on the 5th, at Admiral Seymour's suggestion, a conference of senior naval officers was formed to arrange for co-ordinated action by the different naval

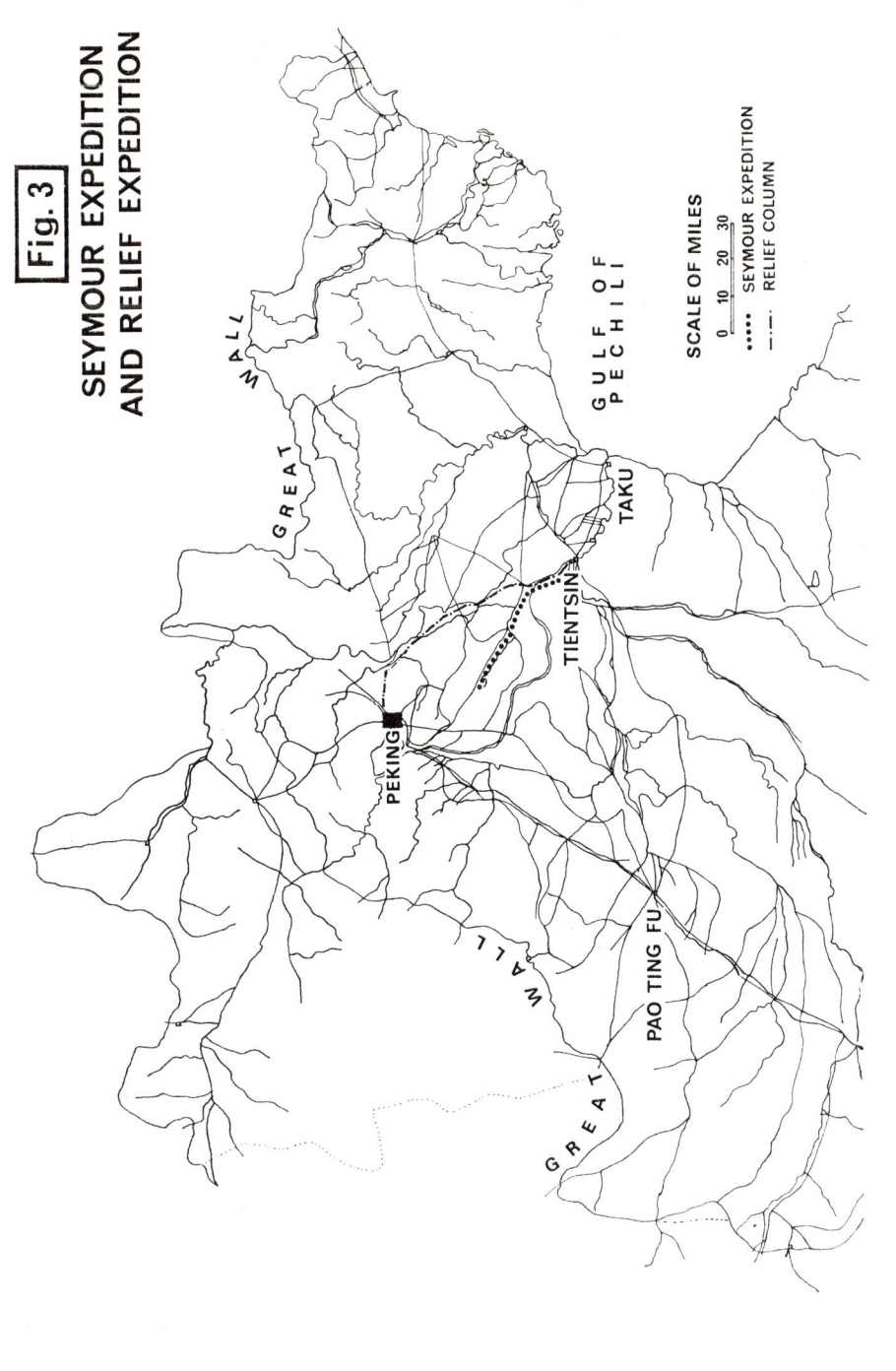

forces, while guard-boats were sent to stand by at the mouth of the Pei Ho, which provided the only accessible gateway to Tientsin and the inland. More significant, at the same time, the foreign admirals were given the go ahead by their governments to take any action felt necessary to save the ministers and foreigners. This matter was discussed by the senior naval officers at an allied meeting held on June the 6th, and it was decided that if Peking was cut off then they would send a force inland to relieve the besieged foreigners. The naval officers were in particular disturbed by the rumours that a rising had been planned for June the 19th, the anniversary of the Tientsin massacre; and by intelligence reports that the Imperial troops were acting with the Boxers.

This system of divided rule, whereby the ministers at Peking and the admirals both had power, although it may have been necessary, was fraught with danger. If either acted precipitately without the fullest information about the situation, the move could embarrass or even endanger the other party.

At the time of the burning of the Race Course this sort of bungling was avoided. Communications were still intact and action taken at Taku could be co-ordinated with measures being taken at Peking. Nevertheless, the subsequent moves made were disastrous and badly managed, mainly because of Admiral Seymour who acted far too hastily and followed a narrow independent line without using to good advantage the allied war council he helped to create.

Time, of course, had something to do with the matter. It was not until 11.30 p.m. on the 9th that Seymour received MacDonald's urgent call for help. In view of the alarm shown by MacDonald, Seymour decided to set out immediately with a force to relieve Peking before it was too late. Instead of calling up his colleagues to discuss the situation, he left notes to inform them of his decision and hoped that they would co-operate by sending following contingents. The British forces were immediately landed under Seymour's personal command and were later joined by other contingents.

It was unfortunate that Seymour chose to lead the force himself. The task of moving a large allied contingent across nearly one hundred miles of hostile territory, with little prior planning was no easy task, and Seymour, who may have been able to keep one of Her Majesty's ships spick and span, certainly had no experience of this style of warfare, nor did he seem to have the intellectual capacity needed to cope with the challenge. His action, in fact, was a typical example of British 'amateurism' that was then being severely criticized in the case of the Boer War.

Indeed it has never been made clear why Seymour chose to leave his flag-ship and move inland. No doubt he was influenced in some way by the heroes who had emerged from the Boer War as siege raisers. Names like Field-Marshal Roberts and General Baden-Powell were on everybody's lips after Mafeking and Ladysmith were relieved, and siege reliefs were the very thing to catch the attention of the Poet Laureate, as the siege of Lucknow had stirred Tennyson and prompted him to immortalize the incident in English literature. In any case, no matter what his motives, Seymour set off with little more than high thoughts and a body of ill-equipped marines, to head for disaster.

Seymour and the British marines left Taku at 6 a.m. on the 10th and arrived at Tientsin shortly afterwards, where he assembled an international force of just over 2,000 men, consisting of 915 British, 450 German, 358 French, 312 Russians, 112 Americans, 54 Japanese, 40 Italians and 25 Austrians.

While these were being assembled, railway trains were being prepared to take the force to Peking, and the foreign consuls at Tientsin made arrangements with Yu Lu, the Governor-General of Chihli, to let the trains leave Tientsin. Permission to do this was granted at 9.30 a.m. and the first train moved off with four others following, loaded with troops, material to fix the railway line destroyed, and provisions for three days which seemed ridiculous in view of the task ahead. However, Seymour expected to reach Peking that day, despite the fact that a large Imperial force under General Nieh, and an unknown number of Boxers lay between Tientsin and the capital.

Progress made by the column was disappointingly slow. Instead of reaching Peking on the 10th, the force travelled only twenty-five miles, to Yang Tsun, having had to repair the line which was being torn up ahead of them.

On the 11th, after leaving small detachments of guards at the various stations passed, the force pushed onwards reaching Lang Fang by the night of the 11th. There the trains were halted by Boxers who were destroying the lines. A small force was sent ahead to scout, but could not get beyond the village of An Ting because of the vigorous opposition by Boxers. There seemed nothing for it but to sit it out and send back to Tientsin for more materials to repair the line, and for supplies. Already, however, disturbing reports had come to hand that the Boxers were active behind the column in between Lang Fang and Tientsin. This, unfortunately for Seymour and the men with him, proved to be true as he soon found out. On the 15th he sent off a supply train to go to Tientsin. It returned after a short while, the crew reporting that there was little left of the line they had built on the way up. Seymour and his 2,000 men were trapped inland with stores running out fast, as well as their ammunition.

In view of the fact that the railway lines were being torn up as fast as they were laid, Seymour decided on the 16th to fall back and make the attempt to relieve Peking by the river route. He therefore evacuated his forces to Yang Tsun along the remaining piece of track, to where the railway line crosses the river. From there he could make his way down stream to Tientsin to regroup. During this operation there was a marked deterioration in his fortunes. The German cavalry reported on the 18th that they had been engaged in a fight with large forces of the Chinese Imperial Army which seemed to have joined in the attack on the column. This news was disastrous. Seymour had hoped at least for their neutrality or at the best for the Chinese army to control the Boxers along the railway line. Instead he now faced two foes. The reason for this change in events, as we shall see later, is that another force was landed from the foreign fleets unknown to Seymour and had attacked the Chinese army on the coast the day before.

Attacks on the trains after the 19th became continuous and Seymour reached the river with great difficulty. There the trains were abandoned and some junks were captured to take the column to Tientsin. Unfortunately the drought was still bad and the river level was so low that the junks could only proceed with difficulty. Consequently the heavy equipment and heavy arms had to be left, thus seriously weakening the effectiveness of the force. In order to move their boats Seymour's force had to clear both banks of the river of enemy forces, while equipped only with light arms. Consequently, before long, the junks were discarded and the column began to march along the river banks. Even then progress was slow. The force was harassed continually by Chinese cavalry and artillery, against which they could do little.

On June the 22nd, after an arduous trek, a large building was seen on the banks of the river. The exhausted force took stock, saw that it was inadequately guarded, and decided to attack it. This was successfully accomplished and Seymour found that he had captured the Chinese Imperial Arsenal at Hsi Ku, not far from Tientsin. More important he had found food, water and other stores, not in great quantities, but enough to ward off disaster. Seymour's force did not move out of the Arsenal. They tried to get messengers out to inform Tientsin of their plight, but these were all caught. Consequently Seymour sat down to wait for rescue. The force remained at the Arsenal on half rations until the 26th when an army of Russian Cossacks found them and escorted them to Tientsin.

The first allied attempt to relieve the Legations thus ended in disaster. Instead of returning to the coast for a triumphal march, the column returned in what was virtually a flight. This defeat of the allies at the outset of hostilities in the north had serious consequences in both the Chinese and allied camp. As far as the former was concerned the Boxers and anti-foreign elements gained a significant psychological victory. The superiorly equipped foreigners had been defeated and expelled. Closer at home, in the allied camp, there were murmurings. Seymour was personally liked, but he had not proved British mettle and Britain's military capacity. When the next expedition was formed, although Britain sent a most competent professional soldier from the Indian Army, he was passed over in favour of a German Commander-in-Chief whose experience was limited to European wars.

The disaster that overtook the column was not wholly Seymour's fault. His main mistake was in moving a large, ill-equipped force inland without taking the precaution of guarding his supply lines and without assessing properly the political situation in Chihli province. He could not be blamed for the furious attacks that were suddenly made on his force on and after the 18th. These were brought about in great part by events in Peking and at Taku, which lay outside Seymour's power and knowledge. These caused not only an increase in confrontation by the Chinese, but also led to a declaration of war by the Chinese Court on the foreign powers.

THE SIEGE OF THE LEGATIONS

EVENTS IN PEKING FROM 9TH TO 17TH JUNE

On the eve of the cataclysm foreigners were scattered about Peking. The bulk of them were in the Legation Quarter, but outside this were the missionaries, foreigners serving in the Chinese Maritime Customs and isolated diplomats such as the Belgians who, strictly speaking, were not in the diplomatic area.

By the 10th of June foreigners in Peking saw the writing on the wall. The streets of the capital were full of wild troops, there were continuous reports of Boxers consorting with them, and Imperial troops were seen mounting cannons on the Ch'ien Men[1] which overlooked the Legation Quarter, and which commanded the street down which the foreign troops would have to march from the railway station. At the same time the telegraph services were cut, as were normal mail services. More important, significant changes took place in the Chinese government. It was announced on the 10th that Prince Ch'ing and other moderates had been removed from the Chinese Foreign Office, which was placed under the superintendence of the noted pro-Boxer, Prince Tuan. In these circumstances the Legations commenced to organize their defences, preparing to hold out till the Relief Column, which they knew was on the way, arrived. A stock of food was taken in which was considered to be enough to last for at least a week.

If these events brought a sleepless rest to many of the foreigners cut off in Peking on the night of the 10th, two items of news on the following day revealed the Boxers in true colours to them.

The day of the 11th began with rays of hope. Before dawn news was circulated to the effect that the foreign troops had arrived at Ma Chia P'u, or were expected there. Consequently a number of foreigners prepared themselves and a number of baggage carts to go down to meet the expected reinforcements. While this was being done, there were already rumours in the city of a large-scale battle further down the Tientsin line and of a Chinese victory, although no foreigner in Peking really believed that the Chinese could have come off best, if in fact there had been a struggle.

The early morning expedition to the station through hostile Chinese crowds proved to be fruitless. No trains had arrived and

---

[1] Men is the Chinese term for gate. The Ch'ien Men was located near the Legation Quarter in the wall between the Chinese and Tartar Cities. For the location of this and other gates in Peking see Fig. 4 on page 74.

none were in sight, and there was no sign of the expected contingent of guards. Consequently most of the foreigners who had made the trip across the city gave up waiting and returned to the relative safety of the Legation Quarter.

On their return they were met with bad news. It was announced that the British Summer Legation in the Western Hills had been destroyed on the previous day and although the gatekeeper had escaped from the Boxers who attacked the building, his wife and children had been killed and the building which contained many of the MacDonalds' personal treasures had been ransacked and destroyed. This news was serious as it indicated that the Boxers would not stop at attacking foreign diplomatic property and that the Chinese government was not capable of protecting Legations.

THE MURDER OF SUGIYAMA

In the afternoon a second and more disturbing piece of news came to hand. One of the foreign diplomats, Sugiyama, the Chancellor at the Japanese Legation, was murdered when he went back from the Legation Quarter to Ma Chia P'u in the afternoon to arrange for the reception of the still expected troops. His action in doing this was extremely unwise. Sugiyama set out alone and unarmed to travel through a hostile population of Pekingese and soldiers who were not in an easy frame of mind. He passed through the city unharmed, but when he arrived outside the Yung Ting Men, the gate in the Chinese city near the railway station, he was attacked by members of Tung Fu-hsiang's Kansu force and killed in brutal circumstances, and his body was mutilated. This crime, strangely enough, was not the work of Boxers. Some of the Legation servants who were in the vicinity of the crime, and whose evidence was borne out by subsequent investigations, revealed that Kansu province soldiers were to blame. The disturbing thing about the murder as far as foreigners were concerned, was that it gave good grounds to believe the rumour that was spreading about the city that General Tung Fu-hsiang and his Kansu force were in Peking to stop foreign reinforcements getting there, and that the General himself was prepared to tear the hearts out of foreign invaders.

The foreign diplomats incomprehensibly did little about the murder. A protest of sorts was made to the Chinese Foreign

Office, and a very unsatisfactory decree was issued stating that the murder was the work of 'desperadoes', concealing the fact that Imperial troops were involved. It is difficult to understand why more was not made of Sugiyama's death. News about it was flashed abroad, but it did not cause much of a stir beyond Tokyo. It seemed to take the murder of a European to raise a world-wide outcry, even though in Sugiyama's case the principle of diplomatic immunity was involved.

BOXER ATTACKS IN PEKING

The situation between the time of the murder of Sugiyama and the 11th gave continual causes for alarm in Peking. The following day, the 12th, was relatively quiet. On the 13th, however, activities started in earnest. That day Boxers were seen in Legation Street, and the German Minister, Baron von Ketteler, who did not mind using his own mailed fist on occasions, himself attacked a group of demonstrators and captured one of the 'red band'. As a result of the appearance of Boxers in the close proximity of the Legations, armed guards were posted and small detachments were sent to guard the Pei T'ang the large Roman Catholic cathedral in the Imperial City, and to the Belgian Legation which lay outside the Legation Quarter, to give them some sort of protection.

There were now to all intents and purposes two groups of foreigners immured in Peking. There were those in the Legation Quarter, or in the area immediately about it, and there was a further group at the Pei T'ang in the Imperial City. The Pei T'ang, in fact, was quite well prepared for the events that followed. The experienced Father Favier who was in charge at the Cathedral, following his warnings to Pichon, had not hesitated to act to protect his church, his colleagues and his flock. Stores, arms and ammunition were laid in after the Pao Ting Fu massacre and consequently the Cathedral was successfully defended throughout the prolonged siege, despite constant and fierce attacks by the Chinese.

In the Legation Quarter preparations were not so carefully made. Flimsy barricades made of furniture were thrown up and outposts mounted, which needed considerable additions later on.

Little was done to bring in stocks of food to sustain the large numbers of people flocking into the area for refuge. The people who were evacuating missions outside the Legation Quarter for the most part arrived empty-handed, although they still had opportunities to bring in with them the stores that existed in their homes and missions.

During the day of the 13th of June the Boxers unleashed a general attack on Christian converts in the city. Many of them were massacred, and at the same time most of the foreign churches in Peking were set on fire, burning far into the night. Following that, further streams of refugees began to pour into the Legation Quarter, threatening to limit even more the amount of food available for all. Room for the refugees was also scarce. The Legation area was already crowded. Chinese refugees were therefore placed in the grounds of Prince Su's Palace near the British Legation, and the defence line was extended to surround and protect them.

That night the Boxers made their first attack on the Legations. Just after dark the foreign guards heard firing and saw lanterns moving in their direction along the street near the Austrian Legation. The Austrians on duty immediately opened fire with their machine gun. The next morning everyone of note gathered to see what damage had been done, but amazingly there were no signs of carnage. There were no bodies, no blood, indeed, no signs of a fight. Morrison of *The Times* blamed it on the Austrian marksmanship. Other commentators were no doubt more correct when they put it down to a Chinese trick of hanging moving lanterns on sticks, to draw fire. In any case, it was a bad affair as far as the foreigners were concerned. It added to the legend that Boxers were invulnerable.

Even after the events of that day and night, there were still isolated foreigners living in the Chinese City. The other major Catholic Cathedral, the Nan T'ang, or South Cathedral, which was situated in the Chinese City, had not been evacuated. During the following three days, the 14th, 15th and 16th, the foreigners in the Legations took the fight out into the enemy camp, sending out patrols to rescue the stragglers. On the 14th, Flecke, a French diplomatic officer, and the adventurous Chamots brought in the residents of the Nan T'ang, which was then seen to go up in flames. More rescues were made on the 15th. A larger foreign patrol of approximately forty went out on the 16th. They found no more refugees, but they came across a Boxer temple, complete with Boxers and Christian prisoners. They took immediate action. The forty-six Boxers were all shot on the spot and the party returned. This skirmish indicated the turn the struggle was taking in Peking and throughout the north. Feelings on both sides were now intense. Neither side found much to admire in the other, and did not look for reasons to spare lives when there were opportunities to do so. The war was becoming a bitter racial struggle.

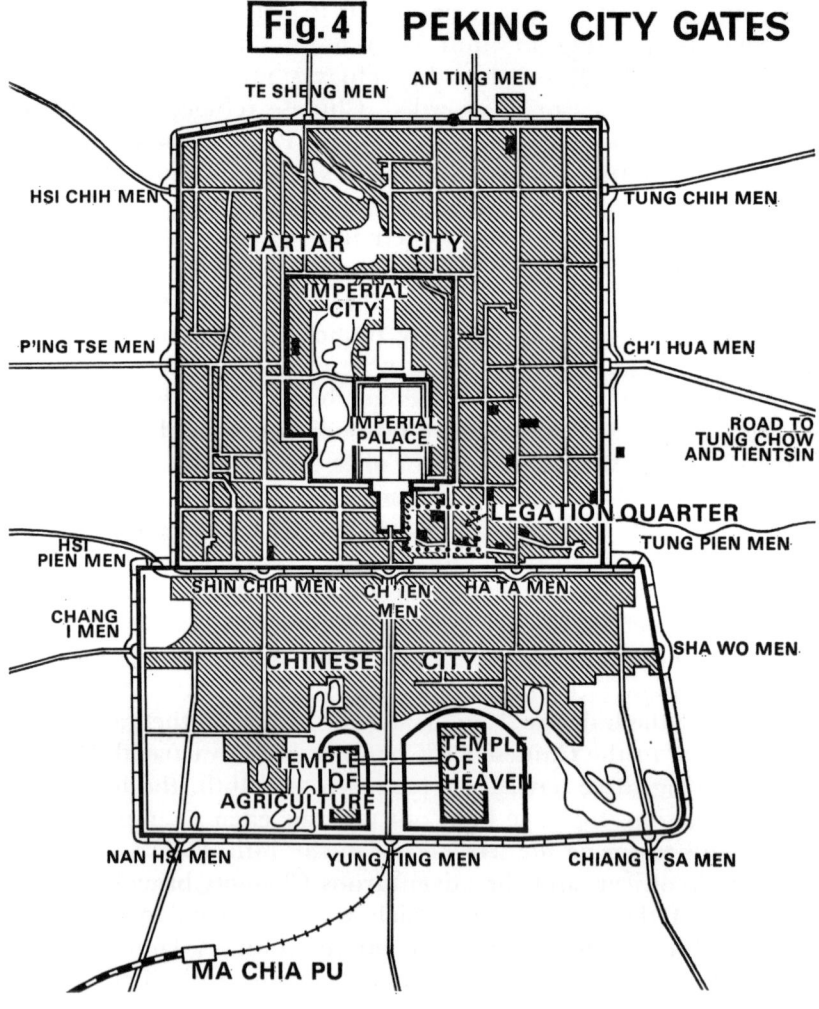

INTRODUCTION: CHINESE ANTI-FOREIGNISM

The Boxers, by the 16th, had been roaming openly about the city for seven days, destroying foreign property and attacking 'foreign devils' and 'second-class foreign devils', and they had been threatening the Legations since the 13th. On the 16th of June a further threat came. Just outside the Ch'ien Men, in the Chinese City, there was a large area containing a variety of stores, theatres, road-side stalls and cafés. For some time past various of the storekeepers there had handled foreign goods, and this soon came to the notice of the anti-foreign rioters.

The destruction of the Ch'ien Men

Boxer attention was turned to this market on the 16th. The first shop to suffer was a drug store, known as the Lao Teh Keh, which was associated with the foreign firm of Llewellyns. This was attacked and set on fire during the morning, and being in the centre of an area crowded with flimsy buildings, the flames soon spread to the other stores and swept on by the wind, moved northwards towards the Imperial City and the Legation Quarter. It was later estimated that some 4,000 stores were destroyed together with a huge quantity of merchandise, books and antiques. During the afternoon the fire still raged and finally reached the famous Ch'ien Men which went up in flames, providing a wonderful spectacle for the foreigners confined in the Legation Quarter. The only thing that saved the Legations from a similar fate was the city wall between them and the closely built up Chinese City. The foreigners gathered behind it drew a sigh of relief.

On the 19th of June, after several days of more restlessness and terror, at the time Seymour's Relief Column was being forced to turn back to Tientsin, the foreign diplomats received a shock. They were suddenly presented with an ultimatum demanding the surrender of the Taku forts on each side of the mouth of the Pei Ho so as to lay the way open to Peking. This followed the methods which the allies had used forty years before when they marched on Peking at the end of the second Opium War. The situation on the coast in fact was much worse than the foreigners in Peking were told. It was because of the situation there that the ultimatum was issued to diplomats in Peking, and Seymour found his column fighting for its existence on the way to the capital.

THE SIEGE OF THE LEGATIONS

THE ATTACK ON THE TAKU FORTS

After Admiral Seymour left the fleet with his forces to go to the aid of the Legations in Peking, a halt was called to the landing of further forces. The foreign powers at that stage had no desire to be committed to a large-scale struggle in East Asia for which they were ill-prepared. Troops reinforcements were distant from the potential war theatre, and were being carefully husbanded close to home in view of the crises in Europe and Africa at the end of the century. In any case there still seemed, even to those immured in Peking, a chance to patch up the trouble. Consequently only the small naval brigade under Seymour was sent off inland in the belief that the trouble would fizzle out as soon as the expected rains fell.

By mid-June two disturbing reports came into the hands of consuls and foreigners on the coast and the foreign admirals at Taku who were responsible for the protection of their nationals in China, which altered the situation in the north. On June the 15th the Boxers who had made for Tientsin from Shantung province, took control of the native city which lay just inland along the river from the foreign settlements, indicating that there was possibly an element of truth in the rumour that an extensive rising was to take place on the 19th of the month. The Boxers seemed to be closing in, and foreigners in Tientsin appeared to be facing the same fate as those threatened in Peking. This fear was made more real by the fact that no news had come from Seymour who was then inland, and in view of the small force that remained in the foreign settlements, there was every reason for foreign residents to believe that Tientsin, which lay some thirty miles from the sea, would be cut off from the coast and besieged and the inhabitants massacred. The loss of Tientsin in such circumstances would have been disastrous to the allied cause. It was not only a large and important foreign economic centre, but was regarded by foreign strategists as the base needed for any large-scale operations further inland, and for the relief of Peking. The fear for Tientsin's safety became more real when reports came of Boxer threats to the railway line between Tientsin and the coast.

On the previous day, the 14th, a second and even more shocking report began to circulate about the China coast. There was no official announcement, but rumour had it that the German

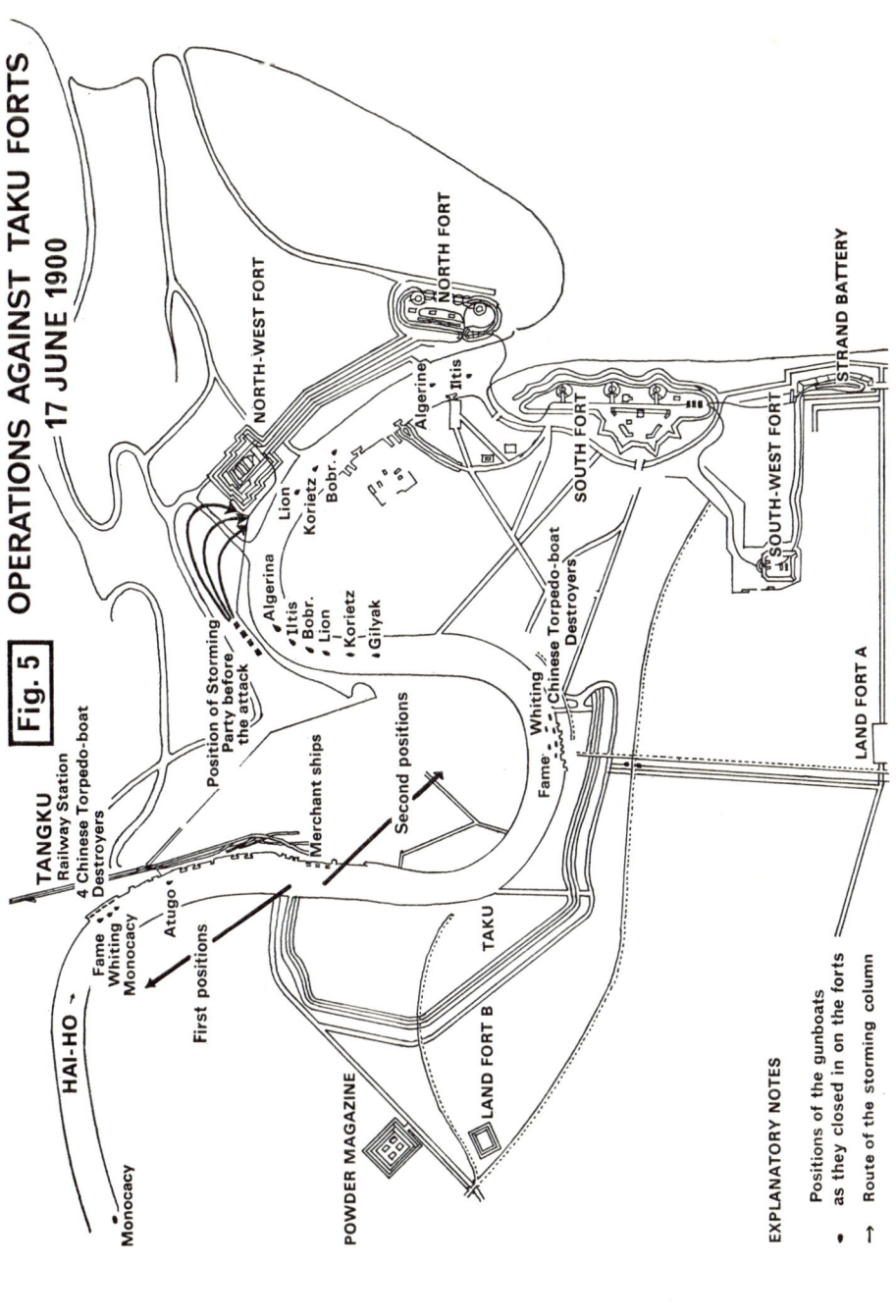

Minister, Baron von Ketteler, had been killed in Peking. The telegraph line to the capital was not working at the time and there was some hesitation about believing the new rumour. News of Sugiyama's death had come out some days previously and although there was a distinct possibility that further murders of foreigners could be expected, there was a feeling that the rumour was a garbled version of the Sugiyama incident or of the destruction of the British Summer Legation.

On the 16th of June it suddenly seemed that the rumour circulated in the previous two days was a fact. That day a news item was printed and sent about the world by the new but reliable Laffan's Newsagency, that Ketteler had been murdered on the 16th. The news immediately appeared in *The Times* (London) and other influential European newspapers, receiving prominent attention, sweeping domestic issues to the lesser important pages, which is certainly more than Sugiyama's death managed to do.

Laffan's Newsagency report remains one of the mysteries of the Boxer Uprising. The release they made was an official one, and was sent abroad by the respectable Exchange Telegraph Company, so there was little cause to doubt the reliability of the report. Ketteler was in fact killed, but actually not until the 20th of June, an error that has never been corrected in *The Times*. Indeed the true facts did not emerge until after the siege of the Peking Legations had been raised, and it has never been made clear how Laffan's got the news before the murder happened and why they of all newsagencies were favoured with advance information.

The admirals who waited on the ships of the allied fleet with the forces did not bother to check the truth of Laffan's report. The news items, for them, were openly depressing. Moreover, close by the fleet they saw for themselves that some sort of trouble was in the air. At the same time as the native city at Tientsin was being invaded by Boxers, Chinese Imperial forces were seen occupying the railway and laying mines at the mouth of the Pei Ho. Obviously as the Boxers had no vessels, it was rightly concluded that the Chinese government was preparing defences against a foreign invasion.

On June the 16th a meeting of admirals, held under the chairmanship of the Russian admiral who was the most senior officer, discussed the situation. In view of what was transpiring they decided to take immediate action to secure the way inland by occupying the Taku forts dominating the mouth of the Pei Ho. In the announcement which they issued they made it quite clear that they were not commencing an offensive. They maintained that they merely wished to preserve contact with the forces that they had already put ashore, and that they wanted to help re-establish order in the north. They also pointed out that the Chinese Imperial forces were in sympathy with the anti-foreign elements, and that China was not abiding by her international agreements and treaties which they were there to help protect. In view of this and the mining of the river, the admirals informed the Chinese authorities at Taku that they intended to occupy the forts with or without their consent by 2 a.m. on June the 17th.

The Chinese authorities could see no merit in the legal and military arguments put forward by the allies. Indeed in view of the edicts and notices which had been issued previously on a number of occasions by the Court, warning officials not to concede territory to encroaching foreigners, surrender would have been fatal for the Chinese officials concerned. The action would have been regarded as treason, and the officials would have been given the same salutary treatment that a British bureaucrat would have received at the hands of his government if he had surrendered Portsmouth or Chatham and the railway access to London to one of Britain's rivals in a time of crisis.

It is difficult to see why the admirals made this decision. The situation on the 16th was actually not impossible, and certainly did not warrant an attack on Chinese government forts. The only real cause for concern was the fact that Boxers controlled the Chinese city at Tientsin which was close to the foreign concessions there. The other items of news were mere rumours. Certainly the mining of the river entrance was a reality and Imperial troops were moving into positions along the railway line, but as yet no attempt had been made to hold up foreigners or foreign troops, or light draft vessels either at Taku or on the way to Tientsin.

The foreign admirals proceeded immediately with their quickly conceived plan. Landing parties were prepared and sent near the forts and eight gunboats were deployed in the river above the forts. The large vessels themselves could not move in close enough to take part in the action. But it was felt that the storming party

THE MANCHU ROYAL FAMILY 1821-1912, SHOWING BOXER AFFILIATIONS

Emperor Tao Kuang (Min Ning)
1821-51
(9 sons)

NAME OF GENERATION*	
Min	Emperor Tao Kuang (Min Ning) 1821-51 (9 sons) — sons numbered 1-9
I	2: Tzu Hsi or Yehenola = Emperor Hsien Feng (I Chu) 1831-62 (Empress Dowager); 5: I Tsung 1831-89 (8 sons); 7: I Huan = Yehenola's sister 1840-91 (5 sons)
Tsai	Emperor T'ung Chih (Tsai Ch'un) 1862-75 (no issue); Tsai Lien (Boxer); Tsai I (Prince Tuan) = Yehenola's niece (**Boxer**); Tsai Lan (Boxer); Emperor Kuang Hsu† (Tsai T'ien) 1875-1908 (no issue); Tsai Feng = Jung Lu's daughter
P'u	P'u Chun Heir Apparent 1900-01; Emperor Hsuan T'ung (P'u I) 1908-12

* The Manchus had generation names to show relationships with kinfolk. When a Manchu of the royal family became emperor, he was given a reign title. These are given in this table instead of his generation and personal name.

† Made emperor although the same generation (Tsai) as the previous emperor.

INTRODUCTION: CHINESE ANTI-FOREIGNISM

of 900 marines and the eight gunboats could tackle the task of capturing the forts if the Chinese did not surrender them.

More than an hour before the ultimatum expired, at about a quarter to one on the morning of the 17th, the Chinese commandant of the forts gave the allied high command his answer. His cannons opened fire on the allied gunboats. Six of these then moved down the river to take up positions near the forts, while the storming parties landed and moved down the left bank towards the northern forts. These soon fell to the invading force and by half past seven on the morning of the 17th, after a hard struggle, Taku and its forts were in allied hands.

There is still some doubt about whether or not the action on the coast led directly to the besieging of foreigners at Peking and Tientsin. Even now, when most of the evidence is available, the answer to that question is not clear. There is some reason to believe that a crisis would have occurred even if Taku had not been captured. What is certain, however, is that the allied action had immediate repercussions inland. Seymour and his relief force were the first to feel these as they were retreating on the 18th, as has been described. Similarly in Peking the Chinese officials began to take a tougher line which culminated in a declaration of war on the allies on June the 21st.

CRISIS IN PEKING, JUNE 19TH

News of the allied victory at Taku actually took some time to reach the Chinese officials at the capital. The Court certainly knew of the ultimatum that had been made by the allied commanders, but in the true fashion of the times in China there was no official who was willing to inform the Court that the Chinese army had suffered a defeat at the hands of the foreigners.

On the 17th, while the struggle was already under way at the coast, the United States Minister was at the Chinese Foreign Office for an interview. The records of the conversation which have been preserved, show quite clearly that the Chinese were trying to prize from him as much information of military value as they could get. They wanted in particular to know about the number of troops on the way, and when they were expected. Conger, of course, had very good answers to these queries. The telegraph had been cut and he knew nothing. But he did impress upon them, as did other foreign diplomats, that if the foreign ministers were killed then Peking would be destroyed.

It was no doubt with this in mind that the ultimatum was issued by the Chinese government at 4 p.m. on the 19th for diplomats to leave Peking within twenty-four hours. Morrison, *The Times* correspondent, in his later detailed reports of events in Peking at the time[1] stated that the powers agreed to evacuate as ordered. This certainly was not the case, and is one of the number of inaccurate statements made by Morrison about the Boxers and the siege. The ministers, in fact, met and decided to play for time. They knew that there was something going on at the coast, and that Seymour's Relief Column had run into trouble and had not arrived, and they were aware that the Legations had few military resources to protect a large number of foreign men, women and children, as well as native Christians, on a march. They therefore decided to ask the Chinese Foreign Office for an interview the following morning, on the 20th, and then to play for more time they would inform the Chinese ministers that as the Chinese admitted that the situation between Peking and Tientsin was unsettled and that the Chinese armies were unreliable, they would not move out of the Legation Quarter until guards other than Chinese arrived.

THE KETTELER'S MURDER

The ministers met at the French Legation at 8.30 a.m. on the morning of the 20th as arranged. Although some time had passed no reply had been received from the Chinese Foreign Office. But this was not disturbing. The Chinese ministers had never been known for their alacrity. Von Ketteler, the German Minister, who had other business to conduct with the Chinese, decided to go on alone to the Chinese Foreign Office which lay to the north-east of the Legations, where it was situated in a side street running off the main Ha Ta Men Street. The other ministers had no objection to Ketteler speaking for them. He was a competent Chinese scholar and knew what he was about, and they knew that he would not take a soft line. He therefore set out at 9 a.m. in a sedan chair, followed by his interpreter, Cordes, who occupied a second chair.

[1] *The Times,* 13 Oct. 1900 and 14 Oct. 1900.

This was certainly a brave move. Cordes had seen the Chinese Foreign Office officials on the previous day, and knew about the Taku affair, and that in these circumstances the streets of Peking were not likely to be safe for foreigners. Indeed it was pointless to expect that Chinese Imperial forces, who were being confronted at Taku and along the railway line, would readily protect foreigners abroad in the streets of Peking or anywhere else in the north.

The two Germans left the French Legation, passed the Imperial Maritime Customs and Austrian Legation, and turned up Chang An Street and then into Ha Ta Men Street. Just north of the Legation Quarter in Ha Ta Men Street was situated the Belgian Legation. Ketteler had just passed this and was near the police station which was situated nearby on the left hand side of the street, when Cordes saw a Manchu soldier who was standing in the street, put his rifle in the German Minister's chair and fire. Cordes immediately shouted to his own porters who dropped his chair and ran, with Cordes scrambling after them. He took a look at Ketteler whom he saw was lying still. The troops then turned on Cordes who was shot in the thigh, but somewhat miraculously he managed to make his escape into the crowded side streets and eventually found his way to the American Mission near the Legation Quarter. This must have been a considerable feat in view of his condition and his lack of familiarity with the confusion of alleys which make up that part of Peking.

When Cordes returned foreign search parties were sent out, but Chinese troops blocked their way and Ketteler's body remained where it was. The Chinese later buried the corpse on the spot where the murder occurred, and it stayed there until Peking was occupied by the foreign powers.

It is difficult to ascertain why Ketteler was killed. Later investigations revealed that the soldier who committed the murder had volunteered after promises of a reward had been made by anti-foreign Manchu officials. One should not ignore the fact that Ketteler was not the most popular diplomat in Peking with the Chinese. He was an irascible man who would tolerate no slight made on his country and did not hesitate to use his walking stick on demonstrators who offended him or Germany. It must also be borne in mind that Germany had demanded a slice of Shantung which caused tremendous bitterness in the metropolitan provinces. In any case, no matter what the cause of his belated death, the murder gave Germany and the Kaiser a special reason to mount an expedition to fight a war for the Cross in China. The German forces, as a result of the loss of Ketteler, were consequently given the leading rôle in the relief expedition and the occupation of the country that followed the fall of Peking, supplying the commander-in-chief of the allied forces.

THE SIEGE AT PEKING

In view of the murder of Ketteler, the foreigners did not move out of Peking, and felt thankful that they had rejected the earlier ultimatum. There is no doubt in view of what was happening at the coast, that they would have suffered the same fate had they been caught in the open. Consequently the foreigners in Peking prepared themselves for a siege in the confined space of the Legation Quarter.

A note was sent to the foreign ministers from the Chinese Foreign Office on the 20th. In this nothing was said about Ketteler's murder. The only reference the Chinese ministers, who must have known of the incident, made about the matter was an oblique reference to the unsettled state of affairs and a warning that the foreign ministers should not come to see them at 9 a.m., as the streets were too dangerous. The note ended with an invitation for the foreign ministers to reconsider the ultimatum, and to find ways to move the foreign representatives and their dependents out of Peking.

Sharp at 4 p.m. the Chinese opened fire on the Legation Quarter. This was returned by the prepared guards and the siege began. The events from then on until August the 14th, when the second Relief Column entered the Legation Quarter, are purely military and are very well described in Giles's diary.

There were two distinct phases in the siege. From June the 20th until July the 14th the defenders were attacked with rifle and artillery fire from all sides. After that, until the end of the siege in August, although there were some ferocious attacks, there was only rifle fire used.

On the 20th of June, after the first attack was over, outposts were called in from the outlying Belgian Legation and American Mission, and the defence line was straightened to make the defenders' task easier. Once this was done work was immediately

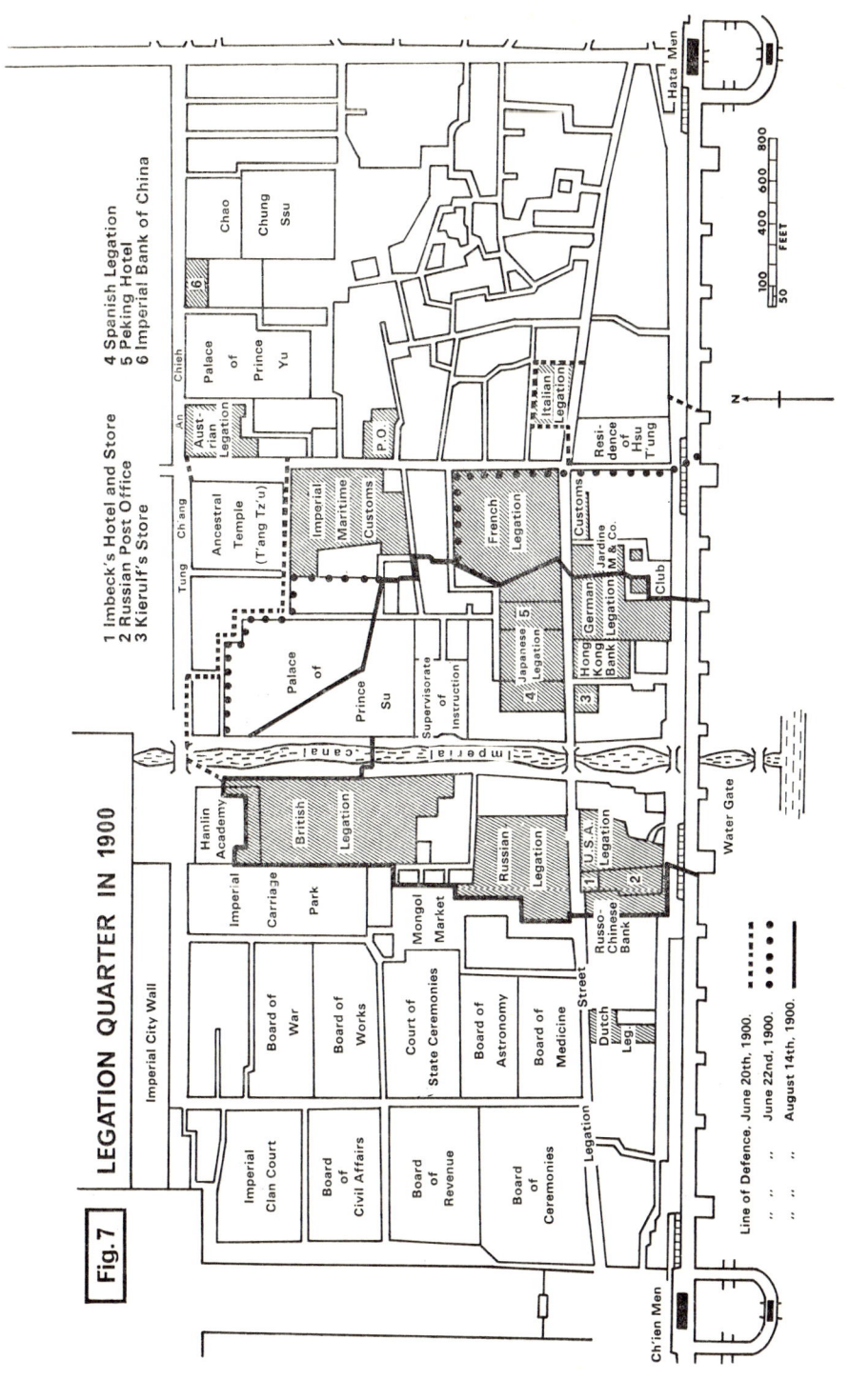

commenced to strengthen the shortened defence works to withstand the expected assaults. Fortifications were built out of sandbags hastily made by the ladies out of any material they could find and commandeer, to replace the flimsy barricades that were thrown up earlier. Loop-holes were knocked in walls, new brick walls were built, and bomb-proof shelters were constructed. Two lines of defence were actually built by the besieged. A heavily defended outside perimeter, shown on the map on page 85, surrounded the Legation Quarter. Inside this the British Legation, which was in somewhat a safe position, was heavily fortified and protected as an inner strong-point to which the defenders could fall back if that became necessary.

In charge of these operations was the British Minister, Sir Claude MacDonald, who had been a regular officer in the Scots Greys, a regiment in the British Army renowned for their pugnacity. To help him he had Squiers, the Secretary of the United States Legation, who was also a former army man, and who served as MacDonald's Chief of Staff. Together these commanded an ill-equipped ragged allied force consisting of 400 assorted guards speaking a variety of languages, and a force of seventy-five volunteers who were known as Thornhill's Roughs, copying the title made popular by Theodore Roosevelt's Rough Riders, but who were better known as the 'Carving Knife Brigade' because of the weapons they had. The latter force was a very amateur one. As one observer stated, the most experienced of the volunteers had once seen a military parade in London. However, both the forces acquitted themselves well, and in the siege Sir Claude proved that whatever he lacked as a diplomat he made up for as a soldier.

In spite of the tightening up of the Legation Quarter's defences the initial pressure put on them by the Chinese proved to be too much. Consequently, on June the 22nd further withdrawals were made. The Austrian Legation and the Imperial Maritime Customs, which proved to be untenable, were evacuated, and the whole of the eastern defence line was shortened, so that the bulk of the French Legation also fell into Chinese hands.

In the western sector, however, advances were made and the situation seemed to be well in hand. This was the result of two measures taken immediately after the initial Chinese attack. First, a defensive area, or glacis, was cleared about the British Legation in particular, by burning and destroying the Chinese homes that lay just outside the Legation Quarter. This *cordon sanitaire* made

Chinese open attacks and infiltration movements much more difficult. Second, the foreign guards captured and held strong points on the city wall near the United States Legation, in the direction of the Ch'ien Men, which made the Legation Quarter relatively safe. If the Chinese had managed to capture the part of the city wall which overlooked the Legation Quarter, the besieged would have had to withstand a withering fire from well-fortified positions which overlooked the whole perimeter, and this would certainly have made the foreign positions untenable. The allies were twice pushed back from their wall barricade under heavy attack, but recaptured the positions and maintained control of the wall which let them dominate the Water Gate, the only direct entrance to the Legation Quarter from the Chinese City, through which the relieving force eventually made its way.

Sir Claude administered the Legation Quarter and the defences by delegating powers and responsibilities to committees. Every foreigner, whether combatant or non-combatant, served on one or more of the committees created for fire-fighting, food rationing, hospital management and a variety of other purposes. It was in this way that the missionaries played their part. Those who spoke fluent Chinese were particularly useful working among the Chinese refugees. Labour in the Legation Quarter was naturally in very short supply with every man rostered to help with the defences. Chinese-speaking missionaries soon remedied this, organizing labour squads of Chinese converts to dig trenches, sink counter-mines and construct fortifications.

The real problem during the siege was food. This was scarce and there was little likelihood of adding to this from outside. However, there was sufficient to last for some months, and none of the besieged really starved. This was due in great part to the proprietors of the Peking Hotel, the Chamots, who worked tirelessly to collect grain, tinned and dried foods and to arrange for its rationing. Besides the dry stores there was a good supply of fresh meat from the riding ponies who had had time to fatten a little since the May races; there was a good supply of drinking water, and from mid-July some fresh foods were being obtained from the Chinese.

On July the 14th there was a new turn of events in the siege. That day the Chinese Foreign Office sent a note into the besieged foreigners, offering to continue diplomatic negotiations. After that life became more tolerable in the Legation Quarter.

Limited quantities of food came in, messages were passed to and fro and news came, more often than not in garbled form, from the approaching relief force.

Although it seems incredible that the Chinese called for a truce in Peking at the moment when they had the Legation Quarter in their power, this was not strange to the defenders. There had been suspicions that the war against the Legations had not been carried out in a whole-hearted manner. Casualties on the foreign side were high and disturbing, but when compared to the number of rounds fired by the Chinese, they were incomprehensibly low. It almost seemed, at times, as if the Imperial soldiers at least were merely putting up a show of attack and seemed content to make things uncomfortable for foreigners, which fitted in with the defenders' theory that Jung Lu, the Army Commander, was not anti-foreign, but was being forced to act as if he were. The besieged did not know the real reason for the truce, although some of them guessed. The assembled Chinese forces had been defeated near the coast; Tientsin had fallen to the allies and Chinese reserves had been sent down from the Peking area to try to save the day and protect the route to the capital.

The truce in Peking lasted until the end of July when the fighting once more started to get bitter. The besieged were again on the defensive and had to put up an increasingly stiff resistance until they were relieved on August the 14th. The first weeks in August were the most dangerous period of the siege. As the Chinese armies fell back from the coast before the allied force, there was every likelihood that they would take their revenge on the besieged garrison of foreigners at the capital. The allied commanders of the relief forces were well aware of this danger and made haste. This was not easily accomplished, nor had the early relief of the diplomats been possible. Peking was not the only problem in north China which the allies had to consider. Tientsin also had to be rescued.

THE SIEGE AT TIENTSIN

Even before the admirals decided to attack the Chinese forts and establish a beach-head on the coast, the foreigners in Tientsin realized that they faced a very uncertain future. By early June it had been made clear that isolated as they were, thirty miles from

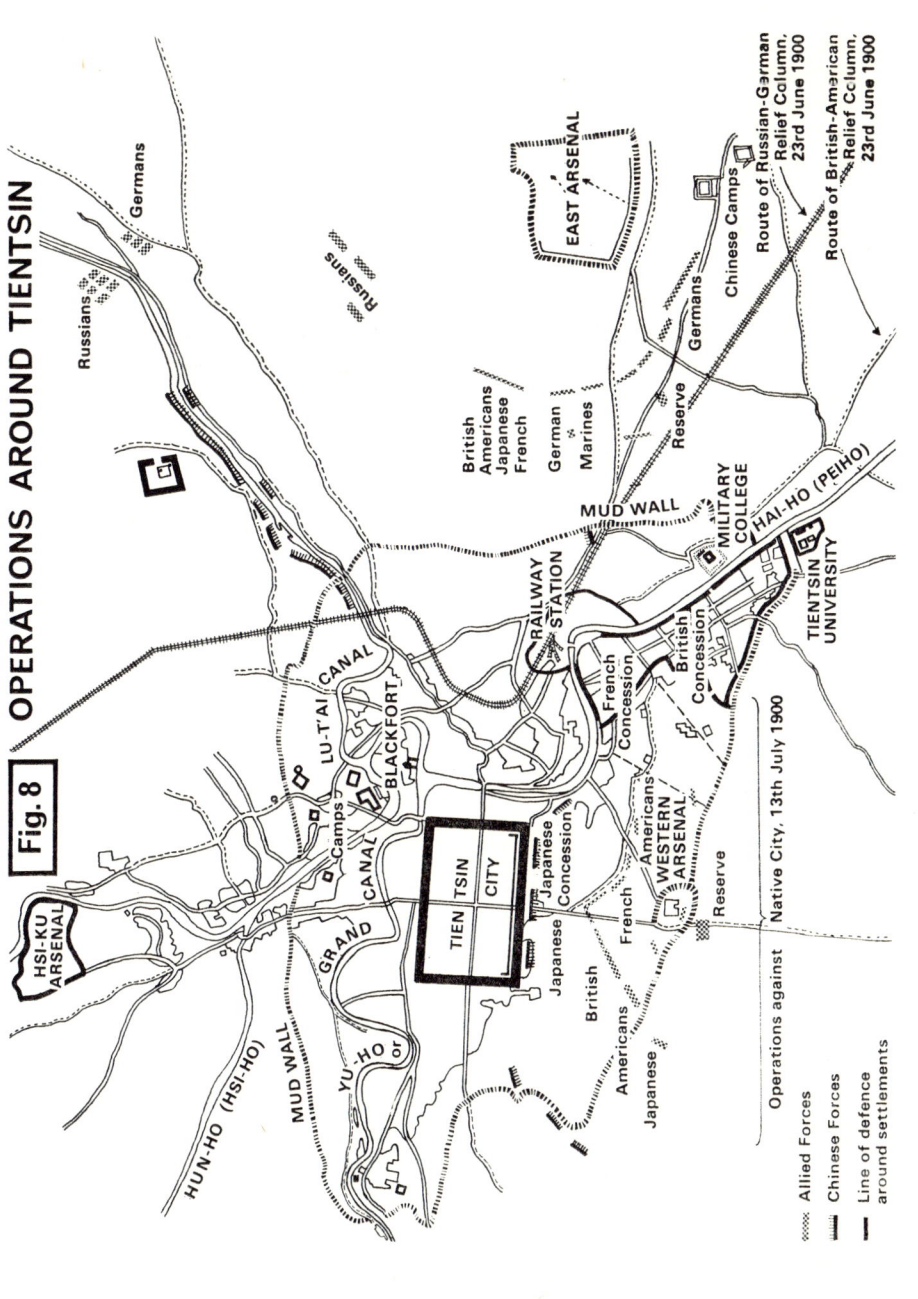
Fig. 8 OPERATIONS AROUND TIENTSIN

the coast up a shallow river that was not navigable in the dry summer, they needed protection. The bulk of the forces that had come up from the coast after the first major round of troubles had gone inland to Peking with Seymour and had disappeared. By the 15th it was apparent that these guards should have been kept in Tientsin itself. That day the same outbreaks of incendiarism that foreigners in Peking were witnessing swept Tientsin. Mission stations, commercial buildings, foreign residences and the French Cathedral in the native city all went up in flames, and cries of *sha, sha* (kill, kill) were heard about the city. Fortunately some Russian reinforcements had arrived several days previously and the situation was somewhat safe, although there was certainly no cause for anyone who saw the black smoke clouds rising beyond the settlements to feel complacent.

The foreigners in Tientsin, even more than those in Peking, did not sit back and wait to be massacred. They immediately started to organize strong defences. The foreign settlements which spread along the right bank of the river below the native city were barricaded and fortified. Bales of cotton goods and merchandise of all kinds, which no one expected would come in use for some time, all went into the defence network. Elsewhere on the inland perimeter earthworks were thrown up, and arrangements were made to evacuate outlying foreigners into the settlements and to house the women and children in the cellars of the Municipal Hall which was the most bomb-proof shelter to be found in the settlement.

An attempt was made by Boxers to attack the railway station on the 15th of June. The station, unfortunately for the foreigners, lay across the river on the left bank opposite the settlements. Luckily a large contingent of Russian troops numbering nearly 1,700 had gone to the station to follow Seymour and were in time to save the place from falling into the hands of the Chinese. There is no doubt that the loss of the station would have been disastrous to the allies in Tientsin. It would not only have affected the psychological attitudes of the defenders, for the loss of an only railway station in 1900 was like the loss of an only aerodrome to besieged forces in the last world war, but would have given distinct strategic advantages to the attackers. French and British defenders in particular would have been caught in a cross fire coming on the one side from Chinese forces on the river banks and on the other from the Chinese held area inland behind the small strip that made up the foreign concessions.

These events in Tientsin were merely a prelude to what was to come. On the 17th, when the Taku forts were being subdued, Tientsin was subjected to a combined attack by Boxers and Chinese troops. Communications with the coast were cut, and as in Peking, the defenders who had drawn in behind their hastily constructed barricades, found themselves facing a barrage of rifle shot and shell.

The situation in Tientsin was somewhat brighter for foreigners than in the capital. There were nearly 2,400 troops in Tientsin to defend the city. However, these like their colleagues in Peking, were not well equipped. They had been sent up from the coast very hastily and had few artillery pieces. They could muster only nine field pieces to confront the Chinese sixty or so modern cannon which fired on them from all sides.

With shell fire sweeping the settlements, the best thing that could be done was to take the fight into the enemy camp. This strategy was commenced immediately. On the 17th an attack was launched by the allies on the Military School near the British Concession, where there was a Chinese battery of 3-inch guns. Eight of these were captured and large quantities of ammunition destroyed, apparently just in time, as a large force of Chinese reinforcements came into the area just after the attack, too late to prevent the devastation.

Pressure on the defences was relieved about the 20th. This was no doubt caused by the Chinese attackers being drawn away from the settlements to create a front against the retreating Seymour who was approaching Tientsin from inland with his large force. Before Seymour arrived, even more acceptable allied reinforcements entered Tientsin. On the 19th a young Englishman, a resident of Tientsin named James Watts, performed a Revere-like ride with three Cossacks, breaking through the Chinese lines to take out the news of the siege, and despite having several horses shot from underneath him he reached the coast and informed the admirals of Tientsin's plight. An advance force of nearly 500 was immediately sent to the city, but were halted about four miles from the foreign settlement, and had to pull back in the face of stiff opposition. On the 23rd an enlarged force of 8,000 allied marines successfully overcame the Chinese forces and entered Tientsin. The arrival of this force immediately enabled help to be sent to Seymour, who was besieged with the remnants of his force at the arsenal at Hsi Ku, just to the west of the city. Seymour finally entered Tientsin on the 26th, as has been indicated, and once his force was refreshed Tientsin was in good shape not only to withstand a siege, but to take the offensive.

As both sides built up forces and grouped at Tientsin, numerous attacks and counter-attacks followed. On the 27th of June the Tientsin Arsenal was destroyed by the allies and a large group of Boxers on the Lu T'ai Canal were defeated and dispersed. Early in July the Japanese succeeded in driving the Chinese from the Race Course which made the foreign positions safer, and on the 9th, as a result of this gain, the nearby Western Arsenal at Hsi Ku was attacked and destroyed, depriving the Chinese of further supplies of ammunition and arms.

By mid-July the fight in Tientsin swung in favour of the allies. A large allied operation was mounted on the 13th to sweep the Chinese from Tientsin. Five thousand allied troops were involved in the move which was aimed at capturing the native city. After a hard and bitter struggle and a great number of casualties, the allies won their objective on the 14th. The Chinese were put to flight and all of Tientsin was in foreign hands, and as further reinforcements moved in from the coast the siege was seen to have been broken.

The fight for the native city in Tientsin was a particularly bitter struggle, one of the most bitter fought in the Boxer war. Both sides fought brutally and neither side gave nor seemed to expect quarter. For the Chinese commanders the war was a last-ditch stand to keep the foreigners from getting to Peking. For the allies it was a war of revenge. Just before the battle occurred, what seemed to be reliable news had come to hand that the ministers in Peking had been killed. Their obituaries were published throughout the world and the allied troops fell on the native city with feelings of revulsion for the Chinese.

There is no doubt that the Chinese lost a great deal when Tientsin fell into allied hands. They were deprived of their great arsenals, the railways from the coast, and the ability to effectively defend Peking. Moreover, during the battle the Chinese lost their most able commander in the north, Nieh Shih-ch'eng, who had been guarding the approaches to the capital.

The allied forces did not follow up their early advantages and break out of Tientsin to head for Peking. There seemed no need to do that in view of the bad news about the ministers. In any case, following Seymour's experience, no one wished to be too hasty. Instead, large-scale reinforcements were called for by the allied commanders to make the proposed expedition inland an assured success. No one was quite sure of the number of troops that would be needed to do this. Estimates varied from fifteen to fifty thousand. Nevertheless, in answer to the calls made for troops, the European powers, Japan and the United States each raised and allocated forces to make up an allied expeditionary force. Most of these could not be got to China before August, and consequently the expedition to Peking was put off by agreement until then, in case Japan and Russia should take advantage of their close proximity to China to send in their forces and get all the honours and the pickings.

Throughout the latter part of July and early August the allies at the coast were busy with two issues. They were building up the different national forces to make an effective striking force; and they were ironing out political difficulties to create a strong united front against China at a time when they were bickering about each other at home. In early August it was eventually decided to appoint a German, Graf von Waldersee, to lead the allied expeditionary force. In the meantime, before he and the rest of the reinforcements arrived, the allies made quite clear their intentions. The Chinese government at Tientsin was dismissed. An allied administration was established and the reforms such as dredging the river channel, which had so long been delayed by the Chinese, were started. China, in fact, was to be taught a new way of life.

THE SECOND RELIEF COLUMN

At the end of July before the reinforcements and von Waldersee had a chance to reach China, a sudden change was called for in the planned programme of the expedition. News came out from the besieged foreigners in Peking, by means of a messenger who managed to get through the Boxer lines, that the ministers were alive and well and wanted to be rescued immediately. An announcement to this effect had actually been made on the 24th of July when the Chinese diplomats who were stationed abroad, announced that they had been in touch with Peking and that all the foreign diplomats were safe. The allies refused to believe this story, regarding the announcement as another Chinese trick to keep the allied army from moving inland. The personal note from the ministers was a different matter, and in the circumstances, with the plea of the beleaguered ministers before them, the allied commanders at Tientsin decided to mount the expedition without delay and not to wait for all the reinforcements.

An immediate advance from Tientsin was out of the question. Peking was a long way inland and very careful preparations had to be made if the expedition was to be successfully launched. The allied troops had proved their mettle at Tientsin and they certainly had the measure of the Chinese forces, but they had little in the way of logistic support. Down to the end of July they had been organized to fight a siege war in Tientsin and to engage in local skirmishes. To do this they had relied heavily upon the railway and river which were open from the coast, and consequently they were not equipped with their own transport.

A start was made immediately to rectify this weakness. At the end of July all moving vehicles and animals that could be found in Tientsin and the surrounding territory were commandeered by the allied force. Although many of the vehicles assembled would have caused misgivings among highly professional soldiers, by the beginning of August the allied force had been made mobile and was prepared to move. At 10 a.m. on the 3rd of August the allied generals held a meeting. At the insistence of the Japanese it was decided to wait no longer, but to move off on the 5th.

There was no holding the allied army back, however. By hard work and enthusiasm all was ready by the day after the meeting, the 4th, and the column, numbering about 17,000 moved out immediately. In front of them, between Peking and Tientsin, was an estimated force of 50,000 Chinese formed up into several army groups. By the first evening without meeting opposition the allies had reached the West Arsenal (Hsi Ku) just outside Tientsin, which they easily occupied and which set them well on the way for an early advance along the river towards Peking.

Japanese cavalry patrols had been sent out since late in July to scout the situation and they had discovered that the Chinese, after their defeat at Tientsin, were regrouping at a place called Pei Tsang, which is on the railway line about seven miles from Tientsin in the direction of Peking. There the Chinese had built extensive earthworks, had dug trenches and were amassed in force preparing to make a stand there. A decision was made to attack the Chinese camp without delay.

Just after 4 a.m., before the sun was up on the morning of the 5th, the allies advanced. By 5 a.m. the first trenches had fallen with little effort. Resistance stiffened but despite this by noon Pei Tsang and the Chinese defences were in allied hands and the Chinese forces were in full retreat. The Chinese had been caught off guard. The allies had attacked at breakfast time before the defences were fully manned, and the Chinese forces had to spend the rest of the morning fighting with empty stomachs.

With the fall of Pei Tsang and the destruction of the assembled Chinese army, the way was opened to Peking. Further effective large-scale resistance by the Chinese from that time was impossible. Chinese military power in the north had been shattered and to make matters worse the Chinese commanders such as Li Ping-heng and Governor-General Yu Lu committed suicide, causing a crisis in Chinese leadership. It was now up to the Boxers and the ragged forces of the Imperial Army that remained to put up the final resistance.

Well aware of the situation, for allied intelligence was good, the foreign force decided to take advantage of the Chinese failures and press on without respite. The story of the allied advance from the 5th until the 14th of August is one of continued allied victories and Chinese defeats. The Chinese were hit daily and the blitzkrieg methods certainly paid off. Yang Tsun, another Chinese fortified place, fell on the 6th. By the 10th of August the allies were half way along the Pei Ho to Peking. On the morning of the 12th the last big obstacle in their way, Tung Chow, fell and was looted.

Peking lay fourteen miles away, almost in sight. Here the allies took stock. Most of the generals expected stiff opposition about the capital and moved cautiously. Scouts were sent out to assess the strength of the forces, but the reports that came in were astoundingly optimistic. The Russian Cossacks had reached the walls of Peking without meeting any resistance whatever. In view of this an allied council of war was called and it was decided to advance on the capital without further delay.

Each of the allied contingents took different routes to the capital and was assigned to attack a different sector of the city wall. The Russians took on the difficult task of attacking the

Tung Pien Men and breaking through into the Chinese City from the east. The Japanese took on the most difficult task and bore the brunt of the fighting, hurling themselves at the Ch'i Hua Men and the Tung Chih Men, and the walls of the Imperial City. Of all the forces the British were the most fortunate. They moved up to the Sha Wo Men and found no opposition. The gates in the Chinese City, in fact, were opened for them and advance units of the British force were despatched with haste across the Chinese City towards the Legation Quarter. When they arrived between the Ha Ta Men and the Ch'ien Men, the Indian and Welsh troops, who made up the advance detachment, saw the foreign flags on the wall. Following the advice of the messenger who had broken out of Peking, the troops passed through the Water Gate or Sluice Gate. At about 3 p.m. the besieged foreigners in the Legation Quarter saw Indian troops marching into the defence area and they knew relief had come.

AFTERMATH

Although the Legations had been saved the fight was not over. There were still anti-foreign forces holding out in the north and as the allied powers had mounted the expedition to shatter Boxer power as much as to relieve the Legations, pursuit continued. On the 14th the area around the Legations was cleared of Chinese resistance. On the 15th the Pei T'ang was relieved and the capital was open for looting and occupation.

The flight of the Court

Early on the morning of the 15th of August while the allies were preparing to move up to the Pei T'ang, the Empress Dowager decided to flee from Peking. There was not much time for her to decide what to leave behind, but one thing she was certain about it would not be the Emperor Kuang Hsu who for so long seemed to hold the favour of the allied powers. Acting quickly the Empress Dowager had Kuang Hsu's favourite wife, Chen Fei, who had opposed the Empress Dowager's wishes, thrown down a well, and the Emperor, surrounded by the Empress Dowager's favourites, was moved reluctantly out of Peking along the hard road to Sian. No preparation had been made for the journey which the Court made. The Emperor later revealed that they travelled 'in patched clothes and with little sustenance'. After an arduous journey the royal family arrived at Tai Yuan, Shensi, on September the 10th and finally at Sian on the 26th of October where they established their Court seat. There two high officials, Li Hung-chang and Prince Ch'ing who the Chinese felt were acceptable to the allies, were appointed to negotiate a peace. But the allies were not yet ready. They made it quite clear that peace would only be talked about once the military situation had been settled to their satisfaction. Consequently they proceeded to occupy north China, and to shatter Boxer power.

There is no doubt that the flight of the Court from Peking brought added difficulties for China and the Chinese. The capital city and Chihli province as well as Manchuria were left in the hands of foreigners who found it difficult to deal with distant officials living in exile. There is no doubt that the Court could have made things easier if it had remained in Peking where they would have had every opportunity to play off the powers, for like most allied occupying powers, they were soon bickering among themselves. Indeed the allies had moved so quickly that they had never discussed their political aims in China. All they had agreed on was that China and the Chinese should be taught a salutary lesson and should reveal that they had changed their ways before the allies would talk about terms of settlement.

RETRIBUTION

The allied occupation powers soon began to make the north Chinese pay for the Boxers. Although some of the actions that were taken were shocking by any standards, there is no reason to whole-heartedly condemn the activities of the forces. They were very much the creatures of their age, and what they did was very much comprehended by their contemporaries. At the end of the nineteenth century Europeans had firm views of punishment and retribution. They believed that punishment was necessary and that it should be given firmly and on the spot. They felt that the best way to deal with children who misbehaved was to apply firm discipline at the scene of the crime, and their penal codes for adults were not known for their leniency. The Chinese were to be given similar treatment.

The folly of anti-foreignism was brought home to the bulk of the Chinese population in the occupied areas by foreign looters. When each city was captured it was opened to the troops of all ranks. A lot of the looting that went on was no doubt in the nature of souvenir hunting, but nevertheless huge quantities of material and treasures must have been taken from China by the troops and foreigners who joined in the looting, which was not frowned upon in those days.

Punitive expeditions

More important, once the allied forces were based inland at Peking and other strategic centres nearer the coast and in Manchuria, they sent out a number of punitive expeditions to areas with a reputation for anti-foreignism, to teach them the lesson of not attacking missionaries and foreigners. On September the 8th the village of Tu Liu Ts'un, about fifteen miles south-west of Tientsin, which was regarded as a Boxer stronghold, was burnt. On the 11th of the month a large column moved down the Peking-Hankow railway and attacked Liang Hsiang Hsien, which lay fifteen miles from Peking. The Chinese resisted stubbornly, to no avail. After the city was subdued the captured were put on trial and 170 were executed, as became the general custom on these expeditions. Numerous of these expeditions were sent out in subsequent months to envelop Boxer nests, and to punish villages, towns and cities where Christians and foreigners had been subjected to violence. The largest-scale operation was naturally directed against the notorious city of Pao Ting Fu. Count von Waldersee had arrived in China on September the 21st and he personally directed the punitive columns sent out. A large allied force gathered outside the city on the 18th of October. General Gaselee unsuccessfully tried to negotiate a surrender, but the opposition was firm and peace efforts failed and the town was vested on the 20th and opened for 'punishment'.

War crimes trials

The fate of Pao Ting Fu, more than any other city, reveals the allied methods used to correct China. A new and innovating system of punishment was devised. The Chinese responsible for the crimes that had been committed were to be put on trial by the victors who claimed that they had come to occupy the country in the name of humanity. The system first used at Pao Ting Fu was generally adopted throughout north China, being applied more or less harshly as circumstances dictated.

A mixed military commission was established in Pao Ting Fu immediately the city was occupied. It recommended after investigation that the Provincial Treasurer and Manchu General should be executed. This was carried out immediately. Besides this the temples used by the Boxers were destroyed, the towers of the city gates were demolished and parts of the city wall razed. Also a fine of 100,000 taels to pay the costs of the occupation was imposed and the sum of 240,000 taels found in the city treasury was divided among the armies, according to the number of troops on the register. Pao Ting Fu admittedly was a guilty city. Fifteen or so missionaries had been murdered in its vicinity, but it is doubtful if the method the allies used was the best way to assure that members of the Christian faith would be welcomed back in the region and rehabilitated.

Continual punitive expeditions were sent out well into the following year. The records of them do not make nice reading. They exacted a harsh and bitter vengeance on the Chinese. But it must be seen, in all fairness, that neither side acted with dignity and restraint. The Chinese acted with equal harshness. The war was as bitter as any crusade or racial struggle, and it remained so until the last resistance by the Chinese had been overcome. By the northern summer of 1901 negotiations for peace were in hand, and the occupation became more peaceful as Chinese Imperial forces took over from the allied occupation armies.

There was now only one source of trouble. The allied structure was cracking. With few 'heathens' left to fight they turned on each other. There was a lot to fight about. Russia seemed to be grabbing territory in the north. The British did not seem to be pulling their weight. The French did not trust the Germans. The Americans were suspicious of the Europeans, and everyone except the Germans had little time for their Commander-in-Chief, von Waldersee. The British in particular objected to him. It was not only national jealousy. Von Waldersee was spending a lot of time with a young Chinese girl whom he had met earlier in Berlin, and this type of fraternization was certainly not approved by people who still regarded the puritanical General Gordon with awe.

The occupation force, by the end of 1901, showed every sign of breaking up.

NEGOTIATIONS FOR A SETTLEMENT

In view of the military actions which were taking place, political negotiations were not easy and, as has been indicated, they were made more difficult by the absence of the Chinese Court from the capital. No one was quite certain of the authority of the powers held by the Chinese officials Li Hung-chang and Prince Ch'ing who had been appointed to handle affairs. Chinese delegates who dealt with foreign powers in the past had not been previously noted for their abilities to make independent agreements which bound their monarchs, and there was no reason to expect a change in 1900. The Chinese negotiators' task would in any event be a difficult one. They would not be able to do much about the terms set before them. All they could do was to see that China somehow saved some face and anything else it could from the ruins.

While they were still fighting in 1900, the allies were not prepared to deal with the Chinese officials or even consider their credentials. They had not at that stage appointed their own delegates. The foreign delegates were selected and assembled during the occupation. In the majority of cases the ministers who had been beleaguered were appointed to dictate the peace terms. There was only one noticeable exception. Sir Claude MacDonald was left off the list. He was replaced by Sir Ernest Satow, Britain's famous diplomat in Tokyo. This was no doubt a personal blow to Macdonald and certainly indicates that the Foreign Office were not impressed by MacDonald's record as a diplomat in 1900. However, care was taken to see that he lost no face and he departed from Peking amidst expressions of gratitude for his leadership in the difficult times.

Before Peking fell three political objectives of the foreign powers had been determined on, even if they had not been formally agreed to. Chinese officials and Boxers were to be punished; China was to pay for the costs of the allied war machine that came 'to restore peace and order'; and there was to be a revision of the existing treaties, which the foreign powers had been trying to effect before the Boxer Uprising.

By late September 1900, after the Chinese delegates had been nominated, these objectives were gradually clarified. In November all the powers had agreed to an eleven-point programme. China was to send a mission to Berlin to apologize for the von Ketteler's murder and erect monuments to him; officials who had encouraged the Boxers were to be executed, and areas where foreigners were killed were not allowd to have Civil Service exams for five years, which was a great punishment for Chinese scholars; monuments were to be erected in foreign cemeteries; China was not to import arms for two years; an indemnity was to be paid to the allies; a defence system was to be built about the Legation Quarter from which Chinese residents were to be excluded; the Taku forts were to be razed to the ground; the powers were to occupy strong points to guarantee communications inland until order was restored; decrees were to be published to the effect that anti-foreignism was a crime punishable with death and that local officials were personally responsible for the lives of foreigners in their territory; China was to agree to new commercial treaties; and the old Chinese Foreign Office, the Tsung Li Ya Men, was to be replaced with a modern Foreign Office under the direction of a responsible minister.

These points were incorporated in a document on the 22nd of December 1900, with a twelfth point added somewhat as an afterthought. China was also to apologize and make reparations to Japan for the murder of her Chancellor in Peking.

These were not put to China in the form of a treaty as could well have been the case. Such a document would have been a fatal blow to the Manchus and their dynasty. Instead the wishes of the allies were made known and the Court was given a chance to carry out some of these points on their own initiative, to save face.

Consequently, before the final protocol for peace was signed in September 1901, a series of decrees were issued which were carefully scrutinized by the allies and which went a long way to meet their demands, although this was done at times with some hesitation.

Already, on September the 25th 1900, just after the Chinese delegates were appointed, a decree had been issued naming the high officials such as Prince Tuan who had been involved with the Boxers, and announcing that they had been punished by removal from office. This question of punishment naturally became the first and most important issue to be settled. The Chinese action was far from what the allies demanded, which was a death sentence, and it seemed to herald ill for the future negotiations, encouraging the suspicions held by foreigners that the Court was going to play a sly game while it operated in distant Sian. On the point of punishing high officials the allies remained firm. They wanted China to give harsh punishment like the ones being dealt out by the occupation authorities.

Some officials had already committed suicide on the battlefield and at the Court in exile. But there were other top Manchus, guilty in the eyes of foreigners, who still remained. Eventually, as a result of firm demands, these were punished by the Court. Prince Tuan and his brother Tsai Lan were banished for life; Yu Hsien, the infamous Governer of Shansi, was executed with two colleagues; Chao Shu-ch'iao and two other officials were ordered to commit suicide, and K'ang-i and Li Ping-heng and the others, who had already suicided, were dishonoured posthumously. Tung Fu-hsiang, whom the allies treated as a misguided soldier rather than a war criminal, was stripped of his rank and offices, which satisfied the allies. With these people removed the way was opened for a general settlement.

A series of other decrees followed these punishments, which were designed to meet the other wishes expressed by the representatives of the foreign powers. On December the 24th 1900 provincial officials were advised by the Court that in future they were to be held personally responsible for the lives of foreigners in the territories under their control. On February the 1st 1901 the Big Sword Society and the Boxer Society were dissolved and anti-foreignism was declared to be a crime punishable by death. On the 29th of May China offered to pay an indemnity of 450 million taels (67.5 million pounds sterling), payable over 31 years at 4 per cent interest. On July the 24th the Tsung Li Ya Men was abolished and a new-style foreign office, the Wai Wu Pu, was opened to take its place. On the 29th of August 1901 China prohibited the importation of arms of war into her territories for a period of two years. Moreover, delegations were sent from Peking to Berlin and Tokyo to apologize for the murder of the ministers, and the Court announced that Chinese Court ceremonies for foreign diplomats, which had always been a point of difficulty, had been altered so that Western and other foreign ministers accredited to the Court at Peking would no longer be treated as if they were tribute bearers. The Manchu Court, it seemed to the allied representatives, was learning fast. In view of these decrees and other measures taken, the Peace Protocol was signed on September the 7th 1901 and the way was prepared, at least on paper, for the re-establishment of friendly relations and a return to 'normalcy'.

INTERNATIONAL QUESTIONS

However, that was not the end of the matter. China had conceded a lot but there still remained the appetites of the powers which had been whetted by the sharp fight. They soon became grouped into two rather ill-assorted camps consisting of 'free-traders' and 'protectionists'. The real point at issue was the 'open door' to the Chinese Empire. Trading nations, such as Britain, throughout the nineteenth century had sought to gain easy access to China and provide equal opportunities for all comers to the Chinese market so that the spirit of competition could flourish, and they had taken care to write these free trade principles into the treaties they made with the Chinese government. By the time of the Boxer crisis the free trade movement was declining and new protectionist powers such as Russia saw little benefit and purpose in supporting the 'open door'. She manoeuvred to establish monopoly areas and spheres of preponderance for herself in parts of the Chinese Empire—in particular in Manchuria which rapidly became a Russian zone. This became increasingly evident as Russian troops continued to establish themselves in the area on the pretext of putting down troubles.

Britain, Germany and the United States of America took the initiative to preserve the 'open door'. The United States of America, in particular, took the diplomatic lead by issuing diplomatic notes calling for a 'hands-off' policy. It was Britain, however, who showed the way to preserve the 'open door'. She had built up her trade in China by means of treaties which guaranteed the equal treatment of commerce entering China. In 1902 she demanded a new sweeping treaty aimed at removing difficulties that had appeared, and that would deal a blow at any monopolies. On September the 5th 1902 the treaty was signed in accordance with the promises made in the Peace Protocol, and China was opened for trade in a manner as it never had been before. In

1903 Japan dotted the i's of the British commercial treaty by getting further concessions which paved more roads for foreign commerce entering China.

But in the north all was still not well. Russia still saw no virtue in having an 'open door' to China and continued her policy of establishing a special sphere all for herself. In September 1900 she had poured thousands of troops into Manchuria which continued to remain under Russian occupation. On March the 26th 1902 Russia and China signed a special agreement about Manchuria which made it seem as if she would be there for a long time. In the document Russia did agree to remove her troops but did not say when; and she made it quite clear that in any case, no matter what happened militarily, her influence would continue to be felt in Manchuria. Unfortunately Japan also had interests and designs on the same territory, and before long these two powers were to be engaged in a battle of supremacy there.

Indeed, as a result of the Boxer crisis, a new international situation appeared in East Asia. In particular a new power had emerged as China crumbled. Japan, which shared with the Western powers the perils of the expeditions to Peking and had borne the brunt of the fighting inland, was admitted to the ranks of the powers as an equal. By 1902 her position was consolidated even more when she signed an agreement with Britain and became Britain's ally.

As this new East Asia developed in the twentieth century memories of the old order and the Boxer Uprising receded into the background. Von Ketteler was forgotten; the monument to his death soon became a meaningless piece of stone. The Legation Quarter in Peking was changed to make it safer and unrecognizable to those who lived there in 1900. Old threads of life were taken up by those who had participated in the actions and the siege soon became a piece of history. As far as the Chinese were concerned, apart from the Boxers themselves, only Graf von Waldersee has remained alive as a memory. He has become a legendary figure kept alive in Chinese novels and historical fiction, for it is not often that a significant military commander in charge of an occupation force forms an alliance with a young and attractive courtesan of a conquered nation.

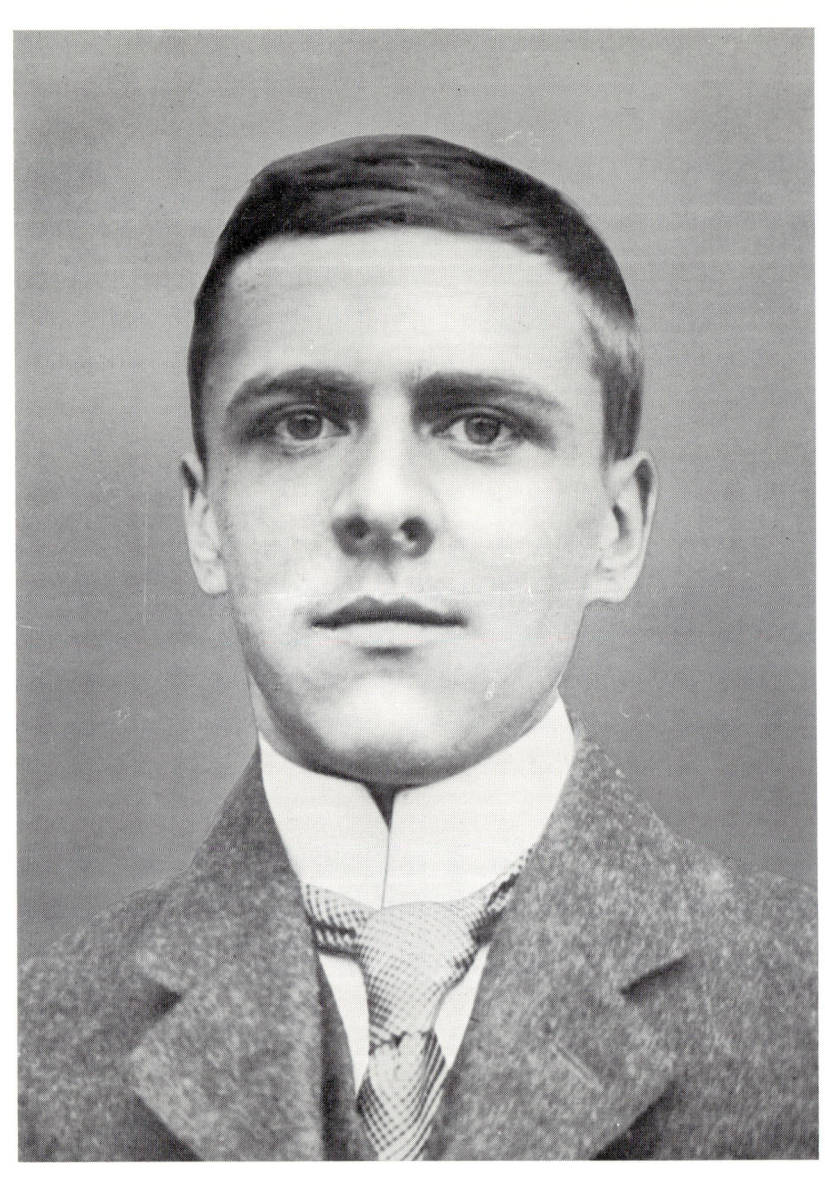
1 Lancelot Giles at the age of 21 (Aug. 1899)

Diary of the Boxer Riots and of the Siege of the Legations in Peking.
June & July 1900.

'The Boxer Sect'
CALLIGRAPHY by LIU WEI-PING

June 4th, Monday

The students decided to follow their usual custom and repair to the Western Hills[1] for the summer. June 2nd was the original day fixed for this migration; but Sir Claude[2] had told us to postpone our departure, giving us permission to start on June 4th. Our carts, bearing away our goods and chattels, started early in the morning, about 6 a.m. Three or four hours later a note came from Cockburn[3] saying that we had best postpone our departure once more and send for our carts to return. This note was due to the arrival of news to the effect that two British missionaries (Messrs. Norman and Robinson[4]) had been murdered by Boxers somewhere between Tientsin and Peking.

The next few days were full of alarming news of the advance of the Boxers. However, we had some 400 foreign troops in Peking, and so felt quite safe, more particularly as the ministers had all telegraphed for reinforcements.

June 9th, Saturday

News came that the Boxers had advanced right up to the city on the west, and had sacked the Race Course grandstand.[5] That afternoon Kirke, Porter, Warren[6] and myself rode out to see what damage had been done. We arrived while the ruins of the stand were still smoking, and found a crowd of men from the neighbouring village[7] looting the bricks etc. etc. We charged them, and scattered them right and left. After a rest we decided to proceed yet further west and see what further damage had been done by the Boxers in their advance. We had not gone more than a quarter of a mile, before we saw the road before us blocked by a dense crowd of Chinese. As soon as they saw us, they began to yell: *'ta, ta'*[8] and *'sha, sha'* (kill, kill). We still advanced till within a hundred yards of them. They then began to dash forward, waving swords and spears which shone ominously in the sun. We promptly wheeled, and galloped off, quickly outdistancing our pursuers, who nevertheless kept up the chase for some time.

On our way back we met Bristow and Drury[9] riding out the same way. We warned them not to go out, telling them what to expect. Both of them are somewhat pigheaded, and obstinately and foolishly they proceeded on their way. They got as far as the Race Course safely enough. But on their return were attacked by a body of Boxers. They escaped these easily enough, though some of the Boxers hurled their heavy swords after them. A little later they fell into an ambush of twelve Boxers, and but for Bristow's promptitude and presence of mind in drawing his revolver and firing point blank at one of them a yard or so off him, they would probably have come to grief. On his firing, however, they wavered and fell back for a moment—sufficient to allow him to clap his heels into his pony's sides and gallop off. After this adventure Sir Claude issued an order forbidding any further rides to be taken by anybody in the Legation.

June 10th, Sunday

Admiral Seymour[10] at Tientsin took over the management of affairs. He seized a train and proceeded to Peking. He got a quarter of the distance, that is to Yang Tsun. Of his further movements we have up to date (July 5th) no news whatever.

June 11th, Monday

A report came yesterday that the troops had arrived at Peking Station (Ma Chia P'u[11]). At 4 a.m., accordingly, fifty carts with a convoy of forty of our marines and any civilian who had a mount, set out to bring them into the city. Some anxiety was caused by a rumour that the Chinese had mounted a Krupp gun on the Ch'ien Men,[12] commanding the entrance to the city from Ma Chia P'u. This, however, was quite unfounded. On our way down we were joined by some Japanese, Italian, and American troops—these last with about twenty carts, so that we formed an imposing procession. On arrival at the station we found that the report of the arrival of the troops was a *canard*. The fact was that each of the ministers thought that one of the others had definite news on the subject. It turned out that the whole thing originated with one of Sir Claude's mafoos!![13] The carts were all brought back to the Legation and are here still.

In the morning definite news came that the Summer Legation had been sacked and burned to the ground. Lady MacDonald is very wrath about it,[14] as many of her priceless treasures (those of a sentimental value) were out there. This Legation was only completed in the spring of this year!

During the afternoon one of the assistants in the Japanese Chancery[15] went down to the station in a cart, accompanied only by his boy. Outside the Yung Ting Men[16] he was set upon by some soldiers, hauled out of his cart and hacked to pieces. The boy escaped. The city gates were immediately closed. The Japanese at first wanted to send some troops to avenge him, but decided not to force matters. Rumour says that they wired for twenty thousand troops.

In the evening the Boxers issued a proclamation, stating the number of guards and guns in the great Roman Catholic mission known as the Pei T'ang[17] and calling on their men to attack it. It was, however, left alone. There were thirty-five French blue-jackets, and ten Italian *ditto* defending the mission; also some hundred armed Chinese. Today our last wire but one got through. The Russian line *via* Kiakta was cut.[18] The only ones to benefit by this are the men in the Chancery. Their work during the last few days has been enormous.

June 12th, Tuesday

The Russian wire was reopened, and Sir Claude sent a wire at once, saying that unless the troops made haste, they would arrive too late to save us. According to a rumour (I am giving an account of the various reports we heard, so that you may the better picture our hopes and fears) the Russians landed 2,000 men at Taku, and the Japanese sent another urgent message for 20,000 men. The people in the know seem to see in this signs of a future war. In fact Dr. Morrison,[19] correspondent of *The Times,* was laying heavy odds on war between Russia and Japan being declared before July 31st. He was also betting on the Japanese occupying Port Arthur before December 31st. His opinion is certainly one to be noted, as he is always to the fore with political news. He sent news of the occupation of Port Arthur to *The Times* before the Foreign Office despatches arrived in London. In the afternoon the two newly elected members of the Tsungli Yamen[20] called on Sir Claude, and gave leave (!) for more troops to be sent up on the condition that they did not leave the Legations or look over the walls. This was probably merely to save their faces.

The teachers say they are hooted when going to and from our Legations; and most of the boys have left, except those who are Christians.

June 13, Wednesday

A t'ing ch'ai[21] of eight years' standing was sent, disguised as a beggar, to find out the whereabouts of the troops. He returned saying he would not leave the city for $100.

The Germans captured a Boxer who was strolling down Legation Street in his full uniform. Later the French shot two others.

At 7 p.m. the Boxers poured in at the Ha Ta Men[22] (see plan no. 1), causing a great scene, and at 7.45 p.m. a loud explosion was heard followed by a report (which proved unfounded) that the Austrian Legation was on fire. There was a fire in that direction, but only among some Chinese houses.

Legation Street had been densely packed with Chinese all the afternoon; but on this rush of Boxers the whole street was cleared by the foreign troops and two barricades erected at the points marked x——x in my plan no. 1; also at the north end of Customs Lane, by the Austrians. As soon as the explosion took place the

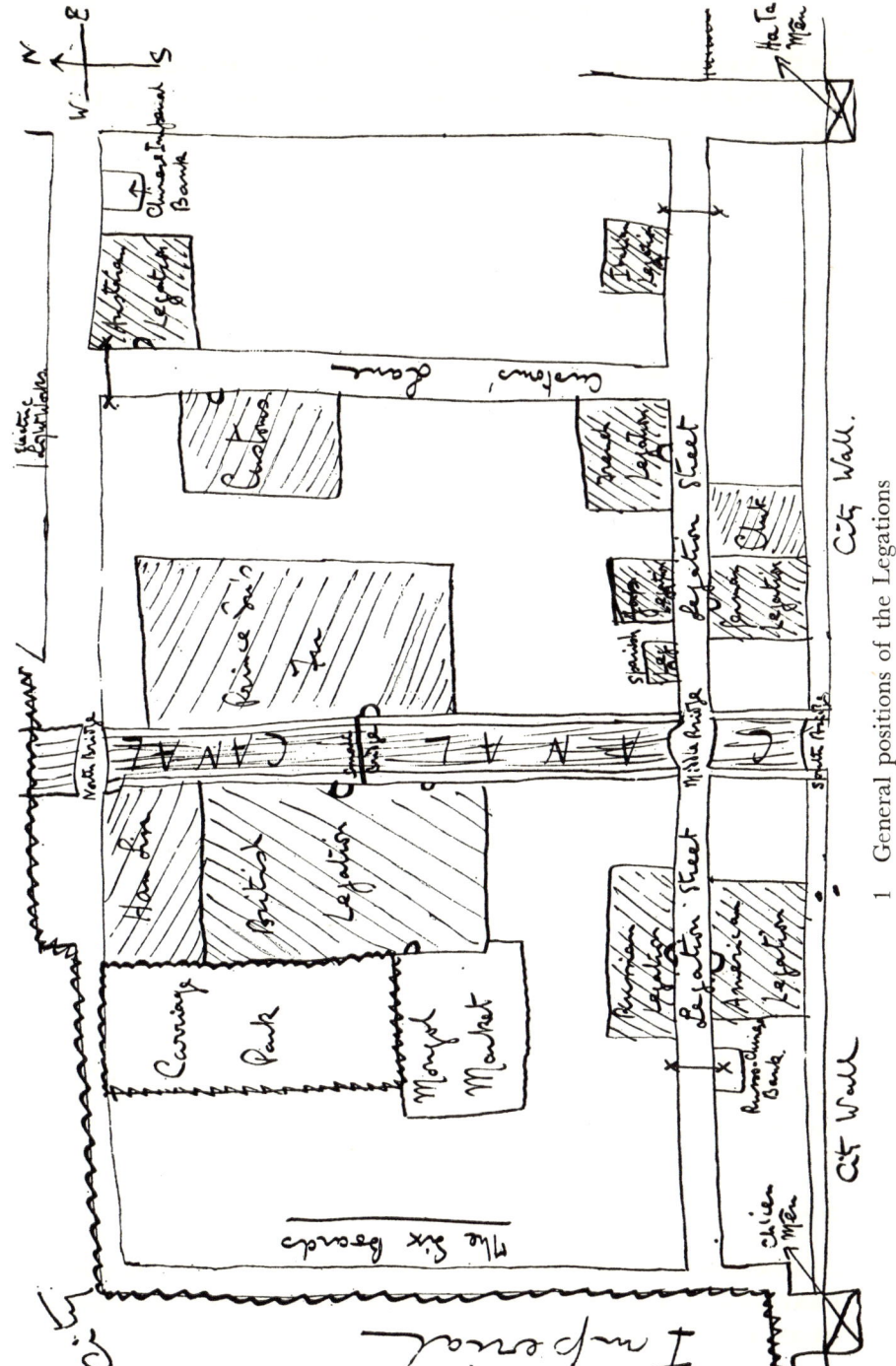

1 General positions of the Legations

The Belgian Legation is to the N.E. of the Austrians.
N.B. The roads along the two sides of the Canal should be considerably broader.

bugle sounded the alarm, and we all dashed to the stations that had been allotted to us. I was in the upper storey of a building situated in the south-west corner of the Legation overlooking the Mongol Market. For an hour we (myself and about eight marines) stood on the alert with loaded rifles ready to fire on anything suspicious in the open square before us.

The west barricade in Legation Street was defended by Russians and Americans; the east barricade was held by French and Italians. The Austrians held their own barricade, while the British had a strong body of men on the North Bridge over the Canal, allowing no one to pass along the roads on either side of the canal.

That night we all sat down to dinner, armed to the teeth; and slept at our posts ready for any emergency.

The Kiakta line was again cut, and we have been completely isolated since then.

During the night the Austrians turned their Colt machine gun on what they thought was a body of Boxers carrying lamps. As a matter of fact the Chinese were making use of an old ruse of theirs, that is planting sticks bearing lamps in the ground and making off. The Austrians also made an attempt to save a woman who was burned to death by torches being applied to her clothing.

During the night the Boxers lighted huge fires, burning down the Roman Catholic mission, known as the Tung T'ang;[23] also the London Mission,[24] and an asylum for blind converts.[25] What affected us perhaps even more was the burning down of an outlying portion of the Customs[26] known as the Pei Yuan and Nan Yuan in the north-east of the city. The Brewitt-Taylors'[27] house was burned to the ground. Their boxes etc. were all ready packed for departure to Swatow. They were only waiting for the railway to be opened. Their losses and those of many of the Customs' junior assistants must be irreparable.

June 14th, Thursday

No Chinese are allowed to pass any of the numerous European pickets without passes signed by some European within the square which we hold in Peking (see plan no. 1). This necessitates an

2 Lady MacDonald's fancy-dress ball, 1900: a group of Students Interpreters

Back: W. P. Thomas, cardinal; W. P. M. Russell, Elizabethan; R. T. Tebbitt, volunteer officer; middle: C. A. W. Rose, statue; H. H. Bristow, the Mad Hatter; front: L. G. C. Graham, early Briton; H. Warren, Knave of Spades; W. M. Hewlett, Gooseberry Fool; G. W. Pearson, Pierrot; L. H. R. Barr, matador

3 The Students' Corps

Back, standing: J. G. Hancock, C. A. W. Rose, H. Porter, A. J. Flaherty, C. C. A. Kirke, H. H. Bristow, W. E. Townsend; front: L. H. R. Barr, W. P. M. Russell, R. D. Drury, W. M. Hewlett, L. Giles

4 Chinese troops crossing the North Bridge on the Imperial Canal before the siege

5 Converts taking refuge in the Fu

6 Boxer handiwork before the siege

7 The barricaded front of the British Legation

8 Enemy loopholes across the Imperial Canal

9 German marines

10 Russian barricade in the Legation Street

11 Chinese positions opposite the Germans

12   A Chinese barricade on the city wall

13   British marines

interpreter being stationed at the outlets of this square. Therefore one of the students is always on duty at the North Bridge held by the British marines. During the day anyone can pass the North Bridge, as long as they do not come south of it; but at night everyone passing over it is stopped and interrogated as to his business there. All day we have a body of about twelve Chinese soldiers (Kansu troops[28]) in gorgeous red uniforms with Mauser rifles, to assist us in holding our position. Each day four students take over the interpreter duties doing two hours at a stretch. Thus each of the four does six hours a day in three spells. I was not on this job till a couple of days after this, being in the last batch of four. I did not find any difficulty in making myself understood or in understanding the talk of the people questioned.

At 11.30 a.m. came the news that the Nan T'ang,[29] a building 278 years old, and of great historical interest, containing as it did a memorial tablet given to the mission by Kang Hsi,[30] was destroyed. It is about one and a half miles from the Legation in a westerly direction. No help could be sent, however. Bishop Scott's[31] place was also burned and looted.

At 12.45 p.m. Captain Wray[32] (Royal Marines), being on duty at the North Bridge, captured a Boxer who was calmly strolling across. He appeared in a half-dazed and mesmerized condition, and was unarmed, or else he would have been shot on the spot. He wore a yellow girdle and had a square piece of red flannel on his chest, hung from his neck. This is supposed to render all Boxers absolutely invulnerable. He was put in the cells, awaiting a decision as to his fate. Several of the Chinese servants forthwith left the Legation for good, saying that this Boxer would breathe fire and burn the place about our ears!

At 7 p.m. the Germans on the city wall saw a large party of Boxers outside the wall. They fired and killed about a dozen. Later in the evening terrific yells and howls were heard in the direction of the Ch'ien Men; the shouting lasted till near midnight. It came from a huge crowd of Boxers who were trying to get into the city. But the gates were closed and held by Chinese troops.

A man was caught trying to fire a part of Legation Street, and two large fires were seen in the West City.

At about midnight some Boxers tried to rush our picket on the North Bridge. One fanatic was hit by a rifle bullet, a revolver bullet, and had a bayonet stuck into him, and was still advancing when the marine holding the bayonet pulled the trigger of his rifle and brought him down! Four men were killed and two wounded amongst the Boxers; no casualties on our side. The two wounded were brought into the Legation (I carried one) and their wounds were tended to. One will never walk again; the other will never talk again. They were sent away a few days later. They were armed only with spears and swords which of course were useless against our rifles.

June 15th, Friday

Russians and Americans went off in a strong body to the Nan T'ang to save native Christians. Many were found roasted alive, and so massacred and cut up as to be unrecognisable. I will spare you the sickening details. It is a noteworthy point that all over the city the Boxers knew which of the Chinese were Christians and where they lived. This points to the Chinese government having a finger in the pie. The houses of the Boxers and their supporters had yellow placards on the doors.

Prince Su's Fu[33] (which I shall hereafter designate as 'the Fu') was seized by the powers as a refuge for the surviving converts. The Japanese and Italians occupy and defend it. It is an important strategical point in our defence, as may be seen by reference to the map no. 1.

Sir Robert Hart[34] started a report that Tung Fu-hsiang's[35] troops were going to attack us at night. This was unfounded; but subsequent events have proved that he knew what he was talking about. Tung Fu-hsiang is one of the leading Chinese generals; the other important ones are Prince Ch'ing[36] and Prince Sung[37] and Jung Lu.[38]

The British also sent out a party to save converts. Captain Halliday[39] was in command and fifty or sixty Boxers were slain, some actually in the act of massacring Christians, so indifferent were they to the approach of our troops. Chinese of all ranks were huddled up in the Fu, absolutely worn out with the fatigues and terrors of the last few days. The unfortunate women with their cramped feet could hardly stand. Added to all this was a fierce scorching sun.

At night more huge fires, and massacring! The Russian troops are said to be at hand. This turned out to be untrue.

Since the night of June 13th I have not slept with my clothes or boots off, ready for the slightest alarm. During the first seventy-two hours of this sort of thing I had only thirteen hours sleep, that is a little over four hours for every twenty-four.

June 16th, Saturday

A mafoo came in from the Pei T'ang saying that it was all right. This is the last we have heard of it up to date (July 5th). We believe it is still all right, as no signs of fire in that direction have been seen.

Five Chinese soldiers were executed this morning for the murder of the Japanese last Monday.

I believe it is absolutely authentic that at a meeting of the Grand Council[40] some time ago, the Empress Dowager[41] strongly urged the instant extermination of all foreigners in Peking. This was opposed by Prince Ch'ing[42] and Jung Lu. The latter left Peking so as to have nothing to do with the matter. At 1.30 that night permission was granted for our troops to come. This was at the time when there were no foreign troops in Peking at all. If the suggestion had been carried out we should have been absolutely helpless, and everyone of us would have perished there and then. This news came in today, and we could only congratulate ourselves on our narrow escape.

To-day twenty British marines, ten Americans and five Japanese went out eastwards and a temple was surrounded, and burst into. Some fifty Boxers were found there. Every one was killed almost without resistance.

A huge fire started to-day just outside the Ch'ien Men in the Chinese City. It extended over acres and acres of the richest trading quarter of the city. All the Chinese silver banks are situated there, and offered fine opportunities for the usual crowd of looters. The fire caught on to the outer gate of the Ch'ien Men.

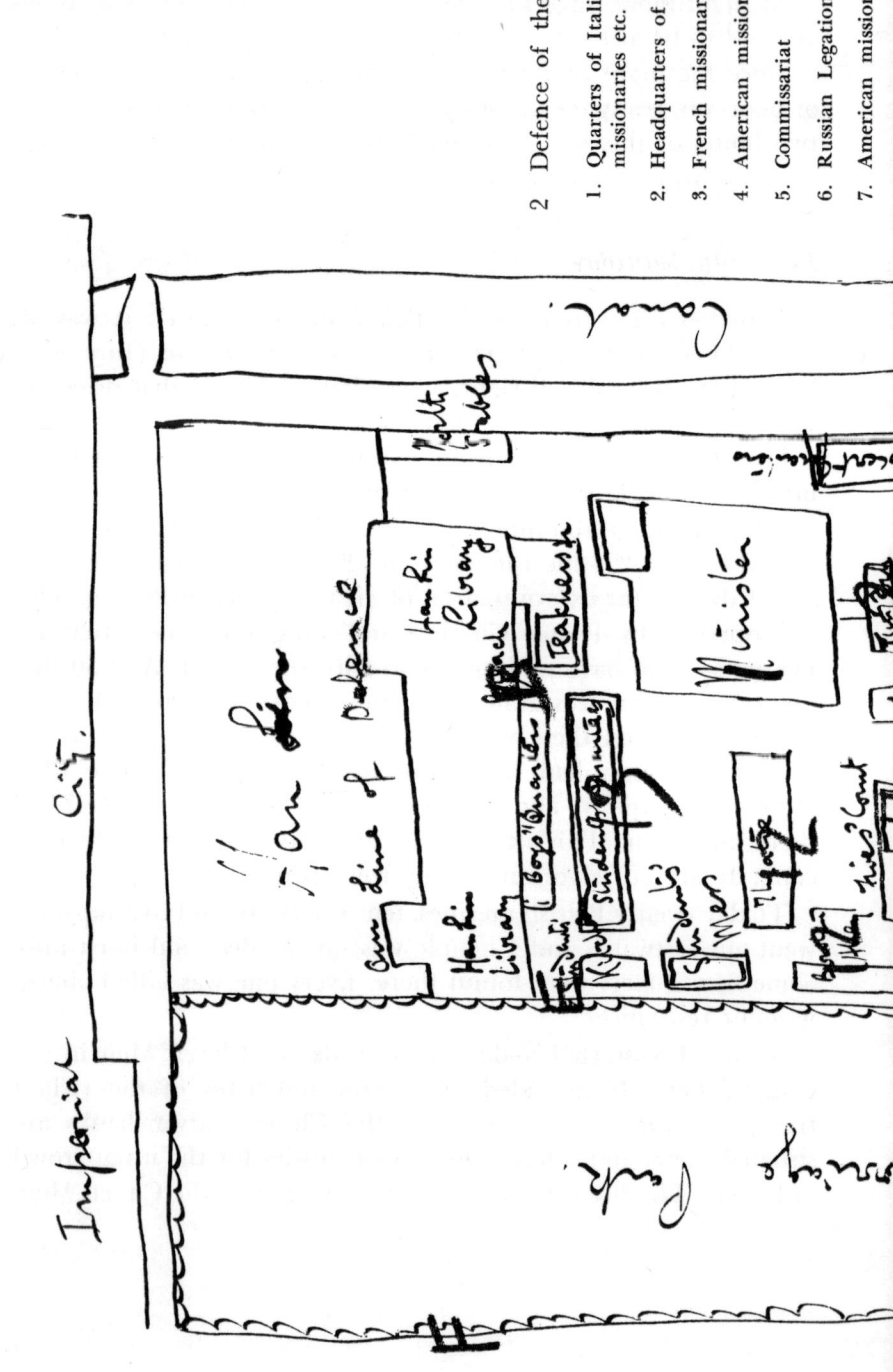

2 Defence of the British Legation
1. Quarters of Italian Legation, missionaries etc.
2. Headquarters of officers
3. French missionaries and nuns
4. American missionaries
5. Commissariat
6. Russian Legation
7. American missionaries

11. Non-coms. quarters
12. Marines barracks
13. Non-conscript refugees, and Japanese Legation
A. Scene of first fire
B. Breach into Hanlin
C. Chinese guns mounted and turned on
D. Stable quarters
E. Breach into Carriage Park for sortie to
F. where heavy fire was opened.

Every gate of the Tartar City has a large square in front of it encircled by a wall like the city wall. On the side opposite the main gate there is another subsidiary gate, never used except by the Emperor. But on either side of the square there are huge arches through the wall, which are used by the outgoing and incoming traffic. The sketch (see plan no. 3) may make it clearer (??).

3   The Ch'ien Men catching fire from the Chinese City

The fire began by Boxers firing separately all shops which sold foreign goods. It got beyond their control and destroyed the goldsmiths', jewellers', curio-, fur-, silk-, lantern-, and fan-shops; also the famous Liu Li Ch'ang (Book Street). The damage cannot be estimated, but must run into millions of taels.[43] The fire caused some alarm in the Imperial Palace, one entrance to which faces the gate; the Imperial Palace Body Guard turned out into the Palace forecourt to watch.

Later (5.15 p.m.) the Russians killed a man of the Chinese Fire Brigade[44] who was putting out a fire which had started in Legation Street; they thought he was an incendiary Chinese soldier, the uniform being similar. The Russians all through showed themselves over eager to shoot at anything and everything on suspicion.

The Russians now began pulling down the houses all round their Legation throwing the refuse into the Canal by the middle bridge.

Ch'ung-li[45] and others accused themselves of not having tried sufficiently to put down the fires. They were deprived of their buttons and official status, but *not* turned out of office. The head of the city police[46] was disgraced; and the government asked whether we wanted any troops to help us. This was declined with thanks, as the troops helping us would be more of a hindrance than anything else.

June 17th, Sunday

In the middle of the day the Austrians (also rather fond of firing) and Germans fired on some of Tung Fu-hsiang's troops who had been throwing stones at the European soldiers. This is most unfortunate, as all wanted to avoid any trouble with the Chinese troops. Bullets began to whiz all over the place, and our picket from the North Bridge was temporarily withdrawn. None of our men fired a shot in return.

Later in the evening Sir Claude and Cockburn had a talk with one of the Chinese officers, and both sides agreed to mutually avoid one another, and to look on the incident as a mistake.

Later a report came that our relief column had met 6,000 of Tung Fu-hsiang's troops and 20,000 Boxers, and had been driven back from Huang Tsun (15 miles from Peking) to Yang Tsun (20 miles from Tientsin). We refused to believe this.

In the early part of the night numerous volleys came from the Americo-Russian barricade.

June 18th, Monday

Same rumour of Russians being in the vicinity. This comes almost every day.

A message came from the Tsungli Yamen to the Russian Minister,[47] requesting him to keep the approaching Russian troops outside the city, as regrettable accidents might occur, now that the Chinese troops were guarding the city walls. They also asked that no more raids should be made on the Boxers, as it irritated the populace. No answer was vouchsafed to this.

Many of the Chinese troops on the North Bridge chatted with the interpreter on duty. They were friendly, and said their object was the same as ours.

The ministers decided and the Chinese authorities agreed that any Chinese (soldier or civilian), seen within or about the foreign *cordon* between 7 p.m. and 4 a.m., was liable, if unable to account for his presence, to be shot.

June 19th, Tuesday

I was on duty as interpreter this morning. At about 5 a.m. a man, carrying a sword and bundle wrapped up in yellow cloth, came strolling across the bridge. The sergeant on duty put his hand on his shoulder to stop him. The Chinaman immediately flung his parcels at the sergeant's chest, and bolted to a neighbouring house which had a small compound in front surrounded by a three foot wall. Here I parleyed with him for a long time, but he refused to come out. So when we (Captain Strouts,[48] our Commanding Officer, and myself) tried to get in to seize him, he bolted and ran round the house, after clearing the wall. However, Captain Strouts ran round one way and drove him right into my hands, in one of which was a loaded revolver. In his parcels were a big sword, and a broadbladed dagger. These were impounded; but the man himself was eventually released.

Meanwhile another man had been walking over the bridge, when this same sergeant caught sight of about an inch of red cloth beneath his jacket. This man too was seized, and found to be garbed in full Boxer uniform. He was, with our previous prisoner of a few days back, eventually shot.

To-day was one of great importance, as at 4 p.m. we received an ultimatum from the Tsungli Yamen to leave Peking within twenty-four hours, as the Taku forts[49] had been bombarded and taken by foreign troops. The Tsungli Yamen promised us safe escort to Tientsin. We were all dead against it, having regard to the historical precedent of Cownpore. Some days later (I know not on what authority) we heard that the Boxers had actually

14 British non-commissioned officers

In white in the middle: Sgt Preston and Cpl Gregory; seated on the ground: Henry Swannell, Signalman H.M.S. *Orlando*

15 British staff

Standing: Cpt. E. Wray, R.M.L.I.; Cpt. Percy Smith; Cpt. F. G. Poole, DSO; seated: Cpt. L. S. T. Halliday, VC, R.M.L.I.; Sir Claude Maxwell MacDonald, Envoy Extraordinary and Minister Plenipotentiary of Great Britain in China.

16 The first Boxer prisoner

17 Kansu (Tung Fu-hsiang's) soldiers who fought with the Boxers against the Legations' defenders

18 A Boxer temple in which forty Boxers were shot by the Allied rescue party
On the right the body of a dead Boxer; pools of blood on the left

19 Those who shot them—the rescue party
At the back of the party G. R. Morrison (correspondent of *The Times*) in round white helmet (l.cr), and Cpt. E. Wray, also in white

20 The Ch'ien Men before burning

21 The Ch'ien Men catching fire from the Chinese City

22 The Ch'ien Men burning

23 The Ch'ien Men enveloped in flames

24 Ruins of the Ch'ien Men from the west

25 Ruins of the Ch'ien Men: a fragment

26 Ruins of the Ch'ien Men from the south

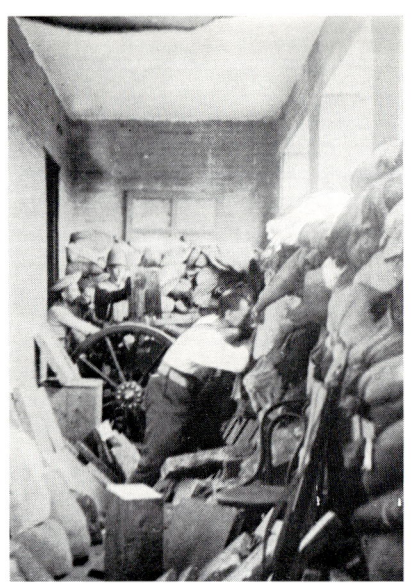

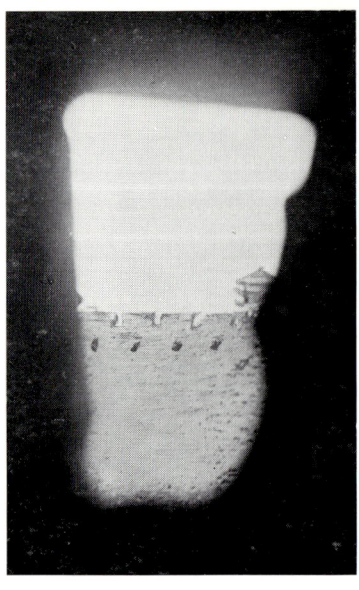

27 A balcony of the British Minister Sir Claude MacDonald's house
A defender firing through a loophole

28 Through a loophole
The Ch'ien Men visible on the right

29 Italian gunner and gun

planned to blow up the boats we should have used on the canal, with torpedoes. In any case it would hardly have been advisable to put any faith in the assurances of the Tsungli Yamen or the protection of the Chinese troops.

June 20th, Wednesday

At 9 a.m. came some very sad news. The ministers were to have gone to a meeting at the Tsungli Yamen. They decided not to go; but the German Minister, Baron von Ketteler, and his interpreter Cordes[50] went in chairs. They had not gone far before they were fired on from all sides by Chinese soldiers. The bearers dropped the chairs and fled. The interpreter, though wounded rather badly, ran for his life; but not seeing von Ketteler, went back; however he found no trace of him, and had to return alone, almost unconscious with the loss of blood, and pain. The t'ing ch'ais with them returned, saying von Ketteler had been shot through the back of the head, and was dead. Let us hope so!

The Tsungli Yamen sent and said they could not recover the body; and although they could not give us means of transport etc. to Tientsin, no extension of the twenty-four hours could be granted.

The ultimatum expired at 4 p.m.; but before then crowds of missionaries, women and children from the Customs, and other Legations had been housed in our Legation. All the morning I was slaving away in the Braziers'[51] house, bringing over all their food and drink and articles of value. It pleases Mrs. Brazier to show much gratitude and all that; but it really was not much for me to do. In fact when the ultimatum was up, we had got everything fairly trim. All the windows had been sandbagged with loopholes for firing; a strong barricade had been built round our front gate. All our other gates had been strongly fortified, and we were ready for the worst.

At the time fixed, almost to a minute, firing was heard in the direction of the Austrian Legation. Immediately 'stations' was sounded on the bugle, and off we dashed to our posts. From this moment—June 20th, at 4 p.m.—the siege of the Legations began.

Another deplorable incident took place this evening. One Professor James,[52] of Peking University—an awfully decent sort—

At the time fixed, almost to a minute, firing was heard in the direction of the Austrian Legation. Immediately "stations" was sounded on the bugle, & off we dashed to our posts. From this moment — June 20th, at 4 p.m. — the Siege of the Legations began.

Another deplorable incident took place this evening. One Professor James, of Peking University — an awfully decent sort — was quite convinced that all this shooting arose from a mistake. So he proceeded to the North Bridge, alone & unarmed, to parley with the soldiers. He was shot at, & fell; but was seen to move afterwards. Some Chinese soldiers went down & carried him off. If he was not dead, goodness only knows what tortures were in store for him. It will not bear thinking of. Of course our outpost at the Bridge had been drawn in previous to this.

In the evening the Austrian Legation was abandoned as untenable; & the Austrians fell back on the French.

was quite convinced that all this shooting arose from a mistake. So he proceeded to the North Bridge, alone and unarmed, to parley with the soldiers. He was shot at, and fell; but was seen to move afterwards. Some Chinese soldiers went down and carried him off. If he was not dead, goodness only knows what tortures were in store for him. It will not bear thinking of. Of course, our outpost at the North Bridge had been drawn in previous to this.

In the evening the Austrian Legation was abandoned as untenable; and the Austrians fell back on the French.

June 21st, Thursday

In the morning an attack was made on the Legation from the further side of the Carriage Park and from the Hanlin.[53]

All day sniping went on. We were all very careful of our ammunition, as our supply is limited; but the Chinese troops are under no such difficulty; they fire a tremendous amount, almost entirely without aiming. They crouch behind a wall, load, point their guns over the wall (without raising themselves) and fire—at nothing in particular. We have grown quite accustomed to the whizzing of bullets overhead, and are absolutely indifferent to them, though we often see them fall to the ground within a few feet of us.

I had a narrow escape to-day. I was firing over the top of some sandbags at some soldiers creeping along the top of the further wall of the Carriage Park. I had brought down one man, and was covering another, who was covering me. We fired almost simultaneously; his bullet cut the top of the sandbag within an inch of my rifle, and cannot have been more than a couple of inches off my head which I had raised to see what had happened. If he had fired that same shot a few seconds earlier, it would have got me while I was aiming. I want no narrower squeaks. A Frenchman, quartered in one of our rooms, (all our sitting rooms are occupied by refugees) was so overcome that he insisted on my taking a glass of cognac. I suppose I must have looked rather washed out and shaky, and no wonder!

The American Methodist Mission, Belgian Legation, Chinese Imperial Bank, and Austrian Legation were burned.

Prince Ch'ing is said to be helping the foreign troops on the wall; while Tung Fu-hsiang's troops are attacking us.

June 22nd, Friday

The Italians had to retire in the morning on to the French Legation. The Italian Minister[54] and his wife were unable to save any property.

At 8.45 a.m. an Austrian under-officer ordered a general retreat on to our Legation. This was only to be done in a case of extreme danger, and as a last move. The French, Italians, Japanese, and Austrians all came in. It was a gross mistake; and they were all ordered to re-take their positions. This was successfully accomplished.

Sir Claude took over the supreme command. At 9.20 a.m., the Russians retired on to our Legation, but were promptly sent back.

The following notice was posted on the notice-board:

> The Germans on the wall have spoken to Ch'ing's troops and found them very friendly. They said they had orders to prevent the Boxers advancing. Ch'ing had given orders for anyone disobeying this order to be shot. Of course foreign troops could go on the wall.

Several fires were seen during the afternoon. In the afternoon the Italian 1-inch gun was placed in an upper room of the South Stables (see plan no. 2) and several shots fired at a wall opposite, which the Chinese had begun to loophole. This gun is the only field piece we have here. The Americans and Austrians have each got an up to date machine gun; while we have a somewhat antiquated Nordenfelt, which generally refuses to work when required. The Americans brought a 3-inch gun as far as Tientsin, and left it there, worse luck. I spent this afternoon in chopping down six trees. Havoc is being made of the Legation trees and walls. Great use has been made of all the missionaries and non-combatants who are housed here, by forming committees and sub-committees who superintend the policing of the Legation. Every Chinese man in the compound has to do two hours work a day for the general good. We have a General Committee; a Fortification, a Sanitation, a Fuel Supply, a Water Supply, a

Chinese Labour, a Fire Defence, etc. etc. Committee. I am on the staff of the Fire Defence Committee.

At 2.30 p.m. a messenger, who had got through to the Tsungli Yamen, returned with a receipt but no answer to the question of why the Chinese troops were firing on us. At 4.20 p.m. the fire-alarm sounded. As I dashed to the spot, I heard one of our 'Tommies' exclaim: 'My God, they have done for us this time!' And indeed it looked rather like it. The Chinese had managed to get quite close up to our west wall, marked A on plan no. 2. A huge fire was blazing away with a strong west wind blowing. Bullets were whizzing over the top of the wall which considerably increased the difficulty and danger of getting the fire under control. For two-and-a-half hours we worked like niggers. I emerged at the end, dripping from head to foot with muddy water, but with the satisfaction of having tided over a very serious danger.

At 6.10 p.m. we suffered our first loss. Private Scadding of the Royal Marines was shot at his post. It was to a great extent his own fault, as he persisted in exposing himself unduly above the sandbags, though bullets were flying all round him.

At 7.30 p.m. Captain Myers of the United States Marines came in with a piece of shell which had burst over the American Legation, and said that the Russo-Chinese Bank had been badly damaged by shells.

At night a patrol was sent into the Hanlin, a gap being made in the north wall of the Legation at B on the map (see plan no. 2).

June 23rd, Saturday

Throughout the day, houses adjoining the Legation were pulled down, as a safeguard against fire.

Throughout the morning our west defence was heavily attacked. We lay low and hardly ever replied to the firing, as we have to be sparing with our ammunition.

Later the north-east defence was heavily attacked, but there were no casualties on our side.

The coolies at work, pulling down the houses outside the south wall, drew a heavy fire from the Chinese. One was killed, but the others stuck to it pluckily.

At 11.15 a.m. a fire was reported in the Hanlin, where the Chinese were entrenched. It was got under, and the Hanlin cleared of Chinese troops.

There was some doubt as to whether we should occupy the Hanlin as a strategic position, and pull down the buildings as a preventive of fires. It was argued, however, that the Chinese would never set fire to so venerable a monument of the country's literature.

This was set at naught by the Chinese setting fire to the various buildings all through the day. The Library was almost entirely destroyed; an attempt was made to save the famous *Yung lu ta tien*[55] but heaps of volumes had been destroyed, so the attempt was given up. I secured volume 13,345 (!!) for myself, merely as a specimen. The pages are one foot by one foot eight inches and the volumes vary from half an inch to one inch in thickness. Each page has eight columns, each column contains two rows of twenty-six characters.

I also picked up a couple of the essays written by some candidate for one of the great examinations.[56]

Within the next few days we completed the work begun by the Chinese and razed the Hanlin to the ground.

Hundreds and hundreds of empty cartridge cases were found behind the Chinese entrenchments. It was calculated that in the first ten or eleven days of the siege the Chinese fired over half a million rifle cartridges.

In the afternoon the Russians and Americans were hard pressed by fires, and help was sent. The Russo-Chinese Bank, containing $80,000 in hard cash was burnt down.

The Customs' men were sent out to help the Japanese in the Fu. Richardson[57] was slightly wounded in the shoulder. All the Customs' houses were found burnt to the ground, including Sir Robert's. Poor old Sir Robert! This is poor thanks for the good work he has done China during the last thirty odd years! He has shown up rather well during the siege. He was naturally invited to mess at Sir Claude's house; but he declined, and insisted on messing with all his junior assistants, eating what they did and nothing better. It must have come rather hard to him, being over sixty-nine. He lost three pounds in weight in a week, which is a serious matter for a man of his years and fragile stature.

During the day the Chinese made four determined attempts to burn us out by lighting big fires in the Hanlin. None succeeded, but we had to work hard at them.

They also gave the Russians a fairly hot time, but were equally unsuccessful.

It is really wonderful how we do manage to keep these fires under, seeing how defective the water supply is, and how feeble our fire-pumps. We are just beginning to make the Chinese coolies perceive how useful a chain is for passing buckets of water. I am a very good organiser of Chinese coolies for this sort of work, being able to trot out some language that makes them sit up!!

June 24th, Sunday

The Chinese turned a 3-inch gun on the Fu. A shell fell into our Legation, and caused somewhat of a panic. The French Minister[58] especially showed himself a poltroon, as indeed he has all through the siege.

Chinese banners were seen all along the city wall to the west of the Ch'ien Men. They are blue with a red border, and have four black characters on them. In the morning the Germans cleared the wall of Chinese troops to within about 100 yards of the Ch'ien Men, which is occupied by the Chinese. An order was issued that every available coolie should proceed to the wall, which must be held at all costs. For if the Chinese can plant their field guns on the wall over the canal, they can lay this Legation in ruins. It would only be a matter of a few hours.

Help was sent over to the Fu during the early part of the morning, as it was being hard pressed. The Japanese Colonel Shiba[59] is in command of the Fu. He is considered the best officer up here, just as the Japanese are undoubtedly the best soldiers. Their pluck and daring is astounding, our marines are next to them in this respect; but I think the Japanese lead the way.

At 9 a.m. there was a fire lighted at the foot of the gate onto the Mongol Market, accompanied by heavy firing on the part of the Chinese soldiers on the further side of the Market. This fire spread further north and south, keeping us very busy for the next three hours. Two sorties were made through our west wall just where the previous fires, at A in plan no. 2, had been. They were led by Captain Strouts and Captain Halliday. Captain Strouts was wounded slightly just below his left ear. The shock knocked him down; but he got up again and led a brilliant charge which did great execution. The other party, headed by Captain Halliday, did fair work. Poor Halliday was shot through the left shoulder. The bullet grazed the top of his left lung. He is slowly recovering, though in some pain. He was considered the best of our three marine officers, being very hardworking and a favourite with the men. After he fell, he killed three men with his revolver, before fainting away. Sir Claude wrote him a congratulatory letter.

The Chinese began to imitate us, and throw up barricades in all the lanes about the Legations, and on the city wall. This renders any sortie more difficult and dangerous.

The Americans were driven from their position on the wall, but retook it later in the afternoon.

There were a couple more fire alarms in the day; but nothing very serious.

A Chinese messenger, sent out by the Japanese, came back and said he had been twenty-five miles down the line to Tientsin, and had seen no Boxers or foreign troops.

At 4 p.m. a notice was posted up:

> Heavy firing constantly heard towards west. Thought to indicate approach of foreign troops.

A marine was hit in the leg, while standing in the middle of the Legation. This shows how liable any of us is to being hit, even when away from the barricades.

A reinforcement was sent to the Americans on the wall in the evening, so as to try and take the Chinese 3-inch gun. It was decided, however, not to make the attempt, as our small numbers did not justify so large a loss of life as was anticipated.

Sixty coolies built a strong barricade on the wall for the American defence. This was effected under cover of darkness.

Most of our ponies were turned out of the Legation into the Fu, mine included. To-day we started on horsemeat. I was glad to be able to start on some fresh meat for a change, for since last

31 Italian gunner in the Hanlin

32 The Nordenfelt

33 Colt automatic gun

34 The front line of defence in the Fu after shelling

35 'Boxer Bill', called also 'Dowager Empress' and 'Old Crock'
An old (1860) Chinese cannon lashed to an improvised gun-carriage. Second from the right American gunner Mitchell

36 The second line of defence in the Fu

37 The gate leading to the Mongol Market

38 The Mongol Market gate barricaded from inside

39 Germans commandeering Chinese labour

40 The last, improved, Russian barricade

41 Students' Quarters seen from the Hanlin

42 Daily food of the besieged

43 The Hanlin: the ruins of the main building

44 The Hanlin: the library

Wednesday we have been living on tinned food. This horsemeat, or rather ponymeat, is really not at all bad; rather like beef, only somewhat tough. Luckily it is hot weather, when one does not require much meat.

In the night the Germans saw two white rockets go up in the south-west. They were probably sent up by the Chinese.

June 25th, Monday

6.30 a.m. Our two Boxer prisoners, (see above), were shot, and their bodies chucked over the wall.

Sir Claude fell ill, and the Italian Minister (Marquis Salvago-Raggi), a very decent fellow and quite young, took his place.

Throughout the day attacks were made off and on at all the barricades, but no great damage was done.

The American captain[60] kept on sending in messages to the effect that the barricade on the wall was untenable. However, they still managed to hold out. Curious people these Americans!

At 4.15 p.m. a board was hung out on the North Bridge with large Chinese characters painted on it. The following is the official translation:

> An Imperial command to protect ministers and to stop firing. A despatch will be delivered at the Yu Ho Bridge.[61]

A reply was sent from us in similar style by a man wearing an official hat. He got as far as the North Bridge (the one mentioned above); but the Chinese troops started calling out: *lai liao, lai liao* ('He has come, he has come'). So this man promptly dropped his board, and fled back to the Legation.

Some mandarins and soldiers came out, and were fired on by the Japanese and Italians in the Fu, who had not yet received the order to *cease fire*.

The Chinese shooting stopped all round simultaneously, which points to the whole thing being properly organised. Meanwhile our fortifications were pushed on with redoubled vigour.

A rumour came in that mandarins were coming to parley; so all the foreign ministers assembled at our main gate at 5.45 p.m.; but it came to nothing.

At 6.15 p.m. some of us (including myself) picked our way over the ruins to the north end of the Hanlin and had a talk with one of the soldiers who came towards us, laying down his rifle and ammunition in the road. Some way behind him (about a 100 yards away) were two to three hundred soldiers of all regiments (Tung Fu-hsiang's, Ch'ing's and Jung Lu's). Their red, green and blue uniforms were very picturesque. This man we talked with gave us repeated assurances that the Chinese troops were there to protect (!) us. He also said that Jung Lu (showing he had come back) had ordered the *cease fire,* and would send despatches. These last never arrived.

In the evening the Chinese were seen building earthworks at the far side of the Carriage Park. We spent a quiet evening, with orders to be especially wide awake and cautious during the night.

At midnight punctually a terrific fusillade began on all sides of all the Legations, and at all the barricades. This also points to organisation; and it only once more indicates what faith may be put in Chinese promises. The fusillade lasted three-quarters of an hour; the number of shots fired was estimated at about fifteen thousand. This is the heaviest firing we have had so far.

June 26th, Tuesday

In the morning the French commanding officer[62] was told to send ten men to reinforce the Americans on the wall. He refused pointblank, so some of our men were sent instead.

The Japanese throughout the morning were destroying the buildings adjacent to the Fu on the north and east sides.

People started making bomb-proof shelters. Personally I would far rather be outside these shelters than in them. They look awful death-traps. But this is a matter of opinion.

There seem to be elements of dissension between the various commanding officers of the various nations. It is a pity. The French and Russians are worst in this respect.

In the evening there was a huge blaze in the vicinity of the French Legation, also heavy volley firing from their barricade.

Later heavy guns were heard some way off in the south.

In the early part of the night heavy firing was heard from the American barricade on the wall. They seem to leave the British pretty much to themselves.

June 27th, Wednesday

Early in the morning (2.45 a.m.) there was some very heavy firing all round the Legation, especially from the north and northwest end of the Hanlin. A couple of volleys from our men in the Hanlin quieted things a bit.

Colonel Shiba wished to force the Chinese barricades just outside the Imperial City. It was, however, considered foolish to irritate the troops there, as they had not yet fired from those positions.

A census was taken to-day of all the foreign *civilians* in Peking at present.

	Men	Women	Children	Total
In the British Legation	191	147	76	414
Outside the British Legation	54	2	3	59

The Chinese within our lines are reckoned at about 3,000.

The Japanese were hard pressed in the afternoon, and reinforcements were sent.

Peachey,[63] who was on duty at one of our gates, was wounded in the thigh. He and Backhouse[64] have taken refuge here. As you may imagine, it is rather humiliating for Peachey to have to come into the Legation again after his previous conduct, which I wrote to you about some time ago. However, we try to make it as pleasant for him as possible.

Colonel Shiba wanted to let the Chinese force their way into the Fu, as they have been trying to do; and then slaughter them. This was considered too risky. He really is a splendid officer.

At 4 p.m. the alarm was sounded and we dashed to our posts. The attack was severe, but as the Chinese never bother to take any aim, no casualties were reported. One death for every 15,000 bullets fired is a poor percentage. Most of the casualties arise from stray shots falling to the ground, or glancing off trees and houses.

The Chinese broke through the wall of the Fu, and got into it. They were swept by a withering fire from the Japanese who were behind loopholed walls. A sortie was then made by our marines, some Customs' men, five Japanese, ten Russians and twenty Italians. The Chinese fired a temple to cover their retreat.

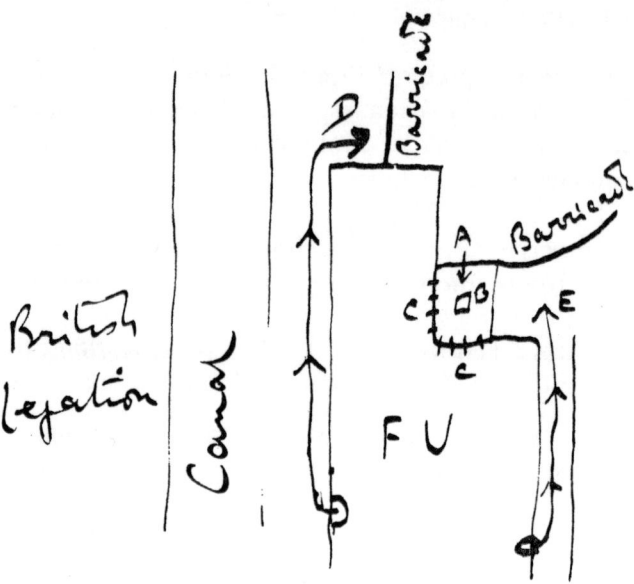

4 A Chinese attack on the Fu and the Allied counter-attack

The above sketch [4] may give you some idea of this strategic movement.

In the evening there was heavy firing from all sides. The Chinese occupied one of the few remaining Hanlin buildings and loopholed the roof, maintaining a steady fire on us. We watched, but did not answer.

At 8 p.m. the Americans reported that the Chinese had forced 200 Boxers to advance on the American barricade, and that they had killed fifty. This proved to be a most gross exaggeration.

8.30 p.m. Heavy guns were heard in the distance in the south. *Query*: troops advancing? I fear me these are vain hopes.

10.30 p.m. Extremely heavy attack on the Americans' and our north front. As usual it fizzled out, and no attempt at a rush was made. The north front, by the way, is where my station is. So I come in for a lot of the heavy firing. Once a bullet whizzed through my loophole just after I had turned aside from it for a moment to speak to someone in the room. Narrow escape number two.

One of our corporals here, Gregory by name, has had three marvellous escapes. His cap was carried off his head by a bullet; the handle of his bayonet at the end of his rifle was shattered; and lastly, when he had his rifle at his shoulder ready to fire, a bullet went clean through his rifle just above the trigger, grazing his right thumb and left cheek a bit. However, all comes to him who waits; he was shot through the instep some days later, and his foot may have to be amputated, poor devil.

June 28th, Thursday

The Chinese mounted a gun (about 3-inch) north-east of the Fu, and started shelling the place. Luckily the Chinese are most incompetent gunners, and seem to have no idea of range; so very little damage was done.

Colonel Shiba with his usual dashing spirit wanted to make a sortie to take the gun. This was postponed for a few days.

A hole was knocked through the Carriage Park wall, so as to be available for sorties. It is in the same place where F. and Abdy[65] made their hole. It is probably the same hole; as, after removing the plaster and a few bricks, it was plain that there had previously been a hole in this place.

In the afternoon a huge fire broke out at the west end of the middle bridge, burning a lot of shops.

Luckily we had looted all these shops, so that there was nothing very valuable to be lost. The origin of the fire is not known, but it was probably accidental.

6.30 p.m. The Chinese started firing a 3-inch and a 1-inch gun at the South Stable quarters overlooking the Mongol Market (see C and D on plan no. 2). They did some damage to the building, but no men were hurt. A piece of shell hit what was considered the best hack in the stables, and killed it. We ate him later! Altogether about twenty shots were fired. The dust raised by one of the bursting shells caused some idiot to ring the fire-alarm.

Owing to the inferior gunpowder in these shells of the Chinese, much less damage was done by the explosions than might have been expected. There were both grape and shrapnel shells.

A notice was posted on the board:

A Chinese of the London Mission[66] has got to Ts'ai Yu (about 20 miles away). He met Boxers flying before the troops who had taken the Taku forts; as he came in he spoke to Chinese troops who said they were tired of fighting the foreigners.

Personally I did not believe a word of it.

June 29th, Friday

Two sorties had been arranged for 3 a.m. today.

1. To enter the Carriage Park at E on plan no. 2, run across to F and burn the houses out there. The cause of this was the report that the Chinese were working behind barricades there. It was feared that they were trying to undermine the walls.

At 3 a.m. five students and five Customs' men and three marines under Captain Poole[67] (of the East Yorkshire Regiment, who is here studying Chinese) were ready to start, when a furious fusillade began just as the first man was about to get through the hole in the wall. It stopped after a few minutes, and as it was considered to be merely an accident, they started again.

They got to within ten yards of their goal when the sentry on watch spotted them, and gave the alarm. He was promptly dropped, but it was too late. A heavy fire started from in front, and a raking crossfire from a barricade to the north. They promptly retreated, firing a few volleys into the barricades. The Chinese were in such a funk, however, that there were no casualties.

2. To go across the Mongol Market and seize the guns which had been shelling us the previous evening. The force, led by Captain Wray, consisted of twenty British, ten Germans, ten Russians, five French and five Italians. They got across near to the position of the gun, when they were told to charge. Here I had better give the words of the marine who related the tale to me. 'Cap'en Wray shouted out "Charge, men, charge! Courage, men, courage!" But did he show us the way? Not 'e, 'e stood be'ind an 'ouse!' Having heard the story from several men independently, I am forced to believe that on this occasion the Captain did not show that reckless courage which is thought to be an attribute of the British officer.

When the charge had been effected, it was found that the gun had been withdrawn during the night. So they set some houses (the wrong ones) on fire, and retreated. I believe Captain Wray was censored on his return for the rotten way in which he carried out the sortie.

Throughout the morning shells were humming over the Legation. It is curious how absolutely indifferent we become to all this shooting and shelling.

All through the day the Japanese and Italians had a very hot time of it, fighting like grim death. Reinforcements were sent over.

2.10 p.m. One of our marines, Phillips, the most popular man of the lot, was killed by a stray shot just outside the guard house by the main entrance to the compound. Anyone might have been standing there. The bullet entered his right shoulder and went through his heart.

In the afternoon the French Legation was hard pressed, and some marines were sent there. The French commander congratulated our marines on their splendid work, as their shooting was excellent and cleared the place.

A French lieutenant was shot at the French barricade.

The French and Japanese are in a critical position. Colonel Shiba says he had to abandon part of the Fu in the north, so he must have been hard pressed.

In the evening there was some heavy firing, but it came to nothing.

The Austrian machine gun was brought into our Legation.

At 10 p.m. a heavy thunderstorm came on, and almost simultaneously a fierce fusillade began from the Hanlin. The effect was magnificent. The rifle fire did not last long; but the jingalls (these are large muskets, firing iron balls, manned by two men) kept going till four the next morning. The Chinese must be running short of rifle ammunition, having to fall back on these antiquated things.

The sentry at the South Stables reported that between ten and eleven at night he saw a steady beam of light moving laterally in the south. It is undoubtedly a searchlight, but it might equally well be a Chinese searchlight as a European one.

June 30th, Saturday

In the morning the big gun began again to the north-east of the Fu. Bits of shell fell in the Legation.

The Japanese sent for reinforcements, as the north wall of the Fu was being battered in. Five students (including myself), a corporal and six marines, and a couple of other men went across. For about a couple of hours we sat crouched behind a hillock along with some Italians and French. It was rather a curious sensation sitting there within fifty yards of this big gun which was booming away, and listening to the shells humming over our heads. The big gun was fired every two minutes which is slow work. We returned without accomplishing anything.

11.30 a.m. Two marines were wounded on the wall. One, with whom I was rather friendly, called Tickner, had one leg frightfully damaged. He was a good footballer, and as he was carried through the gate, he raised a smile and said: 'Well, I stopped that one all right.' He then fainted away.

11.45 a.m. Three Germans were killed and two were wounded on the city wall. The Germans are too reckless, and expose themselves too much over the barricades.

During the day eighty pounds of gunpowder were found in the Fu. They have been stored in Sir Claude's cellar.

2 p.m. Germans reported that Chinese soldiers in great numbers were passing through the Chinese City from west to east.

In the evening the Germans sent up two rockets, but no answer was received.

The night was quiet, except for the usual nightly attack from the Hanlin; we turn out to our posts, and stay there about a quarter of an hour before turning in again.

July 1st, Sunday

9.15 a.m. The Germans at their barricade on the wall were surprised by the Chinese who had crawled up to their position. The Germans promptly retreated. The Americans, seeing the Germans leave their barricade, and finding their rear exposed, also left their position on the wall. There had been no casualties to justify this extreme step, which renders our position most critical. Orders were promptly issued for the positions to be re-taken.

10.10 a.m. The Americans re-took their former positions; but that of the Germans has not been re-captured, as it would entail too heavy a loss of life.

45 The ruins of Customs Lane

46 Under a flag of truce
The Allied party in the foreground watching the arrival of the Yamen
secretary with a message

47 A Chinese messenger, Liu Wu-yüan (age 16), who went to Tientsin and back

48 A scene in the German Legation

49 The Legation Street in ruins

50 The relief
Sir Claude MacDonald in white suit

51 Soldiers of the 7th Rajputs, the first to enter the Legation Quarter

52 The march through the Imperial palace: the British staff with Gen. Gaselee (†)

53 The march through the Imperial palace: the British Marine Corps
Major Halliday (†)

54 The march through the Imperial palace: Graf von Waldersee reviewing the Allied troops

55 The march through the Imperial palace: the Japanese

56 The march through the Imperial palace: the Russians

57 *In memoriam*

Here fell David Oliphant of H.B.M. Consular Service, mortally wounded while cutting down this tree, 11.30 a.m. 5 July 1900, and here Henry Swannell, Signalman, H.M.S. *Orlando,* at the risk of his life stayed by his side and held him until help came to bear him to the hospital.

The American machine gun was brought into the British Legation which is to be held to the last, all troops falling back on it in the last extremity.

Reinforcements were sent to the Americans, and coolies were sent to work at new barricades on the walls. Our own position was temporarily weakened, but the call was imperative.

All the morning all hands were at work making sandbags, as the Americans had just asked for about 400. About 1,000 were made during the morning, so as to have some in hand. The women sewed for all they were worth, while the men filled and carted away the bags.

10.30 a.m. Wagner of the Customs, a ripping fellow, and a great friend of mine, was shot through the head at the French barricade. He is a Frenchman. This is our saddest loss so far as regards my own feelings.

2.30 p.m. Captain Wray was shot through the left shoulder. Not very serious.

3.15 p.m. Five students (Hancock, Flaherty, Bristow, Townsend and Russell[68]) with seven marines were sent across to help Colonel Shiba to take the big gun to the north-east of the Fu. They did not know when they started what they were to do, but when they got there the Italian captain gave them their orders: *'Il faut prendre ce canon.'*

The Japanese went round one way while the British marines, students and Italians went up along the canal to A on plan no. 5. They ought to have gone on to F and G and charged down the lane there. By some mistake they charged from A with a cheer, down to B. As soon as they started they saw in front of them an eight-foot barricade with loopholes. At C.C.C. there were loopholes. They were thus fired on from the front and from the left flank.

At B the Italians and marines turned back in panic and made for E, a hole into the Fu. They dashed at the hole, crowding round it, of course, obstructing each other. Russell kept his head wonderfully, and ordered his four students to stand quietly at D, a small corner where they were out of the line of fire. There they stood, shooting round the corner at the barricade, till all were through E. They then rushed across singly from D to E, and would have all been safe, had not Townsend, in getting through,

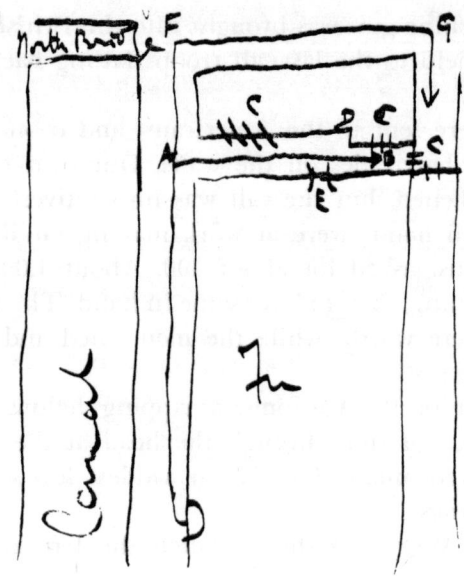

5   The operation designed to take the big Chinese gun to the north-east of the Fu

stumbled and fallen. He was hit in the shoulder and thigh. The rest got through all right. Even the Italian captain dashed through with the rest. I think the students came out of it magnificently, a lot being due to the presence of mind and level head of Russell.

Two Italians were killed, and their commander badly wounded; two marines, a Frenchman and a Japanese were also wounded.

Had the Chinese not been in a mortal funk, and had they known the barest elements of shooting, I do not think a single man would have returned alive.

The Italian commander[69] and Shiba take the whole blame on themselves. Sir Claude was awfully annoyed at the students having been sent on this expedition. He does not want them to be thrown unnecessarily in the way of danger, as he considers himself responsible for them. One or two of these students were very much shaken by this adventure, and were knocked up till the next day.

At 10.20 p.m. a searchlight was again reported to the south.

July 2nd, Monday

The American post was still further fortified. Everything is very quiet. This seems to indicate that the Chinese are running short of ammunition; or that some of the troops have withdrawn. Is it to oppose the relief force?

It rained almost all day. This may account for the falling off in the attack.

The sound of the shots from the big guns seems to indicate that they do not fit the gun.

Sir Claude put up the following notice (I mentioned the incident above).

> Last night between 10 p.m. and 2 a.m. an electric flashlight was seen on south-east horizon; the appropriate distance is from twenty-five to thirty miles. The flashes were regular, and occurred at intervals of about a second, with a pause of from five to ten minutes between each forty or fifty flashes.

Our defences in the North Stables were materially strengthened. The passage up to Sir Claude's front door was protected by a high brick wall on the east side.

The Italian gun was turned on a Chinese barricade at the foot of the Imperial City opposite the Hanlin. It was knocked to pieces.

The Fu was hard pressed during the day; but was left alone during the night, when the Japanese and Italians considerably strengthened it.

July 3rd, Tuesday

At 3 a.m. twenty-five marines, fourteen Americans, and fifteen Russians attacked the Chinese position on the wall towards the Ch'ien Men. They were successful, and captured two Chinese banners, and some rifles and spears. The American commander (Captain Myers) was slightly wounded. Two Americans were killed.

Heavy firing began from the Mongol Market in the early morning. In the Hanlin the Chinese sent up numerous rockets.

4.30 a.m. The big gun near the Fu fired about three shots, and then was silent for the day. Why?

5.30 a.m. Rain fell till 2.30 p.m.

The Canal is filling rapidly and is now about five to six feet deep. French engineers were consulted as to draining it. They could do nothing.

2 p.m. Shells from the 1-inch guns, firing from the Ha Ta Men on the Americans, passed over them and landed amongst the Chinese at the Ch'ien Men.

The halyard of our Union Jack (which has been flying since the ultimatum was up) was cut through, and the flag came down. It was soon nailed to the mast in orthodox fashion.

It is strange how very many points of similarity there are between this siege and that of Lucknow, as described by Tennyson. Quite half the lines in Tennyson's poem apply equally well here.

Five banners were seen near the French Legation. A heavy attack was therefore expected. But nothing happened.

In the evening a furious fusillade was directed against the west defence, but fell off after a while.

The flashlight was seen again in the south, but much brighter and evidently closer. Our signalman could not read anything off it, which points to its being merely a Chinese light.

An unsuccessful attempt was made to burn the Japanese out of the Fu.

July 4th, Wednesday

Casualties up to date are:

	Killed	Wounded	Total
British	2	14	16
Italians	6	7	13
Germans	7	8	15
French	6	5	11
Austrians	3	3	6
Americans	6	9	15
Japanese	4	11	15
Russians	3	11	14
Civilians	3	4	7
Total	40	72	112

The big gun fired off and on most of the day; otherwise it was quiet enough.

Warren and I went round to one of the stores within the cordon and brought in a lot of loot which we shared. We each got about $200 worth. Much better we should get it than the Chinese who were there looting everything they could lay hands on.

In the evening Sir Claude sent out a messenger to try and find the troops. The messenger was a small boy carrying a rice tin with a false bottom. He was lowered over the wall at night. He carried the following message to Admiral Seymour:

> Since June 20th we have been besieged by Imperial troops who have four or five guns—one quick-firing, a 1-inch, a 2-3 inch, and two throwing 14 lb. shells—chiefly used at barricades. The enemy are enterprising but cowardly. Chinese Government, if any, doing nothing to put this down; all their positions very close to ours (our positions were then described). We can hold out, if enemy go on as at present, say ten days; if they attack in earnest, four or five. Haste absolutely necessary, if you want to avoid a horrible massacre. Entrance probably easy; enemy hold gates of city; canal sluices afford easy entrance. We have lost forty killed.

The worst of a siege like this is that there are so many women and children about the place. Also that there can be no suggestion of surrender, seeing what barbarians the Chinese are. We all would shoot ourselves rather than fall alive into the hands of the Chinese. It is too ghastly to think of what would happen were we absolutely concerned. I have no doubt that it would hardly be a red-letter day as regards many Chinese, but that is poor consolation for us. However, we shall stick to it a bit longer yet.

July 5th, Thursday

The big gun seems to have been brought somewhat closer. It has started firing again. I believe it is bearing on the hotel[70] (between the French and Japanese Legations). They say eleven shots went into one room.

Some Japanese rockets were found in one of the stores. They are going to be tried at night.

11.45 a.m. Lots of men were working in the Hanlin cutting down trees, and building walls, when some Chinese started firing from the Carriage Park. Captain Poole whistled to the men to retreat. Oliphant,[71] however, thought he was under cover and went on chopping. Suddenly he dropped with a bullet right through him just below the diaphragm. He was in frightful agony, and died at 3 p.m.

All the afternoon we were at work digging his grave as we did not wish any Chinese to have a hand in it. He was buried at 6.45 a.m. About a couple of hundred people followed the bier.

It is awfully sad, as he was immensely popular with us all. He had just received his step to Second-Assistant. He was quite one of the rising men of the Consular Service, being about the best colloquial Chinese scholar in the place, bar none. He entered at King's Aberdeen the same time Lionel[72] did, but left after one year, for St. Andrews. He had only been out here three years. One of his brothers[73] is here at present, being in the Chinese Imperial Bank.

During the day the Chinese erected a barricade on the Imperial City wall facing the Hanlin, and started firing solid iron shot varying from one and a half inches to two and a half inches in diameter. Several crashed through the north wall of the students' quarters. Barr's[74] room suffered most.

Colonel Shiba gives the relief column another fourteen days from now!

When the Chinese began firing their solid shot, Sir Claude went up to see. He got very keen, as he could see the Chinese manning the gun, and fired five shots out of one of our Martini-Henry rifles. Just then one of the iron shots burst through the wall into the adjacent room, so he cleared out.

The Italian gun was brought to bear on this gun, and silenced it.

5.30 p.m. Gilbert Reid,[75] a missionary, was wounded in the leg, when proceeding from our Legation to the Russian Legation.

Big guns were heard in the distance in the west. Can this be the relief force, or are the Chinese amusing themselves with inspiring us with false hopes?

July 6th, Friday

A very quiet day. The Chinese kept on firing their old muzzle loader at intervals of about a quarter of an hour. Russell and myself sat for some hours, watching them through glasses (they are about 300 yards off). Whenever anyone showed, we fired. Our firing had some effect, because they are very cautious now about showing even a finger! They have erected two doors on the wall. These they fling open when they want to fire, closing them afterwards. Once, when they saw the Italian 1-inch gun trained on them, they got so excited that they fired off their gun without putting any shot in.

The flagstaff over the American Legation was shot away by the Chinese.

A rather disgraceful incident took place to-day. A Russian student, named Kitroff, got frightfully drunk, and then walked out of the French barricade which he crossed, in spite of the protestations of the French officer, and almost before the latter was aware of his intentions. He still went on almost up to the Chinese barricade where he was riddled with the Chinese bullets. However, when he fell, five Chinese rushed out to get in the body. They were all shot down by the French. So the Chinese had to wait till nightfall. The Russian Minister offered a large reward for the body, but with no success as it was mere suicide to show oneself in front of the French line.

A messenger was sent out at night, being lowered over the city wall by the Americans. He returned very quickly, as he was afraid he was being watched.

The night passed quietly except for the occasional booming of the muzzle-loader. A branch which came down with a rush in the Hanlin caused a panic amongst some German volunteers who blazed away at nothing.

Colonel Shiba has raised a corps of thirty Chinese Christians, armed with captured rifles.

July 7th, Saturday

Throughout the day the attack was desultory. The Fu and the French Legation bore the brunt of the attack.

During the morning a big round shot passed through the roof of Sir Claude's dining-room. It caused some alarm in the heart of that worthy.

The following notice was posted:

> The officers commanding the Austrian and French detachments, report heavy cannonading in the south-west, lasting from midnight till this morning.

2 p.m. A fire due east of the French Legation.

3 p.m. Large fire in the Fu. Both these fires were eventually got under.

4 p.m. Heavy firing in north-west. It was suggested it came from the Pei T'ang of which we have had no news since the siege began.

In the afternoon the Americans began to make a gun out of some brass tubing belonging to their old fire-engine. They were wiring the tubes to strengthen them. The Russians had brought up a lot of shells to fit a 9 lb. gun which they had been forced to leave behind in Tientsin. However, later in the afternoon, some Chinese, while digging, struck an old (1860) muzzle-loading cannon. It is about three feet long and can take these Russian shells. It was a glorious find. We put in about half a pound of powder, and then the shell, having first removed the latter from its case, as of course it is meant for a breech loader. The shells explode on concussion, and do good work. The old gun is a bit difficult to train, as there are no sights. It has wakened the Chinese up a bit.

We were also manufacturing lead bullets for use in the Italian gun, as the proper shells for the latter are almost exhausted. We can still use the old cases, which are being diligently hunted for. The lead bullets we make measure about one inch at the base, and are about four inches long, being cone-shaped.

The scene by the main gate of our Legation, throughout the afternoon, presented an animated appearance, being temporarily converted into a small arsenal.

To-day $10,000 were offered by the Russians to a messenger to take a message through to the allied troops, on condition he came back with a receipt before the troops arrived. A man did start,

58 Departure of Gen. Gaselee

59 Prince Ch'ing's arrival for the signing of the Protocol in Peking
The French guard of honour

60 Signing of the Protocol in Peking, 1901: the Allies

The Ministers l. to r.: Dutch, Japanese, Italian, Belgian, Austrian, Spanish (doyen), Russian, German, British (Sir E. Satow), U.S.A. (W. W. Rockhill)

61 Signing of the Protocol in Peking, 1901: the Chinese
Foreground, l. to r.: Li Hung-chang, Prince Ch'ing

62   Students Interpreters before the siege

Back: W. M. Hewlett, G. P. Peachey, C. C. A. Kirke, C. A. W. Rose, H. H. Bristow, H. Porter, A. J. Flaherty, J. G. Hancock; middle: H. Phillips, G. L. C. Graham, R. T. Tebbitt, N. P. Thomas, W. P. M. Russell, G. W. Pearson, J. T. Pratt; front: R. D. Drury, L. H. R. Barr, H. Warren, L. Giles, W. E. Townsend

63   Students Interpreters: the survivors

Back: C. C. A. Kirke, H. H. Bristow, J. L. Flaherty, H. Porter; middle: L. H. R. Barr, L. Giles; front: C. A. W. Rose, W. M. Hewlett

I believe, but did not get any distance. I think the reward was so big that the Chinese imagined it would not be paid.

During the night distant guns were heard. The Japanese heard a rumour that the relief force was at T'ien Tsun, 12 miles to the north-west of the city.

July 8th, Sunday

Throughout the morning the big guns all round were firing at intervals, but did no very serious damage.

10 a.m. A complaint came from the Japanese, to the effect that one of their messengers, who was coming back, had just been shot by the Americans on the city-wall. The lack of discipline among these Americans is astounding.

10.15 a.m. Big fire in the Fu. Colonel Shiba sent for reinforcements. Three students, three Customs' men, and six marines went across. Later there was a heavy fusillade in the Fu, where the position is most critical, the Japanese being driven back inch by inch. Luckily for us it is the Japanese who are defending the Fu. If it had been the Italians or Austrians, it would have been taken long ago; and all would have been UP; for if the Fu be taken the British Legation would be blown to pieces within a few hours.

At midday the Austrian commanding officer[76] was killed by a shell at the French barricade. He was buried at 2 p.m., diplomatic representatives being present. It is strange how callous we get to the way of rushing through funerals, and to death in general.

The old muzzle-loader, variously nicknamed 'Dowager Empress', 'Old Crock', and 'Boxer Bill', when fired for the first time, had such a recoil on it that it burst the ropes which lashed it to its hastily constructed gun-carriage. However, we now put in a smaller charge of powder, and it acts splendidly. Colonel Shiba made use of it during the afternoon, charging it with scrap-iron.

4 p.m. Another big fire in the Fu, burning the converts' refuge, drove the latter back into some other buildings further south. This fire was kindled by the Chinese soldiers fastening large bits of burning tow (previously soaked in petroleum) to long poles and thrusting them up into the wooden eaves of the roof. Our

men actually saw the thing being done, and could not prevent it. This gives you an idea of how closely the Chinese are pressing on the Fu.

5.30 p.m. The Chinese, firing their 1-pounder from the Carriage Park, put two shells through Cockburn's roof.

9.45 p.m. Heavy attack on the Hanlin. Twenty large solid shots were fired from the Imperial City wall.

From this day onward two students and two Customs' men were sent over for twenty-four hours to the Fu, taking two hour watches in four reliefs.

July 9th, Monday

Early in the morning the Fu was heavily attacked. Later the gun, 'Boxer-Bill', was fired from the students' library and did great execution at the Chinese barricade in the north-west of the Carriage Park.

In the morning preparations were made to manufacture an acetylene searchlight.

10.45 a.m. Ten marines were sent to the Fu to replace some Austrians and French who had deserted their posts. The Austrian Chargé d'Affaires (von Rosthorn) was very wrath with his men, threatening to shoot down the next to *look round* from his post!

During the afternoon three Chinese were captured trying to set fire to the French Legation. They were cross-examined, but their answers were so self-contradictory that they were shot.

The Japanese report heavy firing to the south of the city. Colonel Shiba guarantees that the Japanese relief column will be here before July 20th.

In the evening we set fire to some houses in the Mongol Market. When it was too late, we discovered that they were stored with large quantities of valuable silks and furs.

The following notice was posted to-day:

A messenger who went into the Chinese City to-day reports that
(1) there are no Chinese soldiers to be seen in the streets of the Chinese City;
(2) the Ha Ta Men has been closed for many days.
He left the city by Tung Pien Men;[77] and going to the north,

entered the Ch'i Hua Men.[78] At that gate Jung Lu's soldiers were in charge. But at that gate and at the Ha Ta Men he saw many of Tung Fu-hsiang's troops in the streets. Near the Tung Ssu P'ai Lou the streets have their everyday appearance; shopping daily. Emperor and Empress-Dowager in Palace here. Nothing known of the approach of foreign troops. Chinese soldiers much afraid of foreigners. He bought several things at shops and street stalls.

This man was a servant of Squiers,[79] an American secretary. He brought back some chickens, peas, and peaches. He was much slanged for not having purchased a copy of the *Peking Gazette*.[80] Some of his statements are obviously the 'guffs' of teashops and need not be unconditionally believed.

July 10th, Tuesday

Very quiet in the morning, except for a shell which burst on our tennis court, just opposite the house temporarily converted into the French Legation. The French Minister insisted that the Union Jack over the main gate was attracting the fire, and wanted Sir Claude to take down the flag from its prominent position. This, of course, was promptly declined. If the French Minister (Pichon by name) chooses to take refuge in a British Legation, he must put up with the British habit of having the Union Jack flying from the highest convenient place.

The Pei T'ang was reported safe; the Chinese had attacked it, but found it strong. I believe Père Favier,[81] the head of the Pei T'ang, on the first rumour of these troublous times had laid in a stock of ammunition and arms. He was wise in his generation, which is more than can be said of the foreign diplomatic representatives.

In the afternoon there was almost a serious catastrophe. Four marines were sent over to the French Legation. A Norwegian Lutheran missionary, named Nestagaard, volunteered to lead them. He took them right up Legation Street to the Chinese barricade. There the marines saw it was not all right, and took refuge in the archway of the main entrance of the French Legation where they were under cover. The French had to take away the heavy barricade from this gate to let them in. This work took fifteen minutes to do! Every one of those five men might have been picked off with consummate ease (though the loss of Nestagaard would not have actually distressed anybody). For some unaccountable reason the Chinese were evidently not on the watch at this barricade. This man Nestagaard is a well-known character in Peking, being as a rule a harmless lunatic.

In the evening the Italians bolted from their post in the Fu. They were replaced by British marines, and sent to keep watch in the Hanlin. The other marines asked jocularly if the Italians were to be chained up. Hearing that the students were going to be there too, the marines expressed their feelings of absolute safety in that quarter. We students have gained an enviable reputation with the British marines.

Last night twenty Chinese were captured at the French Legation. Three were shot; but then the French corporal, saying it would not do to waste so many precious rounds, killed fifteen with his bayonet. Two were kept to be examined.

The flies about the place are something ghastly, being attracted by the unburied corpses of the Chinese. The heat is very great, especially during the last few days when the thermometer has been up to 103° in the shade. Just imagine having to keep watch in the blazing sun from 12 to 2 p.m. as I had to one of these days! My rifle got so hot in the sun that I could hardly hold it, and had to keep it as cool as possible in the shade that *I* afforded. Add to this steaming heat, a few hundred buzzing flies, and you have my picture.

July 11th, Wednesday

To-day I was one of the two students on duty in the Fu with Flaherty.

9.30 a.m. A messenger was sent out by way of the Sluice Gate under the wall at the south end of the Canal. Immediately on his exit he was fired on by the soldiers on the wall. He came back unhurt.

A Russian officer saw Chinese soldiers to the west of the Russian defences carrying away rice etc. as quickly as possible from various houses, and making off. He heard big guns and volleys in south. Rumour says it is Prince Ch'ing and Prince Tuan[82] fighting each other.

1.15 p.m. While I was on duty in the Fu, the Chinese began shelling a building next to the compound where I was on watch. Shells kept bursting within twenty feet of my post, covering me with dirt and splinters of brick. After about twenty minutes of this game, Colonel Shiba recalled me and stationed me on the next line of defence.

3.10 p.m. Nigel Oliphant, a brother of the man who was killed about a week ago, was wounded in the thigh while at work at some defences in the Fu. Since his brother's death he has been very reckless, absolutely throwing himself in the way of bullets.

During the day two Japanese were wounded and one was killed; a marine was wounded and also two civilians.

7 p.m. Captain Poole, Russell, Bristow and three marines made a sortie from our post into the Hanlin, which they cleared, breaking up a Chinese barricade.

July 12th, Thursday

Yesterday at 4 p.m. the third week of siege was completed. I am getting heartily sick of it.

During the night the Chinese built a barricade on the Carriage-Park wall with sandbags, erecting a banner just behind it.

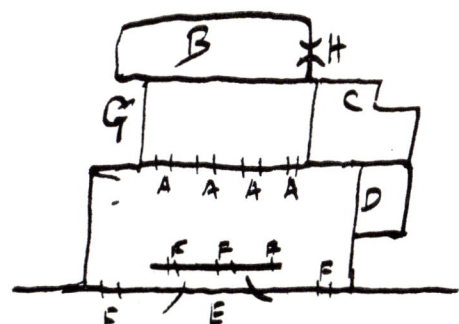

6   The author's encounter with the Chinese in the Fu

6 a.m. I was on watch in the Fu at loopholes marked A A A A [in plan no. 6] with one Japanese volunteer and a couple of

Christian Chinese armed with rifles. B was the position I was in yesterday when the shelling of B was going on. Since the shelling the Japanese had barricaded the wall A A A A.

We were specially on the alert as we saw the Chinese making a hole in the wall at H. We could see the crowbar moving and dust falling, but the man at work was hidden.

All of a sudden as I was looking through my loophole I became aware of the muzzle of a rifle being quietly inserted in my loophole! I leapt to the side and the rifle blazed away into space. If the man had been a second quicker, my head would have been blown off!

The Chinese converts promptly fled, and I was left along with the Japanese. Stealthily getting out my revolver I blazed away through the loophole, without exposing myself. The Chinese on the other side replied without touching me, though I felt the warmth from the rifle on my hand.

I then peered cautiously through the hole and saw the brute quietly reloading. Without a second's delay I fired point blank at his head which was bent down over his rifle. He was silent after that, as you may imagine.

Meanwhile Chinese had occupied all the other loopholes in the compound and commenced blazing away. So the Japanese and I ran across to the little compound marked D, where there was shelter, and then we bolted across individually to E where we occupied the loopholes F F F. The Chinese blazed away for some time without avail, and then set the ruins of B on fire, and then withdrew. The Japanese then set G on fire and conducted it, the fire, to the wall A A A A, thus preventing the Chinese from using that line of defence. About four Chinese were killed.

That was one of the narrowest escapes of the siege so far. It remains a mystery how the Chinese managed to get up to the wall we were guarding in broad daylight without being seen.

During the morning a man was captured at the French Legation with some Boxers. A flag, spears and arrows were also taken. He was examined by Cockburn, and then taken to the American Legation and examined by Pethick, who was Li Hung-ch'ang's[83] private secretary for many years. The prisoner could, or would not give much information. He had been hired by the Chinese to carry the corpses from the French Legation to the Ch'i Hua Men. He got two tiao (about 25 cents) for each body, and was hired by Jung Lu's men.

According to him Tientsin was in great disorder and had been burnt on June 16th. There were 100 foreign ships of war at Taku.

He also said that in the Northern City trade was going on as usual, but not in the Southern City. The Boxers and soldiers fight frequently in the streets over loot. The soldiers, when they have enough loot, desert in numbers.

The government was in the hands of Prince Tuan and Jung Lu, Prince Ch'ing being out of the affair altogether.

The Boxers' headquarters are Prince Tuan's Palace. The Pei T'ang is still holding out, though it had been shelled.

The Chinese were not allowed to use their big modern guns, as they carry too far, and would harm too many of the non-combatants in the city. An edict now authorised the use of cannon of smaller calibre. The muzzle-loading cannon, he says, is 150 years old.

In the afternoon we were at work in the Hanlin when Sergeant Preston[84] thought he would try to capture a Chinese flag which was planted right up against the west side of the Carriage Park wall a little to the north of our line of defence. He got to the top by means of some ruins, but drew a frightful fusillade of bullets and bricks. He was slightly wounded in the right ear. He fell back, and his place was taken by the American gunner, Mitchell, who got hold of the top of the spear to which the flag was attached, and hung on to it like grim death. I was just below him, taking pot shots to skim the top of the wall and prevent any of the enemy leaning over and shooting at him. Meanwhile the Chinese on the other side of the wall were also hauling on to the flag. The issue remained in doubt till some Germans got hold of Mitchell's legs and pulled him and banner down to the ground. The flag is black with a white border, and with big red characters on it.

The French made a sortie and captured a flag, but drew a heavy attack, four men being wounded.

The night passed very quietly.

July 13th, Friday

The Japanese and Italians had to retreat before the heavy shelling of four guns from two barricades. The following notice was posted, signed by Sir Claude:

> A Chinese prisoner, taken by French marines, yesterday stated that the Emperor[85] and Empress Dowager were still in their Palace. Prince Tuan, Jung Lu, and Tung Fu-hsiang are in control of public affairs, Prince Ch'ing taking no part with them. Many Boxers are yet in the city. Their chief patron is Prince Tuan; in his Fu they are registered, fed and paid. Boxers are ridiculed by soldiers because they are not to go under fire at the front in spite of their pretension to be bullet-proof. Tung Fu-hsiang's troops are facing us on the wall, and along our lines. Jung Lu's men are behind the French Legation. Several are killed or wounded every day. There are about 3,000 of Tung Fu-hsiang's men in the city. Direct attack having failed, and our rifles being better than theirs, they have decided to starve us out. Two weeks ago came news that foreign troops from 100 warships had captured Taku forts, and occupied Tung Taku (opposite Tangku railway station). Tientsin city is in a panic. Ammunition is brought here from camp at Nan Hai Tzu. Imperial edicts are issued as usual. Business going on in the north. Market supplies are coming in. The four chief banks (Ssu Ta Hang) are closed. Soldiers believe we have several thousand men here. Prisoner thought we had certainly 2,000.

Throughout the day the shelling was severe. In the Fu an Italian had his head blown off by a bit of shell.

The marines gave up their spare sheets and blankets for making sandbags.

About noon a solid shot entered the back of the ground-floor of the Students' Quarters, and hit the opposite wall just over the bed where a Japanese lady was reclining. She was not hurt.

At 6 p.m. a furious attack began on the Fu, French and German Legations, and more slightly on our west defence. It was accompanied by howls and yells. Part of the French Legation was blown up by a Chinese mine. Two French were killed, also several of the enemy whose curiosity overcame their caution. Reinforcements were sent to the Germans, who now made a brilliant bayonet charge, driving the Chinese down to the South Bridge, where it happened that the Americans were relieving the guard on the wall. The Americans, being in double numbers for this reason, also charged with fixed bayonets and drove the Chinese onto the German bayonets. The enemy only managed to escape up a side lane to some of their loop-holed houses. The Chinese losses were estimated at over 100.

The buildings of the Peking Syndicate[86] were burnt.

July 14, Saturday

Early in the morning the Chinese started a fire in the German Legation stables where they are entrenched. Their flag was captured, and they were driven back by the Germans.

To-day was comparatively quiet, except for occasional shots from 'Boxer Bill', which did great execution from the students' library and the French Legation.

Shiba reports that the Chinese are retreating a little in the Fu.

In the evening Captain Poole and a few others made a short sortie in the Hanlin, but saw nothing much, except a couple of hundred soldiers in various uniforms in the road to the north of the Hanlin.

July 15th, Sunday

In the morning the following notice was put up:

A messenger sent out on July 10th by Mr. Tewkesbury (Chairman of General Committee, and an American missionary) with a letter for our troops, returned yesterday. He is the gate keeper of the Nan T'ang, and a Roman Catholic. He says he was arrested outside the Ha Ta Men and taken to the Wo Fu Ssu (a temple) and his letter taken from him, and he himself beaten with eighty blows. He was later taken to Jung Lu's headquarters in the Imperial City. Here he found a man Yu who formerly knew him as gate-keeper. He was there given a letter purporting to be written by *Prince Ch'ing and others*, and addressed to the British Minister; and told that men would wait at the canal sluice-gate for an answer. The official translation of the letter is as follows:

To Sir Claude Macdonald, British Minister.

In the last ten (!) days the soldiers and militia have been fighting, and there has been no communication between us to our great anxiety. Some time ago (June 25th) we hung up a board expressing our intentions, but no answer has been received, and contrary to expectation the foreign soldiers made renewed attacks (!!), causing alarm and suspicion amongst the soldiers and people. Yesterday the troops captured a convert named Chin Ssu-hsi, and learned from him that all the foreign ministers were well which caused us very great satisfaction (!). But it is the unexpected that happens. The reinforcements of foreign troops were long ago stopped and turned back by the Boxers; and if in accordance with previous agreement we were to guard Your Excellencies out of the city, there are so many Boxers on the Tientsin road that we should be very apprehensive of misadventure. We now request Your Excellencies to first take your families and the various members of your staffs, and leave your Legations in detachments. We should select trustworthy officers to give close and strict protection, and you should temporarily reside in the Tsungli Yamen, pending future arrangements for your return home, in order to preserve friendly relations intact from beginning to end. But at the time of leaving the Legations there must, on no account, be taken any single armed foreign soldier, in order to prevent doubt and fear on the part of the troops and people, leading to untoward incidents. If Your Excellency is willing to show this confidence, we beg you to communicate with all the foreign ministers in Peking, tomorrow at noon being the limit of time; and to let the original messenger deliver your reply, in order that we may settle in advance the day for leaving the Legations.

This is the single way of preserving relations that we have been able to devise in the face of innumerable difficulties. If no reply is received by the time fixed, even our affection will not enable us to help you.

Compliments,
PRINCE TUAN and others
6th moon, 18th day

A reply has been sent to-day declining on the part of the foreign representatives the invitation to proceed to the Tsungli Yamen; and pointing out that no attacks have been made by our troops who are only defending the lives and property of foreigners against the attacks of the Chinese government troops. The reply concluded with a statement that if the Chinese government wish to negotiate, they should send a responsible official with a white flag.

(signed) CLAUDE M. MACDONALD

During the day the Fu endured the usual attack. The Russians made a sortie and strengthened their position by pulling down adjacent houses.

Big guns were heard away in the west, and there was also heavy cannonading from the Pei T'ang.

6.30 p.m. Warren was hit by a bit of shell. It shattered his jaw (upper and lower), also striking his nose. He was patched up; and all was supposed to be going well, when about 7 p.m. a piece of bone from the jaw slipped down his throat. Tracheotomy was performed, and afforded some relief; but at 9.30 p.m. he died. In him I lost my best friend in Peking; I was absolutely overwhelmed by the shock. He and I had formed numerous plans for our enjoyment next winter, when the other batch had gone. He was a good all-round sportsman, a steady worker and promising student. He was very popular in the mess, though not very well-known to Peking society; for he was essentially a man's man, being somewhat reserved with women. His loss leaves a blank in my life here, which nothing but time will fill up.

July 16th, Monday

At breakfast Captain Strouts was with us making a few arrangements with a view to poor old Warren's funeral. Little did he know that it was to be his own funeral! Two hours afterwards he was brought in wounded in the abdomen. He died within a couple of hours. His loss comes hard on us, as he was our senior captain and had been conducting the defence of our Legation splendidly up to now. His tact, cheerfulness, spirit and pluck had made him a universal favourite with his men, with us, and with all the foreign officers and ministers. It was hard that he should not have lived to reap the rewards which would undoubtedly have fallen to him for his brilliant command here.

He and Warren were buried at 6 p.m. All foreign ministers and officers were in attendance. His coffin was borne by six officers,

Warren's by eight students (Hancock, Flaherty, Bristow, Kirke, Porter, Drury, Barr and self).

Dr. Morrison (the brilliant correspondent of *The Times*) was slightly wounded in the leg at the same time and place as Captain Strouts in the Fu.

Fire balloons are being constructed. I gave valuable advice, drawn from my reminiscences of those we used to send up at Tamsui. Perhaps we shall be able to fill them with hydrogen.

The big gun at the Fu was firing throughout the day with intervals.

Our messenger, sent out yesterday, returned to-day with a letter for Sir Claude. The messenger had been again bambooed by these brutes. The note pointed out that there had been no firing all day from the Imperial City, and said that attempts were being made to obtain a 'cease fire' from the Fu. The messenger also bought in to the American Minister (Conger[87]) a note written in cypher which was undated and unsigned. It was:

Communicate tidings bearer.

Now, as the cypher is one only known to the United States Foreign Office and to the ambassadors, ministers etc., it was unlikely that this was a forgery. The only explanation we can make out is that this cypher was entrusted to the officer commanding the American relieving column. In that case he would have used as small a piece of paper as possible—hence the omission of the word *to*. The messenger must have been captured, and the message transcribed.

11.35 p.m. The mad Norwegian missionary, whom I mentioned above, Nestagaard to wit, got up to the sentry's position in the South Stables and began kicking up a tremendous row. The Chinese, evidently thinking he was urging on a charge, fired from the Carriage Park wall, and succeeded in wounding one of our marines. Nestagaard had to be given a sedative and locked up.

During the day thirty marines were sent over to the Fu to give the Japanese a twelve hour rest. The Japanese out of twenty-five men, have eight killed, and thirteen have been wounded. Some of the latter have resumed their duties.

July 17th, Tuesday

Ten-foot trenches are being dug behind our north and northwest defences as a countermine against possible mining. In the Hanlin at G (see plan no. 2) we are digging a mine of our own. We have had to go down a considerable depth, as the soil was too hard for some ten feet down. If we reach our goal, that is beneath the Chinese camp in the north Carriage Park, we shall blow it up with guncotton which is now being manufactured by Mitchell, the American gunner.

Two of Jung Lu's soldiers came in with a message from that worthy and bearing his card. The note said Jung Lu was putting down the Chinese firing. At 6 p.m. the firing absolutely ceased. Many Chinese soldiers laid down their arms and came over to our barricades and chatted. Captain Percy Smith (a retired British officer) with some others went over to the Chinese barricades and gave the soldiers cigarettes and chatted with them.

A Frenchman, named Pelliot, went up to the Chinese barricade in Legation Street and had some tea with the soldiers. The Chinese asked him to go over to their barricade and see their Colonel, one Ma. This he did, and was led to what he thought was the Tsungli Yamen, but what seems from description to be Li Hung-ch'ang's house. There he had a talk with some blue-buttoned officials, who gave him some food, and tried to "pump" him as to the state of our defences and amount of provisions. He seems to have lied beautifully, making us out to be in a splendid way altogether.

He heard that Li Hung-ch'ang was expected here in a few days to take over supreme command of affairs. He was then allowed to return in peace.

An old bandsman of Sir Robert Hart's, now a soldier, came in to-day asking to have his ear, which was wounded, bound up. Just imagine his coolness! He said that the Chinese General Nieh,[88] in command at Tientsin, had refused to fight the foreigners and had been disgraced, and had then committed suicide. He also told us that the foreign troops had won a big victory between Taku and Tientsin, and had occupied that town; and that Tung Fu-hsiang's troops and Boxers had gone to oppose them.

In the Fu the Chinese removed their banners and put up a white flag.

The night passed quietly. Heavy firing was heard in the distance; the direction being south-west, west and north-west. Large bodies of Chinese left the city with carts etc.

July 18th, Wednesday

To-day came our first news (definite) from the outside. As might have been expected, it came through the Japanese. The following notices were put up:

> The Japanese Minister[89] has received news to the following effect. A mixed division consisting of 2,400 Japanese, 4,000 Russians, 2,000 British, 1,500 Americans, 1,500 French, and 300 Germans, leave Tientsin on or about 20th inst. for the relief of Peking. The foreign settlement of Tientsin has not been taken by the enemy.
>
> (signed) CLAUDE M. MACDONALD

The reason why the Germans are in such small numbers is because they have occupied Shantung. The French are said to be embarking 15,000 men from France for China.

> A Chinaman, sent out from Peking on June 30th by the Japanese Minister, has returned here and reports:
> He left by the Ch'i Hua Men on June 30th, proceeding to Tientsin *via* Tung Chow by boat. He arrived at Tientsin on July 5th, but was unable to enter the city, as it was surrounded by Chinese troops. He worked round the city gates, and found a force of Chinese under General Chang[90] posted north of the railway station, cannonading a force of Japanese holding the ground south of the station. On July 9th General Chang was defeated and the messenger managed to get through the Japanese lines on July 12th, and delivered the Japanese Minister's message to the Japanese Consul. While in Tientsin, he gleaned the following news:—that General Nieh was dead; that all missionaries in Tientsin and outlying stations had left for home, and that the Taku forts were taken on June 17th by the foreigners without difficulty. On July 14th the foreign troops took the native city of Tientsin after a two-days' attack. On July 15th the messenger left Tientsin for Peking, being escorted by the Japanese to the 'Second Bridge' (Hung Ch'iao). He returned to

Peking by road. Among other things he mentioned that the Tung Chow Taotai[91] had been lodged in the Board of Punishments,[92] and that previous to his arrival in Tientsin, no news of Peking had reached that place since about the end of June.

(signed) CLAUDE M. MACDONALD

I presume that he meant that his was the only news up to July 15th. Thus you only heard about the first ten days of siege. After looking back over the news of those days, I find that the news was sufficient to cause alarm, which, however, I hope it did not do to any extent.

> A Tsungli Yamen Secretary came this afternoon, sent by Jung Lu. He had no special message, but promised to see whether *Peking Gazettes* could be procured, and a market established for ice, fruit, eggs etc, also to ascertain whether telegrams could be transmitted on behalf of the foreign ministers to their governments. He mentioned that telegraphic communication was interrupted. He expressed the concern of the Chinese government at the doings of the Boxers who had caused the whole difficulty between China and the foreign powers.
> He said nothing had happened to the Pei T'ang.
>
> (signed) CLAUDE M. MACDONALD

This looks rather as though the Chinese were trying to patch up things a bit before the relieving column arrives.

Things have been absolutely quiet all day, except that occasional shots were fired by over-zealous Russians, and one intoxicated American.

We can see the Chinese strolling about outside their barricades, but as long as they do not come too close, we let them be.

July 19th, Thursday

Throughout the day everything was absolutely quiet. We are nevertheless pushing on at our barricades, defence-trenches, and our mine under the Carriage Park.

The Japanese also are digging a mine from their position in the Fu to under the position of the Chinese. Their mine is not progressing so fast as ours.

To-day the Boxers beheaded a Chinaman who had been selling provisions to us. However, the soldiers went for the Boxers in retaliation.

I was in the Fu all the day which passed uneventfully.

July 20th, Friday

The following notice was put up:

> At present only eggs are obtainable at the market opened on the east of the lawn. Distribution at discretion of the Committee—4 cents each.

The notice was put up at 8 a.m. and the market was closed at 9.50 a.m., the stock being then exhausted.

Some days ago the French Minister (Pichon) burned his Legation papers and archives. He was followed shortly after by de Giers, the Russian Minister. Dr. Morrison, of *The Times,* offered Captain Strouts, who was in charge of the burning, $5,000 if he could have a look at the French papers, but $50,000 for a sight of the Russian ones. This was, of course, by way of a joke, but it indicates the respective values that Dr. Morrison sets on these papers.

In the afternoon I was on watch in the Hanlin when we distinctly heard sounds of digging on the other side of the Carriage Park wall. All the bigwigs, including Sir Claude, came over and went down our mine to listen. We came to the conclusion that the Chinese were digging a countermine to our own. This was confirmed by two marines who got up on the Carriage Park wall and looked over. They said the Chinese were digging a trench parallel to the wall right up against it. We therefore stopped work at our mine and only watched; but the Chinese soon knocked off work. We still heard them at work behind their barricades, but this time above ground.

Later at night they started shying over bricks at our advanced post, but did no harm.

During the day translations of numerous *Peking Gazettes* were posted up on the notice-board. I do not transcribe them now, as a limited number (100) copies of all the translations are to be struck off by some process or other. I have put my name down for a copy, so I will insert them at the end as an appendix to these notes.[93]

July 21st, Saturday

The list of killed and wounded up to date is:

	Killed	Wounded	Total
British	3	17	20
Italians	7	7	14
Germans	9	13	22
French	9	7	16
Austrians	4	3	7
Americans	7	9	16
Japanese	8	13	21
Russians	3	11	14
Civilians	7	7	14
Total	57	87	144

Note in this list the small numbers of Austrians who have been hit. This is owing to their habit of—to put it plainly—running away!

The British killed do not represent the work they have done, as the number of the wounded shows. It is merely their luck.

The Russians have had no casualties since July 4th!

The French have a further thirty-five men, and the Italians ten, to account for at the Pei T'ang, this would probably swell their list of casualties.

A messenger who had been sent out on July 20th to find out what was going on in the city, returned and said that Tung Fu-hsiang's troops had left the city to meet our relief column. This was their ostensible purpose. As a matter of fact it is much more likely that they have fled to Kansu, their province.

The messenger also learned that the soldiers who are besieging us, intend to evacuate their positions around us in a few days. This is open to doubt, or why should they still be strengthening their barricades and defences all round?

While our coolies were working away at the trench which is being dug along the north line of our defence in the Hanlin, they struck a pile of stone balls, some quite smooth, others rougher, and some merely hewn to an approximately spherical shape. Many of these balls are broken in half. There is considerable doubt as to what they are. The place where they were found is about twelve feet down, and right under a very ancient-looking tree; so that it seems as though they had been resting there many hundreds of years. There were also found a couple of stone slabs with deep grooves on their surface. These grooves were evidently used to polish up and smooth down the inequalities of the stone spheres, till they became quite smooth and spherical, like some of those that have been found. Various theories have been advanced about these balls. Some think they must have been intended as ornaments on the balustrade of a staircase, or used for something architectural. Others opine that they were used for some sort of a game similar to one that still survives. The chief objection to this last theory is that balls, or parts of the same, were found in various sizes ranging from four inches to one and a half inches in diameter. Perhaps some explanation might be derived from the depths of the *T'u shu*.[94] I have secured several of these spheres and portions of spheres in all states of manufacture, and of all sizes.[95]

We have now had four continuous days with (practically) no firing at all from dawn to dewy eve. It really seems as though we were to have peace and quiet at any rate till our troops arrive. We can be thankful for these few days' quiet.

Fruit and vegetables (chiefly the deadly water melon and equally noxious cucumber), and also eggs are to be bought every day now; but these fruits etc. are, as a rule, carefully avoided by all wise people.

July 22nd, Sunday

The question that occupies us chiefly now is as to what will be done with us after we are able to leave Peking. We expect Chefoo, but hope for Japan[96] for a couple of months; then a clear six months before our exam. I suppose Townsend,[97] who is looking very pale and weak, will be allowed three months or so leave to get over to his people in America.

I see Backhouse occasionally. He strained some muscle early in the siege, and has been laid up ever since. He just manages to crawl about now. He spends his day in a characteristic manner. Every day he reads through from cover to cover Goodrich's Pocket Chinese-English Dictionary![98] He has lost all his property and books (including the famous morocco-bound dictionary). He left them all in his house, thinking they would be safe, being within our lines. However, it was burned down and everything destroyed. However, he means to stick it out here, and recommence his collection of notes etc. of which he had a fair amount.

July 23rd, Monday

During the night it rained in torrents. We unfortunate sentries got soaked to the skin; and, what was worse, our bedding too got sopped. So you may imagine we spent a wretched night. To add to our misery, a portion of the wall of the shed where we sleep came down in the early morning; all the supports having been washed away by the rain. A tremendous lot of big stones and bricks, with a flood of slushy mud, covered all our beds etc. Luckily no one was lying down at the time, or there would have been an accident. Mr. Clarke-Thornhill,[99] a globe-trotter of sorts, who was caught up here by the siege, had just left his long chair for about a minute or so when the wall fell all over it just where his head had been. It was a narrow escape. I had to dig out my bedding with a pickaxe! My poor sunhat got crushed into concertina shape.

The whole compound was in flood. The Canal was full of water, and the Tommies made use of some planks as canoes and paddled about on them.

Two messengers were sent out to-day with letters for the troops. One was the boy of a member (honorary and temporary) of our mess, Sabbione by name.[100] Let us hope they got through all right. They carried one of Dr. Morrison's despatches to *The Times*.

July 24th, Tuesday

In the Fu a coolie at work at the barricades was killed. An

Italian was wounded. As retribution our marines shot three Chinese soldiers who were also at work at the barricades.

A Chinese soldier told Colonel Shiba that their officer had threatened to shoot anyone selling food etc. to the foreigners. However, this man said he had no objection to making some money, though it was a bit risky. He also said that two of our messengers with nine letters in cypher had been captured. Probably they were those sent out yesterday.

In our Legation an extra guard was placed on our west defence, and extra careful watching was done.

A rumour came in that on July 18th there had been a battle at Yang Ts'un between the relief force and Tung Fu-hsiang's men. They say 150 of Tung Fu-hsiang's wounded were brought into the city, and that he himself has returned.

Another rumour came that last night the Pei T'ang had been attacked by Boxers who were only armed with swords and spears.

July 25th, Wednesday

At about 1 a.m. a sharp fusillade began over the Mongol Market. However, it soon stopped. The Chinese must have been frightened at something or other, and started firing. Our men did not respond—as usual.

A Chinese soldier (the same as before) told Colonel Shiba that there had been another fight at Ho Hsi Wu—about 40 miles from Peking—which had lasted from 1 p.m. to midnight. The Chinese had been defeated.

During the night a few shots were fired in the Hanlin and the Carriage Park.

July 26th, Thursday

Colonel Shiba reported that the Chinese had moved their fieldpiece from the Fu in an easterly direction. There was also a rumour to the effect that the Chinese were placing guns on the East City wall.

Shiba's informant stated that the Chinese were making a stand at Tung Chow and that Tung Fu-hsiang was taking 4,800 men to reinforce General Chang's troops.

The day passed uneventfully. Though the Chinese have concluded an armistice with us, and though they have ordered a 'cease fire', between 100 and 200 shots are fired every day.

July 27th, Friday

Drury, who was on watch with us in the west Hanlin, caused somewhat of a diversion by chucking an empty bottle over the Carriage Park wall into the Chinese camp there. They promptly answered with a perfect hail of bricks and stones and even a piece of melon rind! No one was hurt, but Drury got cursed by the rest of us in words long-drawn out.

Colonel Shiba's informant reported that 200 carts and 6,500 soldiers were at the Palace, where the Emperor and Empress-Dowager were preparing for flight. However, as Colonel Shiba pays this man ten taels for each day's news, his information may be looked upon as open to question.

The Empress-Dowager sent a present of ice, melons and other fruit to the British Minister. The Tsungli Yamen also sent a special present of similar articles and bags of flour to Sir Robert Hart, asking him to act as a go-between on behalf of China with the foreign powers. I believe Sir Robert does not intend to accede to their request, seeing that all his property was destroyed, his life's work to some extent undone, and only his diary saved, which, it is said, is to be destroyed in any case at his death. Why was it saved in that case?

July 28th, Saturday

A messenger returned from Tientsin with a message from Carles,[101] which had been the subject of much comment and ridicule. It certainly is not as plain as might be desired, and leaves everything open to doubt. It ran:

> Yours of July 4. 24,000 troops have now landed, and 19,000 here. Gen. Gaselee[102] expected Taku tomorrow. Russians hold Pei Tsang. Tientsin city under foreign government; and Boxer power exploded here. Plenty of troops are on the way, if you can hold out with food. Almost all ladies have left Tientsin.

Does this letter mean that 43,000 troops have reached China, of whom 19,000 are at Tientsin; or that 24,000 troops are in China, of whom 5,000 are between Taku and Tientsin? Is General Gaselee to take over command? If we cannot hold out with food, are plenty of troops on their way or not? Such were the ribald questions which came from every mouth at the publication of this document. Personally I really do not quite see where the difficulty comes in. I made quite an intelligible (and to me the only possible) meaning out of it. It is probably purposely obscured to avoid giving the Chinese any news, if it fell in their hands.

The messenger's report was posted as follows:

Liu Wu-yüan, aged 16, native of Shantung, living in Peking, arrived this morning.
He left Peking with letters on July 5th, disguised as a beggar. Was let down from wall by rope; crept along the moat to the Ch'ien Men; slept under the gate; and in morning walked to the Yung Ting Men; passed through, and went to Ma Chia P'u (the station) without being molested. Hearing nothing there, he went to Tung Chow, and worked his way slowly along main road to Tientsin. At a village near Ho Hsi Wu he was stopped by villagers, and made to do eight days' work. Reached Tientsin on July 18th; first met Russians, then Japanese; and on July 21st met British troops at Pei Yung Men (half a mile from Tientsin city on the Peking road). Delivered his letters to a foreigner in civilian dress who spoke Chinese. July 22nd he was taken to British Consulate. Consul gave him a letter. He was then sent to the foreign outpost at Hung Ch'iao (half a mile west of the city).
July 23rd left Hung Ch'iao, and soon met Chinese troops. Slept that night at Yang Tsun in a locomotive boiler near the railway bridge, which is not destroyed. That day saw only Chinese infantry, the main body was at Pei Tsang. Saw no Boxers.
Night of July 24th slept near Ho Hsi Wu. Saw few soldiers and no Boxers that day.
Night of July 25th slept at Ma Tou. That day few parties of Boxers in villages, but none on road. At Ma Tou and elsewhere he saw that the river was in light flood, few boats moving about, but many moored to banks. July 26th, spent night at Yu Chia Wei (twenty li[103] from Peking). July 27th reached the Sha Wo Men[104] at 10 a.m.

Roads good. Telegraph poles and wires along river all gone. Railway torn up everywhere; rails buried or used for making Boxer swords. He was not stopped at the city gate, though many Boxers and Tung Fu-hsiang's soldiers there. Made his way to Ha Ta Men (closed) and to Water Gate. This was too closely guarded to pass by day. He slept last night near the Ch'ien Men, crawled along moat, and entered Water Gate without challenge before daylight. High road to Tientsin in good condition. Crops everywhere look well. Villagers attending to farms, but Boxer organisation in every village. When he left Tientsin the foreign troops had not advanced beyond the defence wall surrounding Tientsin city at a distance of a half to one mile. All Yamens at Tientsin occupied by foreign troops, chiefly Japanese. All Boxers had left the front at Tientsin, because badly punished in battle, so Chinese soldiers despise them. Chinese army concentrating at Pei Tsang, eight miles north west of Tientsin. The Messenger had $1.00 in his pocket, on reaching Tientsin, but the foreign soldiers took it away from him, in case he should lose it!

General Gaselee's record, as in Whittaker, is as follows:

Gaselee—Co. (Brig. Gen.)—aged 56.
  Sir Alfred, K.C.B., I.S.C., A.D.C.

N.W. Frontier	— '63
Abyssinia	— '67-'68
Bezotis	— '69
Jowaki	— '77-'78
Afghan	— '79-'80
Zhob Valley	— '84
Hazura	— '91
Isazai	— '92
Waziristan	— '94-'95
N.W. Frontier	— '97-'98

—commanded 2nd Brigade Tirah expedition.

Another notice was posted during the day to the following effect:

Chin Tzu-hsi left our lines eight days ago, carrying an official letter to Jung Lu; returned today. He says that he delivered the letter at Jung Lu's headquarters and was locked up there for seven days. Jung Lu goes to the Court every day. Emperor and Empress Dowager both in city. Boxers patrol streets in small bands. Four days ago, a ragged, dirty foreigner, hatless, coatless, of general disreputable appearance was captured by Tung Fu-hsiang's men, and brought to Jung Lu. Medium height, blonde moustache and beard; spoke Chinese. (? Nestagaard) Said he went to find food. Meanwhile Boxers assembled around Jung Lu's house, and demanded the foreigner. But Jung Lu sent him off under guard to the Yamen of the Shun Tien Fu[105] for safe keeping.

This last refers to Nestagaard who escaped from the Legation three days ago; he labours under the delusion that everybody wants to slay him. He returned the next day (July 29th) in a very dishevelled condition, complaining of his maltreatment at the hands of the Chinese. He may consider himself lucky not to have been shot as a spy.

A rather amusing story is going about with reference to Barr. He gets very riled when chaffed about it. He was on watch in the Hanlin one night when the patrol went round. The patrol (a marine), seeing a head above the barricade, called out, 'Who's that?'. Barr hastily answered: 'Ba, ba.' The marine, thinking it was a Chinese soldier rotting him, levelled his rifle, when Barr hastily dashed forward into the light. As the sergeant said afterwards, Barr really should prefix Mr. to his name.

One of the sergeants was strolling down the compound, when Norris, meeting him, said: 'Whither away, sergeant?' With ready wit the answer came: 'I am withering away fast in this heat, sir!'

July 29th, Sunday

In the afternoon the Chinese began building a barricade over the North Bridge so that they might be able to pass to and fro without having to make a long detour by the Imperial City. It was rather curious watching the stones being advanced further and further across, and yet no man visible at all. We fired a few rifle shots, and a few shots from the Italian gun, but they had not much effect. The Italian gunner was wounded in his left hand by a marksman across the canal.

During the night more firing than usual.

Various rumours from diverse sources (1) that 20,000 Russians from Shan Hai Kwan are advancing on Kalgan at The Great Wall, (2) Relief force was defeated at Ma Tou and returned to An

P'ing, (3) About July 27th Yang Tsun was absolutely destroyed by foreign troops who were steadily advancing.

One of the captains of the marines tells us that whenever a marine falls ill, he always puts on his heavy top-coat. Once on the way out, in the Red Sea when the temperature in the shade was one hundred and anything you like, he saw a marine on deck muffled up in his greatcoat. On being asked why he was thus attired, he replied: 'I've got the prickly 'eat something 'orrid, Sir!'

July 30th, Monday

Guns were removed from the Ch'ien Men to Tung Chow.

Two messengers were sent out to the troops, with orders to bring back a reply.

Reports came in about the advance of the relief column from Ma Tou.

July 31st, Tuesday

A despatch was published stating that Yuan Shih-k'ai[106] and his foreign-drilled troops had joined the Germans in Shantung and were sweeping the country.

Shiba's informant reported that fifteen liang[107] of Shansi troops were to arrive at Nan Hai Tzu, and camp there for the night on their way to Tung Chow. These troops were sent on at 7 p.m.

August 1st, Wednesday

Another month begun! Where can the relief force be? We are, however, all very well here, and can hold out another month at this rate.

Shiba's informant said that the foreign troops had been driven out of Chang Chia Wan and Ma Tou to An Ting. This probably meant that our advance guard had met with resistance and had fallen back on the main body.

A few shots from North Bridge and Mongol Market. Also a fire in the north-east Hanlin where the Chinese burned down a house which obstructed the view from their barricades. The

Chinese in the Fu, in the Hanlin, in the Mongol Market, on the west part of the wall, and to the east of the French Legation are still very hostile; whereas those to the east of the German Legation and on the east part of the wall are quite friendly.

In the evening a letter was received by the Japanese saying:

> Your letter of 22nd received; departure of troops from Tientsin delayed by difficulties of transport, but advance will be made in two or three days. Will write again as soon as estimated date of arrival at Peking is fixed.

The letter was dated July 26th.

Sir Robert Hart also received a telegram in cypher; but as the key had been lost when the Customs were burned down, it was not of much use.

The Japanese message rather points to Shiba's informant having given false information, though as a matter of fact he always said that he merely reported the 'guffs' of the camp, and could not guarantee its truth.

List of killed and wounded up to date:

	Killed	Wounded	Total
British	3	17	20
Italians	7	9	16
Germans	9	13	22
French	9	7	16
Austrians	4	3	7
Americans	7	9	16
Japanese	5	13	18
Russians	4	11	15
Civilians	10	7	17
Total	57	89	146

The reason this list differs from previous is because three men have been transferred from the list of Japanese killed, to the list of killed civilians.

August 2nd, Thursday

A Russian soldier very nearly died of strychnine poisoning. He had looted a bottle of the poison from some store, and had drunk it, thinking it was some alcoholic liquor. He recovered, wonderful to relate! It takes more than strychnine to kill a Russian.

To-day we annexed some houses which were only separated from the South Stable quarters by a small lane. These houses extend a little way into the Mongol Market, and strengthen our position not a little.

Letters and telegrams came in to-day, of which I give extracts. Received by the United States Minister:

July 28th from U.S. Consul Ragsdale.[108]
Had lost all hope ever seeing you again. Prospect now brighter. We had thirty days shelling here; nine days siege. Thought that bad enough. Scarcely a house escaped damage. Excitement at home is intense of course. Our prayers and hopes are for your safety and speedy rescue. Advance of troops probable tomorrow.

July 30th from J. S. Mallory (Lt. Col. 41st Inf. U.S.).
A relief column of 10,000 is on the point of starting for Peking, more to follow. God grant they may be in time.

July 30th from Maj.-Gen. A. R. Chaffee U.S.A.[109]
Arrived here this morning.

Received by Mrs. Lowry[110] from her husband.
July 30th. The bearer arrived last Friday p.m. with news from Peking. The 9th and 14th U.S. regiments already at Tientsin; 6th cavalry at Taku on its way up. An advance of several regiments has already started on its way up. There was fighting this a.m. at Pei Tsang. Everything is quiet here now. Word came today that Boxers killing Christians at Tsun Hua, Shan Hai Kwan, and many other places. Russians and Imperial troops have fought at Chin Chow (near Shan Hai Kwan). Tientsin full of foreign soldiers and more coming all the time. Railway open between here and Tang Ku. Many ladies and children were taken to the United States on the transport *Logan*. All property at Pei Tai Ho destroyed.

Another despatch said;

July 29th. Have been trying to reach you since June 21st.
Foreign settlement (of Tientsin) was relieved June 23rd.
Seymour relieved June 24th.
Captured East Arsenal June 26th.
    „   West „   July 10th.
    „   Tientsin City July 14th.

Will advance in two days. Column 10,000 strong. English, Americans, and Japanese follow in few days 40,000 more. Hold on by all means. First column will support and divert enemy from you. There will be eight regiments U.S. Infantry, three Cavalry, and two Batteries. U.S. Marines and 500 Infantry will be in first column. Enemy strongly entrenched seventeen miles north, and at two points further.

This last was in cypher and unpunctuated. It may be read that the English and Americans, 10,000 strong are in first column, and that 40,000 Japanese follow.

The I.G.[111] also received the following from Commissioner Drew.[112]

July 28th. Yours 21st (? June or July) wired carefully home. Keep heart. Aid coming early. Troops pouring in. Enemy at Pei Tsang. Japanese in front, also Russians. Very little rain. Yangtze agitated. Liu[113] and Chang[114] trying to keep order. Li Hung-chang at Shanghai. Doubtful if coming to Chihli. Tientsin governed by joint foreign commission. Manchuria rising against Russia. Russians' hands full there. Newchwang much disturbed. Germany and America each sending 15,000 men. Italy 5,000. Canton, West River, and Ichang threatening. Taylor (? F.E.)[115] appointed temporary I.G. by Viceroy Liu. Earnestly hope rescue of you all.

August 3rd, Friday

Fire in the north-east Hanlin, lighted by Chinese. No danger to us.

In the afternoon Hewlett[116] and self went over to the German and French Legations to take photos. The German Legation has been very heavily shelled and is a bit of a wreck in parts. The German and Chinese positions are separated by a wall, seven or eight feet high and about two feet wide. It is loopholed. The Chinese camp has numerous flags flying—black and white, red and yellow—with the character *chang* in the centre. The Chinese soldiers there are friendly. We climbed up the scaffolding of the new Club[117] building to take photos of the camp. The Chinese soldiers called out 'What do you want?' Hewlett bawled back: 'We want to photograph you' *(Yao chao hsiang)*, to which with signs of fear they said: 'Do you want to shoot us?' *(Yao k'ai chiang ma)*. On our expressing friendly sentiments they stood to be taken, but an officer came out and drove them away.

The French Legation defences are very weak indeed. Half their Legation has been lost and is in Chinese hands.

The top storey of the Hotel is badly damaged.

Sir Claude had a wire from Salisbury[118] asking for news. He replied with a list of killed and wounded. So you know now that I am all right so far.

Edicts issued to-day appointing Jung Lu to escort foreign ministers to Tientsin, and awaiting a letter to fix date of departure; also saying that the Tsungli Yamen was protecting foreigners in Peking, and would forward wires *en clair*.

August 4th, Saturday

Jung Lu's soldiers in the Fu are waiting to escort us to Tientsin. Let them wait! Rumour of big foreign victory at Ho Hsi Wu.

In the evening it poured with rain; and I had to go to my post in the Hanlin through three or four inches of water. In consequence I spent the night with wet feet and clothes. However, it luckily had no ill effect on me.

A Russian was wounded to-day, and died within twenty-four hours.

The French report that the Chinese soldiers there are hiding their uniforms.

The Tsungli Yamen again pressed us to go to Tientsin. Is it because they wish to prevent the troops entering Peking?

August 5th, Sunday

During last night there was pretty smart firing in the Hanlin and in the Mongol Market. The Tsungli Yamen, called upon to explain, said that it meant nothing!

The Tsungli Yamen sent in to say that they had collected carts for our journey to Tientsin. The French Minister only is keen on going.

Three wires came in for Sir Claude, for Conger (American Minister), and for the Germans. Contents unknown.

August 6th, Monday

2 a.m. Twenty minutes heavy fusillading in the Mongol Market, west Legation Street, and in the Hanlin. There was none in Fu or French Legation, or on the city wall. It was accompanied by yells of 'ta, ta'.[119] The Pei T'ang too was attacked, and many Chinese bugles heard. Also there was a short cannonade outside one of the city gates. These are the *friendly* individuals who are to escort us to Tientsin, I suppose.

The Tsungli Yamen sent an apology for the firing, and some frivolous explanation.

August 7th, Tuesday

Heavy volleys and big guns heard in the south and south-west. The census of our Legation is as follows.

Soldiers (British and others)		73	
General Hospital (wounded)		40	113
Legation residents (foreign)	men	191	
	women	147	414
Legation residents (Chinese)	men	180	
	women	107	
	children	69	356
	Total		883

In the afternoon an auction of looted goods was held on the Legation lawn.

A Japanese was wounded in the Fu.

The Tsungli Yamen sent in their condolences on the death of the Duke of Edinburgh.[120]

The chief point of interest now is the form the commemorative medal shall take. Some designs have already been submitted.

11.30 fairly heavy fusillade for a quarter of an hour all round the Legation.

August 8th, Wednesday

Colonel Shiba reports that a messenger came saying that practically all the soldiers in Peking, except five battalions of Jung Lu's men, have been despatched to the front.

During the night three fusillade attacks, all of which were pretty sharp while they lasted.

August 9th, Thursday

Chinese soldiers returned to the Fu, and replanted their standards there.

The Nordenfelt was turned on the Chinese in the Mongol Market and silenced the fire there.

August 10th, Friday

At 3 a.m. furious firing all round the Legation. It lasted about twenty minutes.

Some days ago the ministers asked the Tsungli Yamen, who profess friendliness, for food for the converts in the Fu, as they are absolutely starving. No answer has been received, so some dogs were killed for them.

In the afternoon a messenger came with letters from the troops.

(1) From Lieutenant-General Gaselee—dated Aug. 8th at Tsai Tsung. Strong force of allies advancing. Twice defeated enemy. Keep up your spirits.

(2) From General Fukushima[121]—dated Aug. 8th at camp at Chang Chiang. Japanese and American troops defeated enemy on 5th inst. near Pei Tsang and occupied Yang Tsun on 6th. The allied force, consisting of Americans, British and Russians, left Yang Tsun this morning; and while marching north, I received your letter at 8 a.m. at a village called Nan Tsai Tsung. It is very gratifying to know from your letter that the foreign community at Peking are holding on; and believe me it is the earnest and unanimous desire of the Lieutenant-General[122] and all of us to arrive at Peking as soon as possible, and relieve you from your perilous position. Unless some unforeseen event takes place, the allied forces will be at Ho Hsi Wu on the 9th, Ma Tou on the 10th, Chang Chia Wan the 11th, Tung Chow the 12th and arrive at Peking on the 13th or 14th.

Hurray, relief in sight at last!! The joy over these messages defies description.

The Chinese are moving out of the city in great haste.

9.30 p.m. A very heavy fusillade took place, and we had to stand by. But nothing came of it all.

August 11th, Saturday

The following was posted to-day from the American Consul[123] at Chefoo (July 21st).

> All communications north of this pass thro' this office. So far as I know, excluding army and navy, no Americans have been killed, and but little loss of property south of Tientsin. All trouble confined to Peking and Taku. The high officials doing best to keep order. Very large force of all nations at Taku.

To-day sniping went on practically all day, bursting at intervals into fusillades.

The Tsungli Yamen sent in an offer to open a market for all kinds of eatables. This turned out to be a hoax.

7 p.m. Firing in the Mongol Market very heavy indeed. In the Mongol Market the Chinese post is so close to ours that the orders the officers give can be distinctly heard, and the exhortations to slaughter us.

August 12th, Sunday

A German was shot in the night; also an Austrian, a Russian, and a Frenchman wounded. A Frenchman and a Russian in hospital died of their wounds.

A coolie coming in said there had been a fight at Chang Chia Wan; 3,000 Chinese were surrounded and killed, as the foreigners had been so unsporting as to attack in the rear.

In the afternoon the firing in the Mongol Market was heavy. A Chinese barricade fell down, exposing a Chinese officer and twenty-seven men. The Nordenfelt and any number of rifles were turned on them, and every one of them was slain.

The Austrian machine gun was mounted in the South Stables to rake the Chinese position.

The French captain was killed, when looking over a barricade.

11.30 p.m. Heavy fusillade all round. A big gun also fired from the Ha Ta Men.

The Chinese were using nickel-plated explosive bullets. Fusillades recurred during the night frequently. Very little sleep for anybody.

August 13th, Monday

The [Tsungli] Yamen sent an insolent message about the men who had been killed in the Mongol Market, and said they were too busy to come to the conference which had been arranged for to-day at 11 a.m. Extra careful watches in consequence.

Heavy firing in the afternoon. A splinter from an explosive bullet hit Rose[124] just under his left ear, grazing the skin. Nothing very much.

The [Tsungli] Yamen sent in to say that any man firing at us would be court-martialled. This was in answer to a note saying that, if any woman or child was hurt, the Tsungli Yamen would be held responsible and treated as criminals.

As a consequence this night was the one when we had our heaviest attack of all during the siege. Round shot fell into Sir Claude's bedroom.

We had to stand by thrice during the night for frantically furious fusillades which were something terrific. It was impossible to hear each other talk at the barricades.

The American gunner got his right arm shattered with a bullet in the Mongol Market. It was an awful night.

August 14th, Tuesday

At 2.30 a.m. we heard distant firing and the rattle of Maxims in the distance. Grand indeed!!!!!

Big guns in distance all morning. From the wall we could see shells bursting somewhere eastwards of the city.

At 3 p.m., amidst shouts and howls, a few of the 7th Rajputs[125] entered the Legation, quickly followed by Gaselee and his staff, and we were actually at last relieved!!!!!!!!!!

It was a moment of a lifetime, and can be better imagined than described. Shakings of hands galore! Women in tears! Sikhs patted on the back! Grimy gunners hugged!

The men were almost fainting with fatigue and thirst; but after a quarter of an hour's rest and drink they cleared the Mongol Market of some snipers who actually did not know that the relief was in the walls!!

It was magnificent that the British should be the first to relieve us!

That afternoon I went with the party who cleared the wall, to the Ch'ien Men. Some Chinese soldiers ran out in the yard below the gate and started firing up at us. They were all shot.

Two Maxims were fixed up on Ch'ien Men and turned on a stream of people who were hurrying across the inner Palace yard. About fifty to seventy rifles were turned on them too. Any amount slaughtered.

Every day looting parties go out and get what they can. I have done some splendid looting already. You wait and trust to me, before you speak.

Cannot write more at present, as the excitement is something frantic; and it is difficult even to sit at a table.

Nearly all the ladies are going to clear out by Wednesday.

The students are staying on a bit, being useful. There is some talk of our being sent home on leave.

Your loving son,

[signature: Lancelot Giles]

P.S. I hope you did not have to pay too much for this letter, but there are no stamps in Peking, so you will excuse it this once.

My Life Certificate for June goes by this mail.

NOTES TO THE DIARY

1 Hsi Shan or the Western Hills lie in a north-south line approximately thirteen miles to the west of the Peking city walls. Britain maintained a Summer Legation in these hills at Shih Tzu Wo, Lions' Nest, which was on the heights just above the Hunting Park of the New Summer Palace. In the summer months, when the Court normally retired to the Summer Palace, British diplomatic and consular officials, together with other foreign legation staffs moved to the hills where the climate was more bearable.

   The trip to the Western Hills was an adventure in itself in 1900. The journey was made on horseback or by cart, and took all day. The first part of the route, after leaving the Legation Quarter, lay through the Tartar City. The traveller then passed through the Gate of Just Law, Ping Tze Men, at the west wall, and followed the carriage road to the New Summer Palace. Going beyond this he followed the tracks that led to the temples and villages in the hills.

   The Western Hills, a well-known resort for foreigners, was one of the first places to be affected by Boxers as they approached Peking in June 1900. The British Summer Legation, which had been completed earlier that year, was the first official foreign building to be destroyed by the Boxers. It was never rebuilt.

2 Sir Claude Maxwell MacDonald, Envoy Extraordinary and Minister Plenipotentiary of Great Britain in China.

3 Henry Cockburn, Chinese Secretary at the British Legation in Peking. In 1900 the Chinese Secretary acted as head of the British Consular Service in China, and was responsible for the training of Student Interpreters who were recruited to that service.

4 The Reverend H. V. Norman and the Reverend C. Robinson of the London based Society for the Propagation of the Gospel in Foreign Parts, were attacked by Boxers and killed on June the 1st 1900. For details of the incident see page 59 in the Introduction.

5 The Peking Race Course, Pao Ma Chang, which was a centre of foreign social contacts in 1900, lay a little south of the west of Peking, about ten miles from the city. The main railway from Peking to Hankow, which was being built by Belgians in 1900, passed the Race Course. The newly constructed railway together with the foreign atmosphere that surrounded the Race Course, made the place a prime target for anti-foreign elements and Boxers who moved up the railway line to Peking. For details of this see page 62 of the Introduction.

6 C. C. A. Kirke, H. Porter and H. Warren, Student Interpreters at the British Legation in Peking.

7 This was no doubt the small village of Shi Fang Yuan which was situated to the west of Peking, near the Race Course.

8 Strike, strike, or beat, beat.

9 H. H. Bristow and R. D. Drury, Student Interpreters at the British Legation in Peking.

10 Vice-Admiral Sir Edward Hobart Seymour, Commander-in-Chief of the British Navy's China Station. Admiral Seymour led the first Relief Column which made an abortive attempt to rescue the Legations staffs in June 1900. For details of Admiral Seymour's attempt see page 64 in the Introduction.

11 Peking Railway Station, Ma Chia P'u, was situated just outside the Yung Ting Men in the southern wall of the Chinese City. To reach this from the Legation Quarter, it was necessary to pass through the Ch'ien Men and across the Chinese City. See the map on page 74.

12 The Ch'ien Men was the main gate between the Chinese and Tartar Cities in Peking. The Legation guards who were expected at Ma Chia P'u would have marched along the main thoroughfare of the Chinese City which led to the Ch'ien Men, and then through it to The Legation Quarter. See map on page 74.

13 A groom or stable boy.

14 The MacDonalds spent some of May 1900 at the newly built Summer Legation. The MacDonald children were sent back to the hills in early June, in the care of Lady MacDonald's sister. They returned

to Peking when trouble appeared to be threatening, leaving the buildings and contents to be looked after by the Chinese gatekeeper and his family. For the details about the attack on the Summer Legation see page 71 in the Introduction.

15 Sugiyama Akira, the Chancellor at the Japanese Legation, was killed by Kansu troops who were led by General Tung Fu-hsiang. For details of the attack see page 71 in the Introduction.

16 The Yung Ting Men is a gate in the south wall of the Chinese City, situated between the Temple of Agriculture and the Temple of Heaven. The Peking Railway Station was situated in 1900 just outside this gate.

17 The Pei T'ang or North Cathedral, also known as the Catholic Cathedral and the Cathedral du Saint Sauveur, was situated inside the Imperial City near the West Gate or the Hsi An Men. The Pei T'ang was defended throughout the siege by Bishop Favier, a group of French and Italian marines, and a body of armed Christian converts. For details of this see page 72 in the Introduction.

18 Telegrams from the British Legation to London in 1900 were sent by the Chinese telegraph system from Peking to Shanghai, and then by international sea cable to Britain. The Russian line which went overland through Kiakta to Europe was not used by the British Foreign Office, not only because of the higher costs involved, but also because of London's suspicions of the Russian government which, at the time, seemed to be engaged in conducting a cold war against Britain and her interests in Central and East Asia.

19 George Ernest Morrison, the Peking correspondent of *The Times*, London.

20 The Tsungli Yamen, or more properly the Tsung Li Ko Kuo Shih Wu Ya Men, was the Chinese Office of Foreign Affairs. This was not a fully-fledged foreign office of the type found in Europe. The members of the Tsungli Yamen were temporarily deputed to work there while holding substantive posts elsewhere in the Chinese Civil Service. The two new ministers who called on Sir Claude MacDonald were Ch'i Hsin and Na T'ung. The Tsungli Yamen never seemed to function to the satisfaction of foreigners. After the Boxer Uprising the foreign powers demanded its abolition, and it was consequently reorganized as the Chinese Foreign Office, the Wai Wu Pu, in an Imperial edict of 24th July 1901.

21 An attendant or messenger.

22 The Ha Ta Men, or the Ch'ung Wen Men was a gate situated immediately east of the Legation Quarter, between the Tartar and the Chinese Cities. See map on page 74.

23 The Tung T'ang or East Cathedral, which was also known as Saint Joseph's, was situated to the north of the Legation Quarter in Wang Fu Ching or Morrison Street.

24 This was a mission station maintained by the London Missionary Society in the western section of the Tartar City.

25 The Institute for the Blind, which was maintained by Christian missionaries, was situated near the Ha Ta Men Road, in the Chinese City.

26 The Imperial Maritime Customs or Hai Kuan was established in 1854 as a result of foreign advice. In 1900 the Customs was in the charge of an Irishman, Sir Robert Hart, who had held the post since 1863, and was largely staffed by foreigners. The headquarters of the Customs, the Inspectorate General, and Sir Robert Hart's house were situated near the Legation Quarter.

27 C. H. Brewitt-Taylor, Assistant Chinese Secretary at the Inspectorate General of the Imperial Maritime Customs.

28 Soldiers of General Tung Fu-hsiang's army which was a Kansu corps. See note number 35 on page 183.

29 The Nan T'ang or South Cathedral was situated in the Tartar City, close by the Shun Chih Men, the westernmost gate in the wall between the Tartar City and the Chinese City. The cathedral was built in 1650, and reputedly contained art treasures which included original Castiglione paintings and Italian sculptures.

30 The second Emperor of the Ch'ing dynasty who ruled China from 1661 to 1772. Kang Hsi was noted for his patronage of the arts and scholarship, and for his encouragement and protection of learned Jesuit missionaries who came to his Court.

31 C. P. Scott, the Anglican Bishop for North China, who resided in Peking. The Anglican Mission lay a little north of the Nan T'ang in the western part of the Tartar City.

NOTES TO THE DIARY

32 Captain E. Wray, a member of the marine guard at the British Legation in Peking.

33 Prince Su's residence or palace in Peking, which was known as the Su Wang Fu. Prince Su was a member of the Manchu Imperial family. In later years, from 1907 to 1911, Prince Su served as Minister for the Interior.

34 Sir Robert Hart, the Inspector General of the Chinese Maritime Customs. See note 26.

35 General Tung Fu-hsiang was in charge of the Kansu army corps that was garrisoning Peking in 1900, and which later picketed the Legation Quarter. For details of the Chinese generals and armies which were defending Peking in 1900 see note 36.

36 This reference is somewhat confusing. Prince Ch'ing was the President of the Tsungli Yamen until June 10th 1900, as he had been since 1884. He did have some experience in defence organization, being one of the controllers of the Chinese Admiralty from 1885. However, he could by no means be called an army leader or general. There were in fact only two significant generals with army groups near Peking at the time. These were General Sung-ch'ing (see note number 37) and Tung Fu-hsiang who was mentioned in note number 35. The only other two army men of note with armies in the north were Yuan Shih-k'ai who was using his troops to put down the Boxers in Shantung province, and Nieh Shih-ch'eng who was near the coast in Chihli province, between Peking and the sea.

37 General Sung Ch'ing was in charge of an army, known as the I Chun, which was one of the more modern forces in China at that time, although it was by no means well equipped by European standards. The I Chun army which was guarding the sea approaches to Peking in 1900, clashed with the allied force near Tientsin when they made their advance to Peking.

38 Jung Lu, a Manchu official of high rank, was in charge of the modern army groups in north China in 1900, which he had, as President of the Board of War in 1895, helped so much to create. During the Boxer Uprising Jung Lu was a Grand Secretary and a Grand Councillor, which gave him access to the Imperial Court and made him an adviser with considerable powers. Besides these posts he still controlled the army groups in the north, issuing orders to them.

During the crisis and the siege of the Legation Quarter in Peking, Jung Lu did not take a forceful line. He appeared to play in two camps, and opinions about him among the foreigners were divided. He was not punished after the collapse of the Boxer Uprising, as were the army generals, and he was re-instated to a high official post in 1902, although he had fled from Peking when the allies entered the city, and refused to obey an order of the Court to negotiate with the foreign powers.

39 Captain L. S. T. Halliday of H.M.S. *Orlando,* who was in command of the marine guard at the British Legation in Peking.

40 The Chun Chi Ch'u or the Grand Council, or Council of State as it was sometimes called, was the highest advisory body in the Chinese Empire, serving as a Privy Council for the monarch.

41 Yehenola, or the Empress Hsiao Ch'in, better known as the Empress Dowager, was the Emperor Kuang Hsu's aunt. She violated the dynastic laws of succession by placing him on the throne in 1875. Thereafter, except on several occasions, she remained the real power in Court circles. In 1900 she proved to be conservative and anti-foreign and did little to suppress the Boxers. Although the allies did not demand her punishment, there was a general belief that she was one of the real powers behind the movement. For a discussion of her involvement see page 37ff. in the Introduction.

42 Prince Ch'ing was President of the Tsungli Yamen from 1884 until 10th June 1900, when he was replaced by the more anti-foreign Prince Tuan. Prince Ch'ing later acted with Li Hung-chang as a plenipotentiary to the peace conference between China and the allied powers, which was held in 1901 and 1902.

43 A Chinese unit of coinage. In 1900 the *tael* was quoted at three shillings and a penny sterling.

44 The Hsiao Fang Tui or Peking Fire Brigade.

45 The Superintendent of the Peking police force.

46 The Hsun Ching Tsung T'ing or Central Police Bureau in Peking.

47 Michel de Giers, the Minister Plenipotentiary and Envoy Extraordinary for Russia in China.

48 Captain R. M. Strouts, commandant of the British marine guard at the British Legation in Peking.

NOTES TO THE DIARY

49 The Taku forts guarded the mouth of the Pei Ho (North River) and the approaches to Tientsin from the sea. For details of the allied attack on the forts see map on page 77.

50 H. Cordes, the Second Interpreter at the German Legation in Peking.

51 J. R. Brazier, the Chief Secretary at the Inspectorate General of the Imperial Maritime Customs.

52 Professor Huberty James who was a teacher at Peking University. Professor James was regarded as a sound teacher, but was an idealist who felt he was safe among the Chinese because of his service to them. He was killed by anti-foreign elements when he left the Legation Quarter to confer with the Chinese.

53 The Han Lin Yuan or the National Academy was the highest place of learning in the Chinese Empire. The learned academies in Europe were based on this model which had been described by French missionaries in the eighteenth century.

54 The Marquis G. di Salvago-Raggi, Italy's Minister Resident in China.

55 The *Yung Lu Ta Tien* is the famous Ming encyclopedia consisting of 11,015 volumes. The volume number given by Lancelot Giles could refer to one of the later transcripts of the work. The *Yung Lu Ta Tien* is noted in particular for the copies of rare books which it contains.

56 The Han Lin Yuan was the chief examining body in the Chinese Empire. See note 53.

57 An employee of the Imperial Maritime Customs.

58 S. Pichon, Envoy Extraordinary and Minister Plenipotentiary for France in China.

59 Lieutenant-Colonel Shiba, the Military Attaché at the Japanese Legation in Peking.

60 Captain Myers of the United States Marines, who commanded the guards at the American Legation in Peking.

61 The Canal Bridge, or North Bridge, which lay between the Legation Quarter and the Imperial City.

62 Lieutenant Darcy of the French navy.

63 G. P. Peachey, a former Student Interpreter at the British Legation in Peking. He resigned from the diplomatic service on 28th February 1900. In diaries, written at that time, it was stated that Peachey was having an affair with a married woman in Peking. This would account for his unpopularity.

64 Later Sir Edmund Trelawny Backhouse, who was studying Chinese in Peking. In 1903 Backhouse was appointed to the post of professor at the Peking University. There in Peking he lived the life of a classical Chinese scholar, having few contacts with Europeans. His manuscripts on modern China and its history were destroyed by Japanese when they invaded Peking in 1937.

65 These references made by Giles are not known.

66 The London Missionary Society.

67 Captain F. G. Poole of the East Yorkshire Regiment of the British army, who was in Peking learning Chinese when the Boxer Uprising occurred. During the siege he was placed in command of the volunteers and was made responsible for the northern defences of the British Legation. Captain Poole's brother, Woodsworth Poole, was the surgeon to the British Legation, and was also involved in the siege.

68 J. G. Hancock, A. J. Flaherty, H. H. Bristow, W. E. Townsend, W. P. M. Russell, Student Interpreters at the British Legation in Peking.

69 Lieutenant Paolini of the Italian Navy.

70 The Hôtel de Pékin was situated between the Japanese and French Legations, and consequently was in the front lines during the siege. The Swiss proprietor, Auguste Chamot and his American wife played a gallant part in the siege, defending the perimeter, rescuing people cut off by the Boxers, and organizing provisions for the besieged.

71 David Oliphant was a Second Assistant at the British Legation in Peking. He had just completed his course as a Student Interpreter when the siege occurred.

72 Lancelot's brother, Lionel Giles who became the Keeper of Oriental Books in the British Museum.

NOTES TO THE DIARY

73 Nigel Oliphant who was formerly in the Royal Scots Greys, a regiment in the British army. He later had his diary, which he kept in the siege, published under the title *A Diary of the Siege of the Legations in Peking During the Summer of 1900* (London, 1901).

74 L. H. R. Barr, a Student Interpreter at the British Legation in Peking.

75 Dr Gilbert Reid who was formerly a missionary with the American Presbyterian Mission. In 1900 he was engaged in independent work among Chinese scholars and officials in Peking, endeavouring to interest them in reform and scientific thought.

76 Captain E. Thomann Edlar von Montalmar of the Austrian Navy.

77 A gate in the north-west section of the Chinese City.

78 A gate in the centre of the east wall of the Tartar City.

79 H. G. Squiers was the First Secretary at the United States Legation in Peking. Squiers had served in the United States army and on the death of Captain Strouts of the British marines on 16th July 1900, he was made Sir Claude MacDonald's Chief of Staff.

80 The *T'ang Pao* or *Peking Gazette* contained a selection of Imperial edicts, memorials and other official documents. Copies of this were available in Peking and were also sent to the provinces, thus keeping the bureaucracy and literati informed about the administrative life of the Empire. The Europeans in the Legations in Peking read the *Peking Gazette* to find out the policy of the Court.

81 Monsignor Alphonse-Pierre Favier, a Lazarist, was Vicar Apostolic of Peking and North Chihli. This was a special area under the control of the Congregation of the Mission, commonly called Lazarists. This order was founded by St Vincent de Paul. Bishop Favier organized the defence of the Pei T'ang which held out until a relief column arrived in Peking.

82 Prince Tuan or Tsai I was a member of the Manchu royal family. Conservative in politics, he came to the support of the Empress Dowager who was related to his wife, during the reform movement in 1898 when the Emperor was virtually deposed. Thereafter Prince Tuan was well established in Court as a favourite. In the early part of 1900 his son was named Heir Apparent. His real grievances against the foreign powers who objected to his intrigues against the Emperor, led him to take an active part in the anti-foreign movement

in Peking. He was given ample opportunity to do this when he was ordered to replace Prince Ch'ing, a more moderate man, as President of the Tsungli Yamen on 10th June 1900. Because of the open support he gave the Boxers the foreign powers demanded his execution, but when peace was restored he was exiled to Ili in West China.

83 Li Hung-chang was a prominent Chinese diplomat and statesman. Li was active in diplomacy from 1871, being concerned with the writing of most of China's treaties and agreements with foreign powers from that date. In 1898, however, when the reform movement was under way, he was dismissed from the Tsungli Yamen and his high official posts. He remained in the Civil Service and when the Boxer Uprising occurred he was serving in Canton as Governor-General of Kwangtung province. As he was regarded as being acceptable to the foreign powers, he was appointed by the Court to conduct the negotiations when the Chinese armies were defeated in the north.

84 A member of the marine guard at the British Legation in Peking.

85 Tsai Tien, the ninth emperor of the Ch'ing (Manchu) dynasty, who is better known under his reign title, Kuang Hsu. In 1898 he was associated with the reform party, and because of this he was virtually deposed by the more conservative Empress Dowager. In 1900, just before the Boxer Uprising, the Empress Dowager appointed her own nominee as Heir Apparent, further limiting Kuang Hsu's power in the Court.

86 An Anglo-Italian combination formed in 1897 on the initiative of Commendatore Angelo Luzatti, to exploit China's mineral resources. In May 1898 the Tsungli Yamen granted the Peking Syndicate exclusive rights to mine large areas in north China, and to build access railways which sparked off some anti-foreign feeling. The Peking Syndicate had an office near the Legation Quarter in Peking.

87 E. H. Conger, Envoy Extraordinary and Minister Plenipotentiary for the United States of America in China.

88 General Nieh Shih-ch'eng commanded one of the modernized north armies, the Wu-i Chun, which was created to defend Peking from attack. Nieh's army was stationed at Lu T'ai, near Tientsin, which he was to protect together with the sea-coast eastward. It was with these troops that Admiral Seymour's Relief Column clashed in

NOTES TO THE DIARY

June 1900, although Nieh had previously fought the Boxers. Nieh was killed on 9th July 1900 while defending Tientsin which was being invested by the allied forces.

89 Baron T. Nishi, Envoy Extraordinary and Minister Plenipotentiary of Japan in China.

90 A general in charge of one of the bodies of Imperial troops in Peking.

91 Taotai: an official in charge of a town or district.

92 The Hsing Pu or Board of Punishments was one of the six administrative departments in the Chinese government. The Board was charged with the duty of seeing that punishments were enforced, and had appellate powers.

93 These have not been kept with the diary.

94 Giles could be referring to the Ming encyclopedia, the *T'u shu pien*. There were no encyclopedias of archaeology or science in 1900, although there were some general ones dealing with the origin of things. Consequently Giles would have turned his thoughts to a general reference work such as the *T'u shu pien*.

95 The whereabouts of these is not known. Giles has not kept a photograph of them.

96 Europeans in China always regarded Japan as being a healthy place, and took their short leaves there. Chefoo, on the coast in Shantung, was regarded in somewhat the same way by foreign residents in Peking.

97 W. E. Townsend died on 23rd September 1900, shortly after the relief of Peking.

98 Chauncey Goodrich, *A Pocket Dictionary, Chinese-English, and Pekingese Syllabary* (Peking, 1891 etc.).

99 T. R. Clarke-Thornhill was formerly in the British diplomatic service. He had been appointed to the post of Secretary at the British Legation in Peking in 1897, but he did not take up the position. He was in Peking in 1900 in a private capacity.

100 The person referred to by Giles is not known.

101 W. R. Carles, the British Consul for Peking and Tientsin who resided in the latter city.

102 General Sir Alfred Gaselee of the British Indian Army. He was appointed to command the British division in the Relief Column which left Tientsin in August 1900. For details of that force see page 93 in the Introduction.

103 A Chinese mile which measures approximately 1,890 feet.

104 Sha Wo Men was a gate in the eastern wall of the Chinese City.

105 Shun T'ien Fu, the City Obedient to Heaven, is another name for Peking or the Metropolitan Prefecture. Giles is referring to the administrative office of the prefecture.

106 The Governor of Shantung province who used his modernized army to crush the Boxers in that province. Because of the way he enforced order in Shantung during the troubles in Chihli, Yuan was looked on by some Europeans as the emergent strong man in China. He later became President of the Chinese Republic, and in 1916 tried to establish himself as emperor.

107 A body of twenty-five soldiers.

108 J. W. Ragsdale, Consul for the United States of America at Tientsin.

109 Major General A. R. Chaffee who commanded the United States division in the Relief Column which left Tientsin in August.

110 Mrs Edward Lowry whose husband was an interpreter with the United States division in the Relief Column.

111 Sir Robert Hart. See note 26.

112 E. B. Drew, an employee of the Imperial Maritime Customs who was Commissioner of Customs at Tientsin.

113 Liu K'un-i was Governor-General of the Liang-kiang or lower provinces of the Yangtze River area. In 1900 he acted with his colleague, Chang Chih-tung (see note 114) to keep peace in south China during the Boxer Uprising and the allied expedition against the Boxers. It was his actions and guarantee to protect foreigners that partly served to prevent the Boxer troubles from spreading southwards.

NOTES TO THE DIARY

114 Chang Chih-tung was the Governor-General of the Liang Hu or central Yangtze provinces. In 1900 he joined with Liu K'un-i to guarantee the protection of foreigners and dealt firmly with rebel elements in the territories under his control, thus preventing the spread of anti-foreign troubles to the Yangtze area.

115 F. E. Taylor, Statistical Secretary for the Imperial Maritime Customs. Taylor was based in Shanghai, and was the highest placed official in the Secretariat outside Peking.

116 W. M. Hewlett, a Student Interpreter at the British Legation in Peking.

117 The Peking Club.

118 Robert Arthur Talbot Cecil, the third Marquis of Salisbury, who was Prime Minister of Britain and Secretary of State for Foreign Affairs in 1900.

119 Beat, beat or strike, strike.

120 Alfred Ernest Alfred, Duke of Edinburgh and Duke of Saxe-Coburg and Gotha, the second son of Queen Victoria, who died on July 30th 1900.

121 General Fukushima of the Imperial Japanese Army, who was the Chief of Staff of the Japanese division in the Relief Column which left Tientsin in August 1900 to relieve the besieged Europeans in Peking.

122 Lieutenant-General Yamaguchi of the Imperial Japanese Army, who commanded the Japanese division in the Relief Column.

123 J. Fowler, Consul for the United States of America at Chefoo.

124 C. A. W. Rose, a Student Interpreter at the British Legation in Peking.

125 A regiment in the British Indian Army. The 24th Punjabs entered Peking together with the 7th Rajputs.

LIST OF SELECTED WORKS

OFFICIAL PUBLICATIONS

France. Ministère des Affaires Etrangères. *Documents Diplomatiques Français*, 1871-1914. 1ᵉ Série, vol. 16, pt. 3; 2ᵉ Série, vol. 1, pt. 6.

Germany. Auswärtiges Amt. *Die grosse Politik der Europäischen Kabinette*, 1871-1914. Vol. 16 *Die Chinawirren und die Mächte*, 1900-1902.

United Kingdom. Parliament. Correspondence Respecting the Insurrectionary Movement in China. *Parliamentary Papers*, 1900, vol. 105 [Cd 257].

————. Report from Her Majesty's Minister in China Respecting Events in Peking. *Parliamentary Papers*, 1900, vol. 105 [Cd 364].

United States of America. Congress. Papers Relating to the Foreign Relations of the United States with the Annual Message of the President Transmitted to Congress, December 5, 1899. *House Documents*, 1899-1900.

————. Papers Relating to the Foreign Relations of the United States with the Annual Message of the President Transmitted to Congress, December 3, 1900. *House Documents*, 1900-1901.

MONOGRAPHS

Allen, R. *The Siege of the Peking Legations: being the Diary of the Rev. R. Allen*. London, 1901.

Allier, R. S. P. *Les Troubles de Chine et les Missions Chrétiennes*. Paris, 1901.

Anderson, E. *Persecuted but not Forsaken: an Account of the Journey of Three Swedish Missionaries from Honan to the Coast*. London, 1900.

LIST OF SELECTED WORKS

Anthouard, A. F. I. de Wasservass. *La Chine Contre l'Etranger: les Boxeurs*. Paris, 1902.

Argento, A. *In Perils by the Heathen: account of Mr Argento's Flight from Honan*. London, 1900.

Asiaticus [pseud.] *Die Kämpfe in China in militärischer und politischer Beziehung dargestellt von Asiaticus*. Berlin, 1900.

B [pseud.] *Der gelbe Krieg: ein Selbstschriftenalbum hervorragender Männer der Gegenwart über die Ereignisse und Kämpfe in China*. Leipzig, 1900.

Barascud, A. C. *Campagne de Chine, 1900-1901: Service Vétérinaire du Corps Expéditionaire Français et les Armées Alliées*. Vannes, 1903.

Barnes, A. A. S. *On Active Service with the Chinese Regiment: a Record of the Operations of the First Chinese Regiment in North China from March to October, 1900*. London, 1902.

Bazin, R. F. N. M. *L'Enseigne de Vaisseau Paul Henry*. Tours, 1905.

Beals, Z. C. *China and the Boxers: a Short History on the Boxer Outbreak with two chapters on the Sufferings of Missionaries and a Closing one on the Outlook*. New York, 1901.

Bertrand, P. *Les Atrocités de la Guerre de Chine*. Paris, 1901.

Die Beteiligung der Deutschen Marine an den Kämpfen in China, Sommer, 1900. (N.p., n.d.)

Bigham, C. C., Viscount Mersey. *A Year in China, 1899-1900*. London,

Binder von Krieglstein, E. Baron. *Die Kämpfe des Deutschen: Expeditionskorps in China und Ihre militärischen Lehren*. Berlin, 1902.

Bismarck, H. *Die Belagerung von Peking, 1900: Auszüge aus dem Tagebuch des Herrn H. Bismarck*. Shanghai, 1900.

Bland, J. O. P., and Backhouse, E. *China Under the Empress Dowager*. London, 1910.

―――. *Annals and Memoirs of the Court of Peking from the 16th to the 20th century*. London, 1914.

Ein Blik in Zuid Chan-Si Tijdens de Jongste Vervolging: Verslag van Eenige Missionarissen aan Mgr J. Hofman, Vic. Ap. Met Toelichtingen. Cuyk, 1901.

Boy-Ed, and Krieger, M. *Peking und Umgegend, nebst einer kurzen Geschichte der Belagerung der Gesandtschaften 1900*. Wolfenbüttel, 1910.

LIST OF SELECTED WORKS

The Boxer Rising: a History of the Boxer Trouble in China. Reprinted from the *Shanghai Mercury*. Shanghai, 1900.

Bredon, J. *Sir Robert Hart: the Romance of a Great Career told by His Niece.* London, 1909.

Broomhall, M. *Last Letters and Further Records of Martyred Missionaries of the China Inland Mission.* London, 1901.

———. *Martyred Missionaries of the China Inland Mission: with a Record of the Perils and Sufferings of Some who Escaped.* London, 1901.

Brown, F. *'Boxer' and other China Memories.* London, 1936.

———. *From Tientsin to Peking with the Allied Forces.* London, 1902.

Butterworth, A. E. *The Commission of H.M.S.* Glory, *Flag Ship of Commander-in-Chief, China Station, 1900-1904.* London, 1904.

C., G. *From Portsmouth to Peking via Ladysmith with a Naval Brigade, by G.C.* Hong Kong, 1901.

Carter, W. G. H. *The Life of Lieutenant-General Chaffee.* Chicago, 1917.

Casserley, G. *The Land of the Boxers: or China Under the Allies.* London, 1903.

Chamberlin, W. J. *Ordered to China: letters . . . Written from China while under Commission from the New York 'Sun' during the Boxer Uprising of 1900 and the International Complications which followed.* London, 1903.

Chang Chi-tung. *China's Only Hope.* Translated from the Chinese by S. J. Woodbridge. New York, 1900.

Cheminon, J. M., and Fauvel-Gallais, G. L. C. *Les Evénements Militaires en Chine.* Paris, 1902.

Ch'en, J. *Yuan Shih-k'ai 1859-1916: Brutus Assumes the Purple.* London, 1961.

China Against the World. Reprinted from the *North America Review*. New York, 1900.

China Inland Mission. *Boxer Indemnity and Chinese Education: the Question on the Remission and Allocation of the British Share.* London, 1924.

Chinese War News: How to Read Chinese War News: a Vade-Mecum of Notes to Readers of Despatches. London, 1900.

LIST OF SELECTED WORKS

Ching-shan. *Diary of H. E. Ching Shan.* Translated by J. J. L. Duyvendak. Lugduni Batavorum, 1924.

Clements, P. H. *The Boxer Rebellion: a Political and Diplomatic Review.* New York, 1915.

———. *An Outline of the Politics and Diplomacy of China and the Powers, 1894-1902.* New York, 1914.

Coerper, H. *China und die Missionare. Eine wahre Beantwortung der Fragen: wie hat Europa sich an China verschuldet, und was ist Europa China schuldig?* Hamburg, 1900.

Collin, V. *Un Reportage Belge en Extrême Orient: Guerre Internationale de 1900-1901.* Anvers, 1901.

Coltman, R. *Beleaguered in Peking: the Boxer's War against the Foreigner.* Philadelphia, 1901.

Conger, S. P. *Letters from China with Particular Reference to the Empress Dowager and the Women of China.* Chicago, 1909.

Cordier, H. *Histoire des Relations de la Chine avec les Puissances Occidentales, 1860-1902.* Paris, 1901.

———. *La Revolution en Chine: les Origines.* Leide, 1900.

Cornaby, W.A. *China under the Searchlight.* London, 1901.

Crowe, G. *The Commission of H.M.S. Terrible 1898-1902.* London, 1903.

Daggett, A. S. *America in the China Relief Expedition: an Account of the Brilliant Part Taken by the United States Troops in that Memorable Campaign in the Summer of 1900 for the Relief of the Beleagured Legations in Peking, China.* Kansas City, 1903.

Darcy, E. *La Défense de la Légation de France à Pekin.* Paris, 1901.

Dix, C. C. *The World's Navies in the Boxer Rebellion, 1900.* London, 1905.

Donnet, G. *En Chine, 1900-1901.* Paris, 1902.

Dose, H. *Erlebnisse eines China-Kämpfers vom 4. März 1899 bis Weihnachten, 1900.* Hamburg, 1901.

Douglas, R. K. *Europe and the Far East.* Cambridge, 1904.

Du Bose, H. C. *Are Missionaries in Any Way Responsible for the Present Disturbances in China?* (N.p., n.d.)

Ducrocq, L. *Représailles en Temps de Paix: Blocus Pacifique: Suivi d'une Etude sur les Affaires de Chine, 1900-1901.* Paris, 1901.

LIST OF SELECTED WORKS

Edwards, E. H. *Fire and Sword in Shansi: the Story of the Martyrdom of Foreigners and Chinese Christians.* Edinburgh, 1903.

――――. *Further News of the Massacres in Shansi.* Shanghai, 1901.

Edwards, N. P. *The Story of China with a Description of the Events Relating to the Present Struggle.* London, 1900.

En Chine 1900-1901: Impressions et Souvenirs d'un officier d'Etat Major. (N.p., n.d.)

Fitzgerald, C. P. *Revolution in China.* London, 1952.

Fleming, P. *The Siege at Peking.* London, 1959.

Forsyth, R. C. *The China Martyrs of 1900: a Complete Roll of the Christian Heroes Martyred in China in 1900, with Narratives of Survivors.* London, 1904.

――――. *Narrative of Massacres in Shansi, July, 1900.* Shanghai, 1900.

――――. *Shantung: the Sacred Province of China in Some of its Aspects.* Shanghai, 1912.

Frey, H. N. *Français et Alliés au Pé-Tchi-Li: Campagne de Chine de 1900.* Paris, 1904.

Friederici, G. *Berittene Infanterie in China und andere Feldzugserinnerungen.* Berlin, 1904.

Further News of the Massacres in Shansi. Shanghai, 1901.

Germany. Marine, Admiralstab. *Die kaiserliche Marine während der Wirren in China, 1900-1901. Herausgegeben vom Admiralstab der Marine.* Berlin, 1903.

Giehrl, R. *China-Fahrt. Erlebnisse and Eindrücke von der Expedition, 1900-1901.* München, 1903.

Giles, L. 'Diary of the Boxer Riots and of the Siege of the Legations', *Christ College Magazine,* Cambridge 1900 p. 4-125.

Gipps, G. *The Fighting in North China up to the Fall of Tientsin City.* London, 1901.

Glover, A. E. *A Thousand Miles of Miracle in China: a Personal Record of God's Delivering Power from the Hands of the Imperial Boxers of Shansi.* London, 1904.

Goldmann, P. *Ein Sommer in China.* Frankfurt, 1899.

Green, C. H. S. *In Deaths Oft: a Brief Account of the Lord's Dealings with the Missionaries of Hwai-luh, North China, During the Troublous Times of 1900.* London, 1901.

LIST OF SELECTED WORKS

Green, C. H. S. *Thrilling Experiences of C.I.M. Missionaries in Chihli, 1900.* Shanghai, 1900.

Günther, H. *Die Schreckenstage von Peking.* Hamburg, 1902.

Guillot, M. J. F. *Pékin Pendant l'Occupation Etrangère, 1900-1901.* Paris, 1904.

Guinness, G. W. *A Great Deliverance: Story of the Escape from She-K'i-Tien, Honan.* London, 1900.

Harper, H. *The Handy Man in China: the Expedition of the British Naval Brigade in China from June to September, 1900.* Hong Kong, 1901.

Hart, R. *The Peking Legations: a National Uprising and International Episode.* Shanghai, 1900.

———. *These from the Land of Sinim: Essays on the Chinese Question.* London, 1901.

Heinze, W. *Die Belagerung der Pekinger Gesandtschaften. Eine völkerrechtliche Studie.* Heidelberg, 1901.

Herrings, J. *Das erste Lorbeerreis des III. Seebataillons.* Shanghai (n.d.).

———. *Taku: die Deutsche Reichsmarine im Kampf.* Berlin, 1903.

Hewett, J. W. *In a Chinese Prison: Story of my Escape from 'The Boxers' in Shansi.* London, 1901.

Hewlett, W. M. *The Siege of the Peking Legations.* Harrow on the Hill, 1900.

Hooker, M. *Behind the Scenes in Peking: Experiences During the Siege.* London, 1910.

Institut des Franciscaines Missionaires. *Vie de la Mère Marie-Hermine et de ses Compagnes, Massacrées au Chan-Si, Chine, le 9 Juillet, 1900.* Rome, 1902.

Jefferson, R. L. *China and the Present Crisis.* London, 1900.

Joseph, P. *Foreign Diplomacy in China, 1894-1900.* London, 1928.

Ketler, I. C. *The Tragedy of Paotingfu: an Authentic Story of the Lives, Services and Sacrifices of the Presbyterian, Congregational and China Inland Missionaries who suffered Martyrdom at Paotingfu, China, June 30th and July 1st, 1900.* New York, 1902.

Krausse, A. S. *The Far East: its History and its Question.* London, 1903.
———. *The Story of the Chinese Crisis.* London, 1900.

Landor, A. H. S. *China and the Allies.* London, 1901.

Latourette, K. S. *A History of Christian Missions in China.* London, 1929.

Laur, F. *Le Siège de Pékin: Récits Authentiques des Assiégés.* Paris, 1904.

Legrand-Girarde, E. E. *Le Génie en Chine, 1900-1901.* Paris, 1903.

Leroy, H. J. *En Chine: Au Tché-ly S.E.: une Mission d'Après les Missionaries.* Bruges, 1900.

Leroy-Beaulieu, P. *The Awakening of the East.* London, 1900.

Löffler, O. *Deutschland in China, 1900-1901: Bearbeitet von Teilnehmern an der Expedition.* (Edited chiefly by Captain O. Löffler.) Düsseldorf, 1902.

Loti, P. *Les Derniers Jours de Pékin.* Paris, 1902.

Luzeux, A. F. *Notre Politique en Chine.* Paris, 1901.

Lynch, G. *Impressions of a War Correspondent.* London, 1903.
———. *The War of the Civilizations: Being the Record of a 'Foreign Devil's' Experiences with the Allies in China.* London, 1901.

MacCarthy, M. J. F. *The Coming Power: a History of the Far East, 1895-1905.* London, 1905.

McIntosh, G. *The Chinese Crisis and Christian Missionaries: a Vindication.* (N.p., n.d.)

McLeish, W. *Tientsin Besieged and After the Siege, from the 15th of June to the 16th of July, 1900.* Shanghai, 1901.

Mahan, A. T. *The Problem of Asia and its Effect upon International Policies,* London, 1900.

Martin, W. A. P. *The Siege in Peking: China against the World by an Eyewitness.* New York, 1900.

Mateer, A. H. *Siege Days: Personal Experiences of American Women and Children during the Peking Siege.* New York, 1903.

Matignon, J. J. *La Défense de la Légation de France, Pékin, du 13 Juin au 15 Août, 1900.* Paris, 1902.
———. *Dix ans au Pays du Dragon,* Paris, 1910.
———. *Superstition, Crime et Misère en Chine.* Paris, 1902.

Michie, A. *China and Christianity.* Boston, 1900.
———. *Political Obstacles to Missionary Successes in China.* Hong Kong, 1901.

LIST OF SELECTED WORKS

Miner, L. *China's Book of Martyrs: a Record of Heroic Martyrdoms and Marvellous Deliverances of Chinese Christians during the Summer of 1900.* New York, 1903.

Mitford, A. B. F. *The Attaché at Peking.* London, 1900.

Monitor [pseud.] *Der Weltkrieg um China.* Berlin, 1900.

Monnier, M. *Le Drame Chinois, Juillet-Août, 1900.* Paris, 1900.

Müller, A. F. A. G. von. *Die Wirren in China und die Kämpfe der verbündeten Truppen.* Berlin, 1900.

Newman, H. *The Indian Contingent in China.* Calcutta, 1900.

Oliphant, N. *A Diary of the Siege of the Legations in Peking during the Summer of 1900.* London, 1901.

Parker, E. H. *China and Religion.* London, 1905.
———. *China, Her History, Diplomacy and Commerce from the Earliest Times to the Present Day.* London, 1901.
———. *China Past and Present.* London, 1903.

Pélacot, C. B. de. *Expédition de Chine de 1900 Jusqu'à l'Arrivée du General Voyron.* Paris, 1903.

Pettit, C. *La Femme qui Commanda Cinq Cents Millions d'Hommes: Tseu-Hsi, Imperatrice de Chine, 1835-1908.* Paris, 1928.

Pichon, S. *Dans la Bataille.* Paris, 1908.

Pigott, C. A. *Steadfast into Death: or Martyred for China: Memorials of Thomas Wellesley and Jessie Pigott.* London, 1903.

Pott, F. L. H. *The Outbreak in China: its Causes.* New York, 1900.

Purcell, V. W. W. *The Boxer Uprising: a Background Study.* Cambridge, 1963.

Ransome, J. *Story of the Siege Hospital in Peking and Diary of Events from May to August, 1900.* London, 1901.

Rauch, F. von. *Mit Graf Waldersee in China: Tagebuchaufzeichnungen.* Berlin, 1907.

Reid, G. *The Sources of Anti-Foreign Disturbances in China with a Supplementary Account of the Uprising of 1900.* Shanghai, 1903.

Reinhardt, Lieutenant. *Mit dem II. Seebataillon nach China, 1900-1901.* Berlin, 1902.

Ricalton, J. *The Boxer Uprising, Cheefoo, Taku, Tientsin: a Part of Underwood and Underwood's Stereoscopic Tour Through China Personally Conducted by James Ricalton.* New York, 1902.

Ricalton, J. *China through the Stereoscope: a Journey at the Time of the Boxer Uprising.* New York, 1902.

———. *Pekin; a Part of Underwood and Underwood's Stereoscopic Tour Through China Personally Conducted by James Ricalton.* New York, 1902.

Roberts, J. H. *A Flight for Life and an Inside View of Mongolia.* Boston, 1903.

Robinson, C. N. *China of To-Day: the Yellow Peril: an Album of Pictures and Photographs Illustrating the Principal Places, Incidents and Persons Connected with the Crisis in China.* London, 1900.

Ruffi de Pontevès, J. de. *Les Marines en Chine: Souvenirs de la Colonne Seymour.* Paris, 1903.

Russell, S. M. *The Story of the Siege in Peking.* London, 1901.

S., M. [pseud.] *La Chine et les Alliés, 1900-1901 par M.S.* Paris, 1903.

Sabatier, A. *Etudes sur les Etablissements Militaires Créés par les Etrangères 1900-1907.* Paris, 1909.

———. *La Génie en Chine: Période d'Occupation, 1901-1906.* Nancy, 1910.

Saillens, M. M. P. *Campagne de Chine: Mai à Septembre, 1900: Journal d'un Officier.* Paris, 1901.

Saunders, A. R. *A God of Deliverances: the Story of the Deliverances of a Party of Missionaries when Compelled to flee from Shansi, North China.* London, 1901.

———. *In Weariness and Painfulness: Being the Account by A. R. Saunders of his Flight from Pingiao to Hankow of Himself and Party.* London, 1900.

———. *Two Child Martyrs, Jessie and Isobel Saunders.* London, 1901.

Scheibert, J. *Der Krieg in China, 1900-1901.* Berlin, 1901.

Schlieper, P. *Meine Kriegserlebnisse in China: die Expedition Seymour.* Minden, Westfalen, 1902.

Schott, E. *Die Wirren in China und ihre Ursachen.* Leipzig, 1900.

Seymour, E. *My Naval Career and Travels.* London, 1911.

Sheeks, R. B. *A Re-examination of the I Ho Ch'uan and its Rôle in the Boxer Movement.* Harvard, 1947.

Silbermann, Caporal Leon. *5 ans à la Légion étrangère, 10 ans dans l'infanterie de marine, souvenirs de campagne, par le soldat Silbermann . . . Algérie, Dahomey, Madasgascar, Tonkin Quang-Tchéou-*

Wan, Chine, Siam, Cochinchine. Avec une lettre-preface de M. le général Gallieni . . . 2. éd. Paris, 1910.

Smith, A. H. *China in Convulsion*. Edinburgh, 1901.

Smith, S. P. *China from Within: or the Story of the Chinese Crisis*. London, 1900.

Soulié, G. *Tseu-Hsi: Impératrice des Boxers*. (N.p.), 1911.

Steiner, P. *Tage der Drangsal in China: Züge aus der chinesischen Verfolgungszeit*. Basel, 1901.

Stewart, N. R. *My Service Days: India, Afghanistan, Suakim '85 and China*. London, 1908.

Stoecker, H. *Deutschland und China im 19. Jahrhundert*. Berlin, 1958.

Tan, C. C. *The Boxer Catastrophe*. New York, 1955.

Tanera, C. *Deutschlands Kämpfe in Ostasien, 1900-1901*. München, 1901.

Thomson, H. C. *China and the Powers: a Narrative of the Outbreak of 1900*. London, 1902.

Tissier, R. *La Croix-Rouge Française et les Navires-Hôpitaux Pendant la Campagne de Chine, 1900-1901*. Paris, 1903.

Townley, S. *My Chinese Note Book*. London, 1904.

Valli, M. *Gli Avvenimenti in Cina nel 1900 e l'Azione della R. Marina Italiana*. Milano, 1905.

Vandenbossche, A. *Au Pe-tchi-li: Deuxième Campagne de Chine 1900-1901*. Lyon, 1906.

Varè, D. *The Last of the Empresses*. London, 1936.

Varg, P. A. *Missionaries, Chinese and Diplomats: the American Protestant Missionary Movement in China, 1890-1952*. Princeton, 1952.

Vaughan, H. B. *St. George and the Chinese Dragon: an Account of the Relief of the Peking Legations*. London, 1902.

Velde, Oberstabsarzt. *Rückblick auf die Ereignisse in Peking im Sommer, 1900*. Berlin, 1906.

Vereshchagin, A. V. *Quer durch die Mandschurei in den Kämpfen gegen China, 1900-1901*. Mülheim, 1903.

Voskamp, C. J. *Konfuzius und das heutige China*. Shanghai, 1900.

LIST OF SELECTED WORKS

Voyron, General. *Rapport sur l'Expédition de Chine, 1900-1901.* Paris, 1904.

Waldersee, A. H. K. L. Graf von. *Denkwürdigkeiten des Generalfeldmarschalls Alfred Grafen von Waldersee.* Stuttgart, 1923-1925.

———. *A Field Marshal's Memoirs: from the Diary, Correspondence and Reminiscences of Alfred, Count von Waldersee,* condensed and translated by F. Whyte. London, 1924.

Walton, J. *China and the Present Crisis.* London, 1900.

Weale, B. L. P. *Indiscreet Letters from Peking, 1900.* London, 1907.

Wegener, G. *Zur Kriegszeit durch China, 1900-1901.* Berlin, 1902.

Wen Ching [pseud.] *The Chinese Crisis from Within.* Ed. by G. M. Reith. London, 1901.

Weulersse, G. *Chine Ancienne et Nouvelle: Impressions et Réflexions.* Paris, 1902.

Will, A. S. *World Crisis in China, 1900: a Short Account of the Outbreak of the War with the Boxers and Ensuing Foreign Complications.* Baltimore, 1900.

Wilson, J. H. *China: Travels and Investigations in the Middle Kingdom: a Study of Its Civilization and Possibilities Together with an Account of the Boxer War.* New York, 1901.

———. *Under the Old Flag: Recollections of Military Operations in the War for the Union, the Spanish War, the Boxer Rebellion.* New York, 1912.

Winterhalder, T. von. *Kämpfe in China, 1900-1901. Eine Darstellung der Wirren und der Beteiligung von Osterreich-Ungarns Seemacht, 1900-1901.* Wien, 1902.

Wojcick, C. *Ursachen und Verlauf der Wirren.* Wien, 1902.

Wu Yung. *The Flight of an Empress.* London, 1937.

Zabel, R. *Deutschland in China.* Leipzig, 1902.

INDEX

INTRODUCTION

Africa, 2
Allied force, *see* Foreign expeditionary force
American Legation, *see* Legations
American Mission, 84
Americans, 10, 35-6, 54, 67, 93, 99, 103
An Ting, 67
Anti-Christian literature, 11-12, 15, 29-30
Anti-Christian movement, 5, 14ff., 28ff., 46ff.
Anti-colonialism, 1, 13
Assent (Swiss), 58
Austrian Legation, *see* Legations
Austrians, 67, 73

Balkan states, 1
Barbarians, 10, 45
Belgian Legation, *see* Legations
Belgians, 53, 55
Bible, 12
Big Sword Society, *see* Ta Tung Hui
Boer War, 2, 67
Boxer temple, 74
Boxers, *see* I Ho Ch'uan
British, 10, 13, 17, 19, 26, 31, 34, 36, 40, 47-8, 54, 67, 69, 96, 99, 103
British-Chinese commercial treaty, 103
British forces, 66-8
British India forces, 69, 96
British Legation, *see* Legations
Brooks, Rev. S. P., 31, 35-6, 39-40, 42; memorial tablet, 42
Buddhism, 27, 29
Burma, 13

Canton, 15
'Carving Knife Brigade', 86
Chamot, A., 56, 73, 87
Chang An Street, 83
Chang Shia Tien, 31
Chang Shui Tien, 53
Ch'ang Hsin Tien, 55, 57
Chao Shu-ch'iao, 61, 102
Chartered Bank, Tientsin, 52
Chefoo, 18, 23

Chen Fei, 96
Ch'i Hua Men, 96
Chiang Chia Chuang, 43
Ch'ien Men, 70, 75, 87, 96
Chihli, 32ff., 41-6, 48, 52, 57, 69, 97
China Station, British Navy, 17
Chinese attitudes, 9-13, 45
Chinese City, 71, 73, 75, 96
Chinese City wall, 87
Chinese Civil Service exams, 101
Chinese forces, 21, 37, 50, 57-8, 60-2, 66, 68-70, 79, 82-3, 88, 91, 94-5; *see also* Kansu forces
Chinese Foreign Office, *see* Tsungli Yamen; Wai Wu Pu
Chinese foreign wars, 3, 13, 19, 25, 27, 75
Ch'ing dynasty, 22
Ch'ing, Prince, 38, 50, 60, 70, 97, 100
Chinkiang, 14
Cho Chow, 61
Christian converts, 15, 19, 29-30, 33, 43, 46, 52-3, 62-3, 72-3, 87
Christian literature, 5, 11
Christian missionaries, 3, 18, 25, 29ff., 35, 41, 43, 46, 64, 90, 99
Christian orphanages, 15
Chun Chi Ch'u, 61
Ch'ung Li, 52
Ch'ung Wen Men, *see* Ha Ta Men
Chungking, 14, 17
Cockburn, H., 60
Colonialism, 1; *see also* Anti-colonialism
Concessionaires, 25
Conger, E. H., 35-7, 81
Cordes, H., 82-3
Coup (1898), 26
Court, *see* Manchu Court

Darwinism, 7
Darwinism and China, 8, 11
Death Blow to Corrupt Doctrines, *see* Pi Hsieh Chi Shieh
Decrees, Imperial, 35-6, 38-9, 41-2, 50, 52, 61, 72, 101-3, *see also* Edicts

205

Diedrichs, Adm. von, 22
Diplomats, see Foreign diplomats
Dragon Boat Festival, 50, 52, 59
Drought, 33-4
Dubois, Eugène, 8
Dupree (Australian), 56
Dynastic laws, 39

Edicts, Imperial, 35; see also Decrees
Exchange Telegraph Company, 78
Empress Dowager, see Tzu Hsi, Empress
Europe, 1, 10, 13, 17-18, 31, 93

Famine, 33
Favier, Bishop A. P., 46-7, 72
Feng Tai, 53, 55, 56
Flecke (Frenchman), 73
Fleming, P., 47
Foreign attitudes, 6-9
Foreign buildings, 5, 34
Foreign-Chinese wars, see Chinese foreign wars
Foreign diplomats, 36, 38, 40-1, 47, 51-2, 54, 60, 63-4, 66, 71, 75, 82, 84, 92-3
Foreign expeditionary force, 42, 54, 84, 91-4; see also Relief Column
Foreign literature, 5, 25
Foreign naval forces, 42, 47, 54, 59-60, 63-4, 66, 76, 78-9, 81, 93
Foreign naval stations, 24; see also China Station, British Navy
Foreign occupation, 97ff.
Foreign penetration, 4-6, 13, 18-19, 21-2, 26
Foreign powers, 38, 40-1, 69, 76, 97, 99, 103
Foreign treaties, 3-5, 19, 103
French, 13-14, 17, 21, 40, 44, 47, 54, 56, 67, 99
French Legation, see Legations

Gaselee, Gen. A., 98
German East Africa, 2
German forces, 22, 68-9, 84
German Legation, see Legations
Germans, 22, 26, 31, 40, 44, 67, 99, 102-3
Giers, M. de, 47-8
Governor of Peking, 45
Grand Council, see Chun Chi Ch'u
'Great forward movement', 19

Ha Ta Men, 96
Ha Ta Men Road, 82
Hai Kuan, 70, 83, 86
Hanlin, see Han Lin Yuan
Han Lin Yuan, 41
Hankow, 14, 34
Hindu cult, 2

Ho Jun-sheng, 61
Hôtel de Pékin, see Peking Hotel
Hsi Ku, 69, 92, 94
Hsi Shan, 50, 62, 71
Hsiao Ch'in, see Tzu Hsi, Empress
Hsun Ching Tsung T'ing, 52
Huang Ho, 20
Hunan, 14
Hupeh, 14

I Ho Ch'uan, 2, 4, 17-18, 21, 26ff., 38, 40-50ff., 102
Ichang, 17
Imperial City, 72, 75
Imperial decrees, see Decrees, Imperial
Imperial edicts, see Edicts, Imperial
Imperial Maritime Customs, see Hai Kuan
Indemnity, 102
Indian forces, see British India forces
Indonesia, 2
Italian Legation, see Legations
Italians, 47, 54, 58, 67, 96

Japanese, 17, 19-21, 37, 54, 67, 93, 101-2, 104
Japanese-Chinese commercial treaty, 104
Japanese Legation, see Legations
Java, 8
Jesuits, 6, 25
Jesus, 11
Jung Lu, 37-8, 44, 51, 55, 88

K'ang-i, 102
K'ang Yu-wei, 25
Kansu, 51
Kansu forces, 51, 62, 71
Kao Lao Hui, 15
Ketels, Consul, 58
Ketteler, Baron von, 72, 78, 82-4, 101, 104; monument, 101, 104
Kiaochow, 22
Kuang Hsu, Emperor, 25, 37-9, 96
Kutien, 17

Laffan's Newsagency, 78
Lai Shui, 51
Landor, A. H. S., 30
Lang Fang, 68
Legation guards, 26, 38, 42, 47, 52, 54, 60, 87
Legation Street, 72
Legations, 2, 24, 26, 33, 44, 48, 54-5, 63, 69, 70-2, 75, 82-3, 86-8, 96, 101, 104; Austrian, 83, 86; Belgian, 72, 84; British, 73, 86; French, 82-3, 86; Japanese, 71; United States, 87; Summer, 62, 71; British Summer, 78
Li Hung-chang, 97, 100
Li Ping-heng, 30, 95, 102

Liang Hsiang Hsien, 98
Liang Hu, 14
Liu Li Ho, 53
Liang Shiang, 61
Lu Han railway, 34-5, 43, 45, 51-2, 55, 60, 64, 98
Lu Ko Chow, 53, 56
Lu T'ai Canal, 92

Ma Chia P'u, 54-5, 70-1
MacDonald, Sir C. M., 34, 36, 47-52, 60, 63-4, 66, 71, 86-7, 100
Manchuria, 33, 97, 103-4
Manchu Imperial family, 38, 80
Manchus, 15, 18, 27, 29-30, 37, 44, 61, **83**
Manchu Court, 35-6, 40, 47, 50-2, 60-1, 64, 69, 79, 81, 96-7, 100-3
Marco Polo Bridge, see Lu Ko Chow
Margary, A. R., 4, 13
Meng Kuang-wen, 31
Militia, 37
Messengers, 88
Ministers, see Foreign diplomats
Missionaries, see Christian missionaries
Morrison, G. E., 48, 73, 82

Nan T'ang, 73
Naval forces, see Foreign naval forces
Newchwang, 18
Nieh Shih-ch'eng, 61
Nordenfelt (gun), 54
Norman, Rev. H. V., 59, 64
North Borneo, 2
North China Herald, 44
North River, see Pei Ho

Old Testament, 11
'Open door to China' policy, 103-4
Orphanage, see Christian orphanages

Pai Lien Chiao, 27
Pao Ma Chang, see Race Course
Pao Ting Fu, 43, 45, 50-5, 57-60, 64, 98-9; massacre, 45-6, 72
Peace mission, 61
Peace negotiations, 97ff.
Peace Protocol, 101-3
Pei Ho, 42-4, 60, 64, 66, 75, 78-9, 90, 95
Pei T'ang, 72, 96
Pei Tsang, 94-5
Peking, 2, 18, 24, 26, 33, 35-7, 39-40, 43-5, 50, 52-7, 59, 61-2, 66-7, 70ff.
Peking Gazette, see *T'ang Pao*
Peking-Hankow railway, see Lu Han railway
Peking Hotel, 56, 87
Peking Police force, see Hsun Ching Tsung T'ing
Peking relief, 95-6

Peking relief column, see Relief Column, first, second
Peking siege, 84ff.
Peking Syndicate, 41-2
Peking-Tientsin railway, see Tientsin-Peking railway
Pi-hsieh Chi-hsieh, 11ff., 15
Pichon, S., 46-7, 50, 63
Placards, anti-foreign, 48-9
Proclamations, Imperial anti-Boxer, 52; see also Decrees, Imperial
P'u Chun, 38-9
Punitive expeditions, 98-9

Race Course, 44, 62, 66
Railways, 6, 13, 24, 34, 50, 52-3, 55, 90; see also Lu Han railway; Tientsin-Peking railway
Red Lantern Society, 28
Reform movement, 13, 25-6
Relief Column, Peking: first, 63ff., 70, 75-6, 82, 90-2; second, 84, 88, 93ff.; Tientsin, 54, 91-2; see also Foreign expeditionary force
Richard, Timothy, 25-6
Riots, southern, 3, 13ff., 39, 51
Robinson, Rev. C., 59, 64
Russian-Chinese agreement, 104; see also 'Open dor to China' policy
Russian forces, 59, 69, 78, 90-1, 95
Russian Legation, see Legations
Russians, 26, 40, 43, 47-8, 54, 67, 78, 99, 103-4

Salisbury, Third Marquis of, 41-2
Salvago-Raggi, Marquis de, 47
Satow, Sir E., 100
Seymour, Sir E. H., 63-4, 66, 68-9, 75, 77, 81-2, 90-2
Shan Hai Kwan, 34
Shanghai, 5
Shansi, 41-2, 102
Shantung, 20, 22, 26-7, 30ff., 36, 41-2, 48, 76, 83
Shensi, 97
Sian, 96
Sikh police, 14
Sino-Japanese War, 19, 25, 27
Sluice Gate, see Water Gate
Society for the Propagation of the Gospel in Foreign Parts, 31
Spring Race Meeting, 44-5, 63, 87
Squires, H. G., 86
Su, Prince, 73
Sugiyama Akira, 71-2, 78, 101
Summer Legations, see Legations, Summer
Summer Palace, 50

Ta Tung Hui, 27, 102
Tai Yuan, 97

INDEX: INTRODUCTION

Taku, 42, 59, 63-4, 67, 69, 75-6, 79, 81, 83, 88, 91, 101
T'ang Pao 41-2
Taoism, 27
Telegraphs, 49-50, 52, 54, 66, 81
Tientsin, 2, 18, 23-4, 34, 41-5, 52-9, 61-2, 64, 66-9, 75-6, 78-9, 81, 94; administration, 93; Arsenal, 92; massacre (1870), 4, 13, 18, 45-6, 50, 66; siege, 88ff.
Tientsin-Peking railway, 34, 55, 60, 62, 67, 70
Tientsin Relief Column, *see* Relief Column, Tientsin
Tientsin-Shan Hai Kwan railway, 34
The Times (London), 48, 78, 82
Tonking, *see* Vietnam
Treaty ports, 2, 5, 7, 14, 18, 24, 32, 34, 51, 59
Truce, 88
Tsai I, *see* Tuan, Prince
Tsai Lan, 102
Tsung Li Ko Kuo Shih Wu Ya Men, *see* Tsungli Yamen
Tsungli Yamen, 36, 50, 52, 60-1, 70-1, 81-4, 87, 101; *see also* Wai Wu Pu
Tu Liu Ts'un, 98
Tuan, Prince, 37-9, 70, 101
T'ung Chih, Emperor, 39
Tung Chih Men, 96
Tung Chow, 43, 62, 95
Tung Fu-hsiang, 51, 55, 62, 71, 102
Tung Pien Men, 96
Tung Tien River, 57
Turks, 58
Tzu Hsi, Empress, 25-6, 37, 39, 44, 51, 61, 96

United Kingdom, *see* British
United States of America, *see* Americans

Vietnam, 2, 13

Wai Wu Pu, 102, *see also* Tsungli Yamen
Waldersee, Graf von, 84, 93, 96, 99, 104
Wang, *see* Governor of Peking
War crimes trials, 98ff.
War declaration, 81
Water Gate, 87, 96
Watts, J., 91
Weiheiwei, 23
West Arsenal, *see* Hsi Ku
West River, 13
Western Hills, *see* Hsi Shan
White Lily Sect, see *Pai Lien Chiao*
Wusueh, 17

Yang, Brig., 51
Yang Tsun, 67-8, 95
Yangtze River, 13-14, 17, 57
Yellow River, *see* Huang Ho
Yen Chow, 22
Yu Hsien, 30-1, 38-9, 41, 102
Yu Lu, 67, 95
Yu Tu (god), 48-9
Yuan Shih-k'ai, 26, 31, 42
Yung Ch'ing, 52, 59-60
Yung Ting Men, 71
Yunnan, 13

INDEX

DIARY

Allied force, see Foreign expeditionary force
American Legation, see Legations
American Methodist Mission, 123
American Presbyterian Mission, 187
Americans, 109, 112, 114-15, 119, 124, 126, 128-31, 136-7, 139-40, 143-5, 147, 151, 153, 156, 158-9, 161, 163, 170-2, 175-7, 185, 187-8
An P'ing, 168
An Ting, 169
Anglican Mission, 182
Anti-Christian movement, 107ff.
Austrian Legation, see Legations
Austrians, 112, 119, 124, 135, 144-6, 161, 170, 176, 187

Backhouse, E. T., 131, 163, 186n.
Barr, L. H. R., 142, 156, 168, 187n.
Belgian Legation, see Legations
Belgians, 180
Board of Punishments, see Hsing Pu
'Boxer Bill' (cannon), 144-6, 153
Boxer temple, 115
Boxers, see I Ho Ch'uan
Brazier, J. R., 121, 185n.
Brewitt-Taylor, C. H., 112, 182n.
Bristow, H. H., 108, 137, 149, 156, 180n., 186
British, 112-13, 115, 130-1, 134, 136-8, 145-7, 158, 161, 166, 170, 172, 175, 178, 181
British forces, 108-78 pass., 183, 186-7
British India forces, 177, 190-1
British Legation, see Legations

Canal, see Imperial Canal
Canton, 172
Carles, W. R., 165-6, 190n.
Carriage Park, 123, 130, 133-4, 142, 146, 149, 151, 156-7, 159-60, 164-5
Casualty census, 140-1, 161, 170
Chaffee, General A. R., 171, 190n.
Chamot, A., 186n.
Chang Chia Wan, 169, 175-6

Chang Chiang, 175
Chang Chih-tung, 172, 190, 191n.
Chang, Gen., 158, 164
Chefoo, 162, 176, 189
Ch'i Hsin, 181
Ch'i Hua Men, 147, 151, 158
Ch'ien Men, 109, 113, 115-18, 127, 139-40, 166-7, 169, 178, 180n.
Chihli, 172, 183, 187, 190
Chin Chow, 171
China Station, British Navy, 180
Chinese City, 115, 136, 146, 151, 153, 180-2, 187
Chinese City wall, 113, 118, 124, 127-8, 145, 148, 164, 174, 177
Chinese Civil Service exams, 126, 185
Chinese forces, 115, 119, 125, 130-151, 158, 167, 171, 174, 183, 188; see also Kansu forces
Chinese Foreign Office, see Tsungli Yamen; Wai Wu Pu
Chinese Imperial Bank, 123
Ch'ing, Prince 114-15, 124, 130, 149, 151-3, 183, 184n., 188
Christian convrets, 111-12, 114, 121, 143, 150, 154, 171, 175, 181
Christian missionaries, 107, 121
Chun Chi Ch'u, 115, 184n.
Ch'ung Li, 119
Ch'ung Wen Men, see Ha Ta Men
Clarke-Thornhill, T. R., 163, 189n.
Cockburn, H., 107, 119, 146, 150
Committees, 124-5, 153, 160
Conger, E. H., 156, 171, 173, 188n.
Cordes, H., 121, 185n.
Court, see Manchu Court
Customs Lane, 110

Darcy, Lt, 131, 135, 186n.
Decrees, Imperial, see Edicts
Diplomats, see Foreign diplomats
Drew, E. B., 172, 190n.
Drury, R. D., 108, 156, 165, 180n.
Duke of Edinburgh, see Edinburgh, Duke of

209

Edicts, Imperial, 152, 173, 181
Edinburgh, Duke of, 174, 191n.; commemorative medal, 174
Empress Dowager, see Tzu Hsi, Empress

Favier, Bishop A. P., 147, 181, 187n.
Fire Brigade, Peking, see Hsiao Fang Tui
Flaherty, A. J., 137, 148, 156, 186n.
Foreign diplomats, 109, 120, 129, 154-6, 159-60, 173-4
Foreign expeditionary force, 176, 189; see also Relief Column
Foreign powers, 165, 181
Foreign treaties, 188
Fowler, J., 176, 191n.
French, 109-10, 112, 123-4, 130, 134-8, 140, 143-8, 151-2, 158, 160-1, 170, 173, 176, 181, 185-6
French Legation, see Legations
Fukushima, Gen., 175, 191n.

Gaselee, Gen. A., 165, 167, 175, 177, 190n.
German Legation, see Legations
Germans, 110, 113, 119, 127, 129, 134, 136, 143, 151-3, 158, 161, 169-70, 172-3, 176
Giers, M. de, 119, 143, 160, 184n.
Giles, Lionel, 142, 186
Goodrich, C., 163, 189n.
Grand Council, see Chun Chi Ch'u
Grand Secretariat, see Nei Ko
Gregory, Cpl, 133

Ha Ta Men, 110, 140, 146-7, 153, 167, 176, 182n.
Ha Ta Men Road, 182
Hai Kuan, 112, 126, 131, 134, 145-6, 170, 185
Halliday, Cpt. L. S. T., 114, 128, 184n.
Hanlin, see Han Lin Yuan
Han Lin Yuan, 123, 125-7, 130-2, 135-6, 139, 142-3, 146, 148-9, 151, 153, 157, 160, 162, 164-5, 169-70, 172-4, 185n.
Hancock, J. G., 137, 156, 186n.
Hart, Sir R., 114, 126, 157, 165, 170, 172, 182, 183n., 190
Hewlett, W. M., 172, 191n.
Ho Hsi Wu, 164, 166, 173, 175
Hôtel de Pékin, see Peking Hotel
Hsi An Men, 181
Hsi Ku, 171
Hsi Shan, 107
Hsiao Ch'in, see Tzu Hsi, Empress
Hsing Pu, 159, 189n.
Hsiao Fang Tui, 118, 184n.
Hsun Ching Tsung T'ing, 119, 184n.
Huang Tsun, 119
Hung Ch'iao, 158, 166

I Ho Ch'uan, 107ff.
Ichang, 172
Imperial Canal, 112, 140, 148, 163
Imperial City, 131, 139, 142, 146, 153, 156, 168, 181, 185
Imperial edicts, see Edicts, Imperial
Imperial Maritime Customs, see Hai Kuan
Imperial Palace, 118, 165, 178
Indian forces, see British India forces
Institute for the Blind, 112, 182n.
Italian Legation, see Legations
Italians, 109, 112, 114, 124, 129, 131, 134-9, 142, 144-5, 148, 152, 164, 170, 172, 181, 185-6

James, Prof. H., 121, 185n.
Japanese, 109-10, 114-15, 124, 126-31, 135-41, 145-6, 149-50, 152, 156, 158, 161-2, 166-7, 170, 172, 174-5, 185-6, 189, 191
Japanese Legation, see Legations
Jung Lu, 114-15, 130, 147, 151-3, 157, 159, 167-8, 173-4, 183-4n.

Kang Hsi, Emperor, 113, 182n.
Kansu, 113, 161
Kansu forces, 119, 130, 147, 152, 157, 161, 164, 168, 181-3
Ketteler, Baron von, 121
Kirke, C. C. A., 107, 156, 180n.
Kitroff (Russian), 143
Kuang Hsu, Emperor, 147, 152, 165, 167, 184, 187, 188n.

Legation census, 131, 174
Legation guards, 107, 109-10, 180
Legation Street, 110, 112-13, 118, 147, 157, 174
Legations, 107, 110, 154, 180; Austrian, 110, 121-3; Belgian, 123; British, 107ff.; French, 124, 130, 135, 140-53, 170, 172-4; German, 152-3, 170, 172; Japanese, 141, 181; Russian, 119, 142; United States, 125, 143, 150, 185; Summer, 107, 109, 179; British Summer, 179, 180-1n.
Li Hung-chang, 150, 157, 172, 184, 188n.
Liang Hu, 191
Liu K'un-i, 172, 190n., 191
Liu Li Ch'ang, 118
Logan (ship), 171
London Missionary Society, 112, 134, 182, 186
Lowry, Mrs E., 171, 190n.
Lu Han railway, 180
Lu T'ai, 188
Luzatti, A., 188n.

Ma Chia P'u, 108-9, 166, 180n., 181
Ma Tou, 166, 168-9, 175

MacDonald, Lady, 109, 180-1n.
MacDonald, Sir C. M., 107-10, 119, 124, 126, 128-9, 136, 138-9, 141-2, 144, 147, 152-6, 158-60, 165, 173, 177, 179n., 180-1, 187
Mallory, Lt-Col, J. S., 171
Manchuria, 172
Manchu Imperial family, 183, 187
Manchu Court, 167, 183-4, 187
Maxim (gun), 177-8
Messengers, 128, 134, 141, 143-6, 148, 153, 156, 158, 161, 163-7, 169-71, 174-6
Mines and countermines, 152, 157, 159-60
Ministers, see Foreign diplomats
Missionaries, see Christian missionaries
Mitchell (gunner), 151, 157
Mongol Market, 121, 127, 133-4, 139, 146, 164, 169-71, 173-8
Montalmar, Capt. E. T. E. von, 145, 187n.
Morrison, G. E., 110, 156, 160, 163
Morrison Street, see Wang Fu Ching
Myers, Cpt., 125, 129, 139, 185n.

Na T'ung, 181
Nan Hai Tzu, 152, 169
Nan T'ang, 113, 114, 153, 182n.; memorial tablet to, 113
Nan Tsai Tsung, 175
Nan Yuan, 112
Nei Ko, 183
Nestagaard (missionary), 147-8, 156, 168
Newchwang, 172
Nieh Shih-ch'eng, 157-8, 183, 188-9n.
Nishi, Baron T., 158, 189n.
Nordenfelt (gun), 124, 175-6
Norman, Rev. H. V., 107
North Bridge, 112-13, 114, 119-20, 123, 129, 168-9, 185n.
North River, see Pei Ho
North Stable, 139
Notices for besieged, 124, 129, 134, 144, 146, 152-3, 158, 160, 166-7, 176

Oliphant, D., 142, 186n.
Oliphant, N., 142, 149, 187n.
Orlando (ship), 184

Pao Ma Chang, see Race Course
Paolini, Lt, 138, 186n.
Peace negotiations, 184
Peachey, G. P., 131, 186n.
Pei Ho, 185
Pei Tai Ho, 171
Pei T'ang, 109, 115, 144, 147, 151, 155, 159, 161, 164, 174, 181n., 187
Pei Tsang, 165-7, 171-2, 175
Pei Yuan, 112
Pei Yung Men, 166

Peking, 107ff.
Peking Club, 172, 191
Peking Gazette, see *T'ang Pao*
Peking-Hankow railway, see Lu Han railway
Peking Hotel, 141, 173, 186n.
Peking Police force, see Hsun Ching Tsung T'ing
Peking relief, 177-8
Peking relief column, see Relief Column, first, second
Peking siege, 121ff.
Peking Syndicate, 153, 188n.
Peking-Tientsin railway, see Tientsin-Peking railway
Pelliot (Frenchman), 157
Pethick (secretary), 150
Phillips (marine), 135
Pichon, S., 127, 147, 160, 173, 185n.
Ping Tze Men, 179
Poole, Cpt. F. G., 134, 142, 149, 153, 186n.
Port Arthur, 110
Porter, H., 107, 156, 180n.
Preston, Sgt, 151
Prisoners, 129, 148, 150, 152

Race Course, 107-8, 180n.
Ragsdale, J. W., 171, 190n.
Railways, 112
Relief Column, first, 110, 139, 141-2, 145-6, 156, 180, 188; second, 158-9, 164-9, 171-2, 175, 190-1; see also Foreign expeditionary force
Reid, Gilbert, 142, 187n.
Richardson (Imperial Maritime Customs), 126
Robinson, Rev. C., 107
Rockets, 129, 136, 141
Rose, C. A. W., 177, 191n.
Rosthorn, von, 146
Russell, W. P. M., 137-8, 143, 149, 186n.
Russian forces, 115
Russian Legation, see Legations
Russians, 110, 112, 114, 118-19, 124, 126-7, 130-1, 134, 139, 144, 148, 155, 158-61, 165-6, 168, 170-3, 175-6, 181
Russo-Chinese Bank, 125-6

Sabbione, 163
Salisbury, Third Marquis of, 173, 191n.
Salvago-Raggi, Marquis de, 124, 129, 185n.
Scadding, Pte, 125
Scott, Bishop C. P., 182n.
Searchlight, 135, 138-40, 146
Seymour, Sir E. H., 108, 141, 171, 180n.
Sha Wo Men, 166, 190n.
Shan Hai Kwan, 168, 171
Shanghai, 172
Shansi, 169

Shantung, 158, 169, 183, 189-90
Shi Fang Yuan, 107, 180n.
Shiba, Lt-Col, 127, 131, 133, 135, 137-8, 142-3, 145-6, 149, 164-5, 169-70, 174, 185n.
Shih Tzu Wo, 179
Shin Chih Men, see Shun Chih Men
Shun Chih Men, 182
Shun T'ien Fu, 168, 190n.
Sluice Gate, see Water Gate
Smith, Cpt. Percy, 157
Society for the Propagation of the Gospel in Foreign Parts, 179
Sorties, 125, 127-8, 131-4, 137, 149, 151, 153, 155
South Bridge, 152
South Stable, 124, 133, 135, 156, 171, 176
Squiers, H. G., 147, 187n.
Ssu Ta Hang, 152
Strouts, Capt. R. M., 120, 128, 155-6, 160, 184, 187
Student Interpreters, 107, 134, 136-8, 145-6, 148, 152-3, 178-9
Su, Prince, 114, 183
Su Wang Fu, 114-15, 126-33, 135,40, 143-6, 148-9, 152-3, 155-7, 159-60, 163-4, 170, 173-5, 183n.
Sugiyama Akira, 109, 115, 181n.
Summer Legations, see Legations, Summer
Summer Palace, 179
Sung Ch'ing, 183n.
Sung, Prince, 114

Taku, 110, 120, 134, 151-2, 157-8, 165, 171, 176, 185n.
Tamsui, 156
Tang Ku, 171
T'ang Pao, 147, 159-60, 187n.
Taotai of Tung Chow, see Tung Chow
Tartar City, 118, 151, 179-80, 182, 187
Taylor, F. E., 172, 191n.
Telegraphs, 107, 109, 112, 159, 167, 170-1, 173, 181
Tewkesbury (missionary), 153
Tickner (marine), 136
T'ien Tsun, 145
Tientsin, 144, 151-2, 157-9, 165-7, 171-3, 176, 183, 189-90; administration, 165, 167, 172; Arsenal, 172

Tientsin-Peking railway, 128, 171; road, 154, 159, 166-7
The Times (London), 110, 156, 160, 163
Townsend, W. E., 137, 162, 186, 189n.
Truce, 129-30, 155-6, 165
Tsai I, see Tuan, Prince
Tsai Tsung, 175
Ts'ai Yu, 134
Tsun Hua, 171
Tsung Li Ko Kuo Shih Wu Ya Men, see Tsungli Yamen
Tsungli Yamen, 110, 119-20, 121, 125, 154, 157, 159, 165, 173-7, 183-4, 181n,. 188; see also Wai Wu Pu
T'u shu pien, 162, 189n.
Tuan, Prince, 149, 151-2, 154, 184, 187-8n.
Tung Chow, 158-9, 164, 166, 169, 175; Taotai, 159
Tung Fu-hsiang, 114, 119, 124, 130, 147, 152, 157, 161, 164, 167-8, 181-2, 183n.
Tung Pien Men, 146
Tung, T'ang, 112, 182
Tung Ssu P'ai Lou, 147
Tzu Hsi, Empress, 115, 147, 152, 165, 167, 184n., 187-8

United Kingdom, see British
United States of America, see Americans

Wagner (Imperial Maritime Customs), 137
Wai Wu Pu, 181n., see also Tsungli Yamen
Wang Fu Ching, 182
Warren, H., 107, 141, 155, 180n.
Water Gate, 148, 153, 167
West Arsenal, see Hsi Ku
West River, 172
Western Hills, see Hsi Shan
Wo Fu Ssu, 153
Wray, Cpt. E., 113, 134-5, 137, 183n.

Yamaguchi, Lt-Gen., 175, 191n.
Yang Tsun, 108, 119, 164, 166, 169, 175
Yangtze River, 172, 190-1
Yu Chia Wei, 166
Yuan Shih-k'ai, 169, 183, 190
Yung Lu Ta Tien, 126, 185n.
Yung Ting Men, 109, 166, 180, 181n.